NATURAL HAZARDS

2ND EDITION

Steve Frampton, John Chaffey,
John Hardwick, Alistair McNaught

Hodder & Stoughton

A MEMBER OF THE HODDER HEADLINE GROUP

Acknowledgements

Jill Rankin and A Jeanes for supplying many of the original resources and slides on which the New Zealand section in Chapter 5 was based; the New Zealand Government for permission to use several extracts from *Tephra*, their hazard management journal, and especially Dallas Moore at the Ministry for Civil Defence, Wellington, New Zealand. James Few and Royal Global Insurance for supplying data on windstorms.

The author and publishers thank the following for permission to reproduce material in this book:

Associated Press Ltd, Figure 3.1; Cambridge University Press, Figures 1.3, 3.4; *The Daily News*, California, Figure 5.17; *Dorset Evening Echo*, Figures 5.6, 5.7, 5.14; Hensmen, Brocklesby, Henmen, Figure 3.11; *The Independent*, Figure 6.2; International Federation of Red Cross and Red Crescent Societies, Figure 1.2; Reprinted with permission from *Nature* copyright 1995, MacMillan Magazines, Figure 3.24; Penguin, Figures 5.19, 5.22, 5.23; Prentice Hall, Figure 3.50; Routledge, *Environmental Hazards*, Keith Smith, Figures 1.11, 1.14; UCL Press, Figures 3.12, 3.42, 4.4, 4.5; US Geological Survey, Figure 3.23;

Reprinted by permission of John Wiley & Sons Inc, *The Way the Earth Works*, Wyllie Figure 3.6.

The publishers would also like to thank the following for giving permission to reproduce copyright photographs in this book:

AP Photo/Javier Casella, Figure 3.27; Associated Press, Figure 3.44, 3.52; Associated Press/Topham, Figure 3.25; Hulton Getty, Figure 3.13; Mary Rae, Figure 2.28; PA News, Figures 3.32, 3.33; Popperfoto, Figure 3.38; SPA/ESA, Figure 2.7; Trip/W Jacobs, Figure 3.8b; USGS, Figures 3.8d, 3.16, 3.22; Reg Vincent, Figure 5.5; Johan Witteveen, Figure 2.11.

The front cover is reproduced courtesy of Volcano Watch International/Steve O'Meara.

All other photos belong to the authors.

Every effort has been made to contact the holders of copyright material but if any have been inadvertently overlooked, the publisher will be pleased to make the necessary alterations at the first opportunity.

British Library Cataloguing in Publication Data

Natural hazards: causes, consequences and management

1. Natural disasters 2. Natural disasters – Forecasting
I. Frampton, S. (Steve)
551

ISBN 0 340 74944 X

First edition published 1996
Impression number   10 9 8 7 6 5 4 3 2 1
Year   2005 2004 2003 2002 2001 2000

Typeset by Fakenham Photosetting Limited, Fakenham, Norfolk.
Printed for Hodder & Stoughton Educational, a division of Hodder Headline Plc, 338 Euston Road, London NW1 3BH by Oriental Press, Dubai.

NATURAL HAZARDS

2ND EDITION

Contents

4 Mass movement hazards

5 Case studies of Managing Natural Hazards

6 Conclusion

Appendix

Index

1

INTRODUCTION

A classification of extreme events and natural hazards

How to maximise your use of this book

The 1990s have been declared by the United Nations (UN) to be the International Decade for Natural Disaster Reduction (IDNDR). Contemporary events make this an all too appropriate selection. Many observers have suggested that 1998 was one of the most hazardous years for the global population (see Figure 1.1). The late 1990s is also a turning point for post-16 Geography education with the advent of the new A-level Geography syllabuses, many of which take either a modular or people-environment approach to the subject, and feature hazards as a key theme.

The focus of this volume is without doubt one of the most topical and interesting of all the people-environment interactions; human efforts working to understand and reduce the impact of natural hazards. For many it may be fascinating due to the spectacular scenes of volcanic activity and power of these natural forces. Dramatic media images of floods, cyclones and earthquakes dominate news broadcasts or make headlines in our daily papers. This book will not just focus on the 250 000 deaths and US $40 billion of damage per annum, or the human tragedy associated with such disasters. It will attempt to focus on defining terminologies; try and explain their varied causal processes; explore their consequences on people and environments; and investigate how humans respond to such events.

The authors hope that you will enjoy working with this book, that you find the material informative, challenging and interesting, and that it motivates you to accept the responsibility for your own learning. The book, although comprehensive, is designed to act as a secure foundation upon which you can build through your own investigations and research. You will be encouraged to explore your own case studies by keeping a research file of topical events, and develop the key skills essential in developing your full potential.

We also hope that you become more aware of the factors underlying the UN designation of the 1990s as the International Decade for Natural Disaster Reduction, with the key aims of improving human safety and welfare for our global population.

Structure of the book

The book is physically organised into six sections.
A A brief introductory chapter where terminology and classifications are discussed and a clear route for enquiry set out.
B A major review of the three main types of natural hazard: i) **Climatic**; ii) **Geological**; iii) **Land Instability**. All consider the causal processes and consequences of these hazards.
C Detailed cases studies at various scales, focusing on attempts to reduce the impact of natural hazards, are considered:
i) The Chesil Sea Defence Scheme, Portland, Dorset;
ii) The Los Angeles urban Region;
iii) Flooding in Northern Italy;
iv) A National scale study of hazard management in New Zealand.
D A brief conclusion considers whether natural hazards are on the increase and reviews the main generalisations of the book.

Additionally you will find a comprehensive list of references and a glossary to explain key terms.

STUDENT ACTIVITY 1.1

Your first research tasks
1 Test the hypothesis that '1998 was one of the most hazardous years for the global population?' Study Figure 1.1 to begin with, but then gather further materials from a range of sources that could include:
- The Philips Geographical Digest;
- Almanacs in your library;
- The International Federation of the Red Cross – World Disaster Report (see Figure 1.2).
2 How does 1998 compare with this year?

Tornadoes
Worst season for 15 years in US.
Over 100 people were killed in events in Tennessee (Nashville) and Alabama. Meanwhile a small tornado struck Selsey, W. Sussex in the UK.

Freak Weather Hits N. and S. America
N. York suffers from massive snowfalls. Drought and fires sweep across Brazil, and in Texas temperatures hit 100°F for a record 29 consecutive days.

Flooding in Europe
In the UK large areas of the Midlands and S. Wales were flooded over Easter. Worst hit were Northampton where 1500 homes were affected, Stratford and Shrewsbury. Heavy rains and mudslides were responsible for large numbers of deaths in the Black Tides' disasters in S. Italy.

Flooding in Bangladesh
Over 2/3rds of the population were affected by the worst floods of the century, which lasted for over 3 months.

Tectonic Hazards
Earthquakes caused 4000 deaths in Afghanistan, but the most devastating tectonic event occurred in Papua New Guinea where one of the world's largest tsunamis claimed numerous deaths.

Hurricanes
Hurricane Bonnie caused significant damage in the USA. Hurricane 'Mitch' is being called the worst this century. Much of Central America was hit by this hurricane that claimed 10 000 deaths in Nicaragua.
The long-term social and economic impacts may yet prove to be more devastating. Current figures suggest over 20 000 people are dead or missing; 1 million homes were lost and 3 million people lost their livelihoods.

Flooding in China
A state of emergency was declared by the Chinese authorities as 400 million people were threatened in the Yangtze basin. Over 1000 people were killed and millions made homeless.

FIGURE 1.1 The Global Planet – a hazardous place to live in 1998

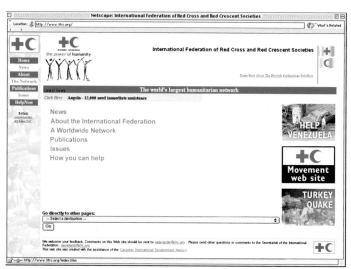

FIGURE 1.2 The International Federation of the Red Cross – world disaster report

Defining terms – Hazards and Disasters

Disasters and so-called 'natural hazards' are an integral part of our human history and can be studied from a number of viewpoints. A sociological or humanistic viewpoint states that the severity of a natural hazard depends upon who you are, and what society you belong to at the time of the disaster. Marxist theory argues that droughts and earthquakes do not kill or strike people in the same way and that it is the poor and oppressed who suffer most; society is differentiated into groups with different levels of vulnerability. A more geographical approach focuses on describing and explaining these natural uncontrollable physical events, and trying to understand their causes and consequences.

Disasters may be newsworthy and studied in various ways, but more importantly what is the difference between a natural process or event, a hazard and a disaster? Secondly are there actually any 'natural hazards'? These are by no means easy questions to answer.

John Whittow, in his classic book *Disasters: the Anatomy of Environmental Hazards*, suggested that, '*A hazard is a perceived natural event which threatens both life and property – a disaster is the realisation of this hazard.*'

Disasters are extreme events which cause great loss of life and/or damage to property and create severe disruption to human activities. They can be created by human actions, (e.g. transport accidents and industrial explosions) or natural processes (e.g. earthquakes). A natural hazard is when extreme natural events or processes occur in an area of human settlement and cause loss of life and damage to existing constructed resources and infrastructures.

Spatial variability and vulnerability

Unstable hill slopes, low-lying coasts and plains, volcanic zones, active faults and other parts of the earth's physical surface have an increased risk to extreme natural events. Some socio-economic and political areas of the earth's surface have an increased vulnerability due to poverty.

Hazards can be sub-divided or classified into similar groups for ease of study based on a wide range of criteria including magnitude, numbers of people killed (see Figure 1.3), frequency and causal processes. All natural hazards, however, do share common diagnostic criteria:
- the origin of the hazard event is clear and produces characteristic effects;
- warning time is normally short, except in droughts, i.e. they are rapid-onset unscheduled events;
- most losses to life and property are suffered soon after the event;
- the risk to exposure is involuntary;
- the impact on the human population has an intensity and scale to justify an emergency response.

Thus deforestation, desertification and rising sea levels are long-term environmental problems and

FIGURE 1.3 Ranking of natural hazard events by characteristics and impacts

Overall rank[b]	Event	Grading of characteristics and impacts[a]								
		Degree of severity	Length of event	Total areal extent	Total loss of life	Total economic loss	Social effect	Long-term impact	Suddenness	Occurrence of associated hazards
1	Drought	1	1	1	1	1	1	1	4	3
2	Tropical cyclone	1	2	2	2	2	2	1	5	1
3	Regional flood	2	2	2	1	1	1	2	4	3
4	Earthquake	1	5	1	2	1	1	2	3	3
5	Volcano	1	4	4	2	2	2	1	3	1
6	Extra-tropical storm	1	3	2	2	2	2	2	5	3
7	Tsunami	2	4	1	2	2	2	3	4	5
8	Bushfire	3	3	3	3	3	3	3	2	5
9	Sea level rise	5	1	1	5	3	5	1	5	4
10	Icebergs	4	1	1	4	4	5	5	2	5
11	Dust storm	3	3	2	5	4	5	4	1	5
12	Landslides	4	2	2	4	4	4	5	2	5
13	Debris avalanches	2	5	5	3	4	3	5	1	5
14	Tornado	2	5	3	4	4	4	5	2	5
15	Snowstorm	4	3	3	5	4	4	5	2	4
16	Flash flood	3	5	4	4	4	4	5	1	5
17	Thunderstorm	4	5	2	4	4	5	5	2	4
18	Lightning strike	4	5	2	4	4	5	5	1	5
19	Blizzard	4	3	4	4	4	5	5	1	5
20	Ocean waves	4	4	2	4	4	5	5	3	5
21	Hail storm	4	5	4	5	3	5	5	1	5
22	Localised strong winds	5	4	3	5	5	5	5	1	5
23	Subsidence	4	3	5	5	4	4	5	3	5
24	Mud and debris flows	4	4	5	4	4	5	5	4	5
25	Rockfalls	5	5	5	5	5	5	5	1	5

[a]Hazard characteristics and impacts are graded on a scale of 1 (largest or greatest) to 5 (smallest or least significant).
[b]Overall rank is based on average grading.

not natural environmental hazards. Hewitt and Burton (1971) suggested the following measures could be used to more precisely define a natural hazard:

1   Property damage – must affect more than 20 families or losses must exceed US $50 000 (1971 prices).
2   Death of more than ten people or more than 50 serious injuries.
3   Disruption to social services: communication failures; infrastructure disruption; closure of essential services (schools, airports); severe stress on personnel, finances and equipment for the police, fire and hospital services.

Why classify Hazards?

Hazards have been classified using a wide range of criteria and approaches, and for a variety of purposes and user groups. The purposes of classifying include:

1   assessing risks;
2   understanding spatial patterns;
3   understanding how hazards impact on people;
4   aiding our understanding of processes and their inter-relationships;
5   helping to manage responses to hazards.
In all classifications there is a need to balance simplicity with accuracy, and different user groups will have varying requirements and uses for their classifications e.g. Researchers, Planners, Insurance Companies and Hazard Managers including the emergency services.

STUDENT ACTIVITY 1.2

Defining and classifying natural hazards
1   Using Figure 1.3 attempt to classify natural hazard events into groups based on their causal processes:
a) climatic;
b) geological;
c) land instability.
2   Using this data and Figures 1.4 and 1.5 suggest what are the problems with such a simplistic classification?
    Which of these are the most potentially serious natural hazards? Justify your decision.
3   Review your own definitions of natural event, natural hazard and natural disaster and use examples to highlight the critical differences between these three related terms.
4   Explain why natural hazards should not be called 'Acts of God!'
5   Using the data in Figures 1.4–1.6 assess the validity of the statement: *'it is the poor and oppressed who suffer most; society is differentiated into groups with different levels of vulnerability.'*

Hazards have been classified by their spatial distribution, e.g. MEDC/LEDC or by continent, or even by tectonic occurrence (e.g. Plate situation) or climate region. Other commonly used methods are by origin/causal process (see Fig. 1.7a), or impact on people (1.7b). More recently more complex classifications have been proposed based on the scale of impact on people, using combinations of the

FIGURE 1.4 Annual average number of disasters by region and type

	Africa	Americas	Asia	Europe	Oceania	Total
Earthquake	2	6	11	4	2	25
Drought & famine	7	2	3	1	0	13
Flood	11	22	36	9	5	83
Landslide	1	5	7	1	1	15
High wind	4	28	35	11	7	85
Volcano	0	2	2	0	1	5
Other	17	8	13	7	1	46
Total	42	73	107	33	17	272

Source: *Red Cross – World Disaster Report*

FIGURE 1.5 Annual average estimated damage by region and by type over ten years (1987–96) in thousands of US dollars

	Africa	Americas	Asia	Europe	Oceania	Total
Earthquake	30 920	2 913 486	12 006 577	47 213 990	146 763	62 311 736
Drought & famine	9 874	314 440	8 276	218 860	520 840	1 072 290
Flood	157 577	2 463 027	13 522 541	8 806 790	34 860	24 984 795
Landslide	0	2 620	28 330	50 000	0	80 950
High wind	69 297	7 474 687	5 603 058	7 520 826	318 388	20 986 256
Volcano	0	1 000	22 089	1 650	40 000	64 739
Other	4 700	465 290	189 889	281 039	0	940 918
Total	272 368	13 634 550	31 380 760	64 093 155	1 060 851	110 441 684

Estimates of damage, recorded as financial loss, need to be treated with caution. Earthquakes always rate high on such listings, as figures reflect the cost of rebuilding infrastructure or damage reported through insurance companies. Economic damage to individual households is badly under-reported, hence the very low figures for famine and drought.
Source: *Red Cross – World Disaster Report*

Country	Killed	Affected	Killed 1997	Affected 1997	Country	Killed	Affected	Killed 1997	Affected 1997
AFRICA					EUROPE				
Ethiopia	951	4 026 399	297	1 051 200	Soviet Union	6 794	284 189	–	–
Mozambique	725	629 167	252	32 176	Russian Federat.	1 022	36 774	252	–
Burkina Faso	415	290 592	1 953	16 775	Turkey	305	23 584	–	–
Sudan	358	1 489 703	–	–	Greece	130	1 750	70	–
Seychelles	0	0	5	250	United Kingdom	112	351 296	20	1 000
TOTAL	8 601	12 731 564	8 327	5 935 170	Ukraine	83	69 112	16	–
					Georgia	76	17 717	–	–
AMERICAS					Poland	75	0	115	162 500
Peru	1 313	626 819	479	32 800	France	74	31 172	46	10 000
USA	516	182 699	160	306 390	Azerbaijan	72	275 045	31	75 000
Brazil	420	459 641	46	600	Norway	61	400	55	–
Ecuador	355	39 332	62	35 000	Italy	58	1 780	52	130 000
Mexico	294	73 910	472	622 955	Spain	47	2 051	46	750
Venezuela	110	6 397	99	15 000	Germany	32	10 380	30	15 000
Dominican Rep.	93	122 770	–	–	Belgium	27	142	10	–
Chile	92	35 005	44	108 350	Portugal	27	305	11	–
Cuba	78	130 366	56	7 000	Sweden	24	0	–	–
Bolivia	64	51 077	–	108 000	Switzerland	5	720	–	–
Canada	34	5 457	–	30 600	Ireland	4	350	–	–
Montserrat	1	1 000	32	4 000	Austria	4	0	–	–
TOTAL	4 547	3 029 403	1 581	1 667 195	Iceland	3	6	–	–
					TOTAL	9 542	1 717 626	874	488 975
ASIA									
Bangladesh	44 014	18 574 280	463	3 468 738	OCEANIA				
India	5 063	56 563 631	2 540	392 690	Papua New Guinea	47	25 940	102	703 000
Iran	4 293	40 725	2 754	151 658	Australia	39	2 283 391	41	400
China, P. Rep.	4 135	99 073 268	1 389	16 832 527	New Zealand	3	1 626	3	340
Philippines	2 556	3 690 032	119	486 765	TOTAL	109	2 368 316	418	709 340
Indonesia	848	153 898	1 262	215 000					
Nepal	783	200 768	20	–					
Pakistan	748	1 407 065	528	837 228					
Japan	676	124 347	49	68 200					
TOTAL	67 130	185 798 713	10 551	24 516 489					

The ratio of killed to affected in disasters reflects the type of disaster and the degree of disaster preparedness in a country; more preparedness means less lives lost. Floods affect many but kill few. The ratio of killed to affected is far greater for earthquakes. Source: CRED.

Source: *Red Cross – World Disaster Report*

FIGURE 1.6 Annual average number of people killed or affected by disaster by selected countries and also regions, over ten years (1987–1996)

Saffir Simpson Scale with the Mercalli and Richter Scales. This method may additionally involve either a damage index which incorporates Loss of Life: Property Damage ratios, or a risk index based on the magnitude and frequency of the hazard event(s). A final classification that interests geographers is the extent to which hazards can be classified by the degree of human impact involved in the causal process (Fig. 1.7c).

Risk Assessment

Hazards are ever-present, and every day some degree of personal risk from floods, transport accidents or theft and vandalism to property is faced. Risk is often used synonymously with hazard, but risk carries the additional implication of the probability or chance of a particular hazard actually occurring. The relationship between the severity of an environmental hazard, probability and risk can be seen in Figure 1.10.

Grist in his 1978 study of the UK showed the risk from natural hazards to be very low despite the high media profile for such events. He showed that of the 640 000 deaths each year, out of a total population of 54 million in the UK,

STUDENT ACTIVITY 1.3

Further classification of hazards
In Student Activity 1.2 you were asked to do a simple classification of hazards. Now study Fig. 1.7 and explain:
1 What are the problems and limitations with attempting to classify hazards?
2 Why are there different approaches?
3 Who would find these useful? Why?
4 How would you classify a Jokulhlaup (Fig. 1.9)?
5 Some workers have argued that hazard profiles are more useful (Fig. 1.8). Why?
6 A proforma for an individual event can be completed based upon a range of criteria including magnitude, speed of onset, duration, areal extent, recovery rate, frequency, damage and deaths. These can then be collated for hazard types at a range of scales/locations to produce benchmarking data. Who would find these interesting and why might these be more useful? Produce 4 hazard profiles for three contrasting recent hazard events. Ensure you have a balance of scale/location and hazard types.

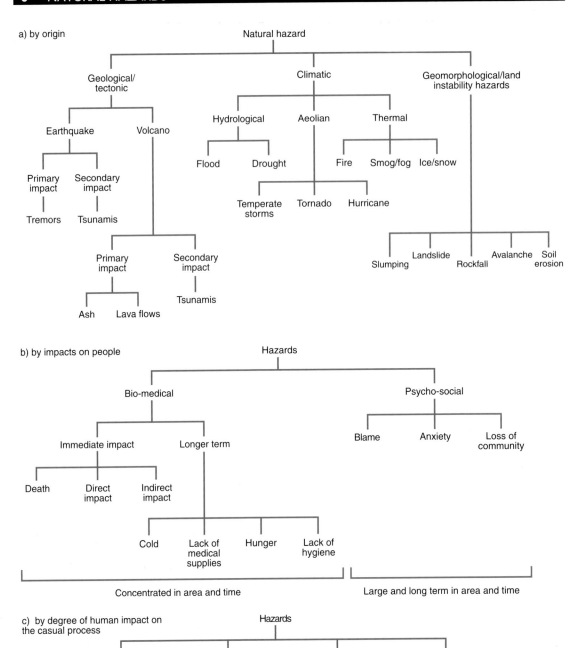

FIGURE 1.7 Classification of hazards (a) by origin (b) by impacts on people (c) by degree of human impact on the causal process

a) by origin

b) by impacts on people

c) by degree of human impact on the casual process

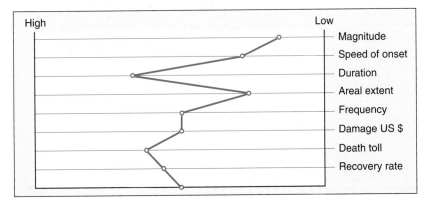

FIGURE 1.8 A typical hazard profile

about 90 per cent were due to familiar Western medical disorders. Accidental deaths actually only constitutes 3 per cent of the overall total, and most of these were due to road accidents. He concluded that risk in the UK is strongly age-related. On a global scale the work of Starr (1979) (Figure 1.11) and Dinman (1980) (Figure 1.12) suggests that although natural hazards are not frequent and an everyday cause of death or damage, they are high risk because of their potential for unexpected

FIGURE 1.9 A glacier burst flood event caused by rapid drainage of an ice-dammed lake in Iceland

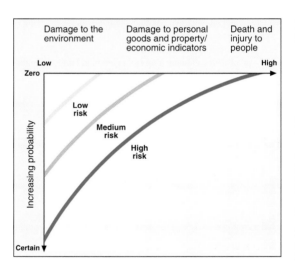

FIGURE 1.10 The relationship between the severity of a hazard, probability and risk

Hazard	Annual rate per 1000 households
Floods	3.4
Hurricanes/tropical storms	3.4
Tornadoes/windstorms	10.0
Earthquakes/severe tremors	1.8
Any of the four hazards	18.7

Source: *data from random-digit-dialling telephone survey;*
N = 13 006

FIGURE 1.11 Annual rates of selected natural hazard incidence causing injury or property damage in American households, 1970–80

catastrophic loss. Risks of specific natural hazards will obviously vary spatially and through time with changes in physical exposure and human vulnerability.

FIGURE 1.12 Federally declared disasters within the USA, 1965–85

STUDENT ACTIVITY 1.4

Risk assessment
1 Using the data in Figures 1.11–1.13 compare and contrast the risks associated with natural hazards in the USA and UK. What factors might help explain these differences?
2 Will all parts of the UK and USA display the same degree of risk? Justify your viewpoint.
3 Do you think that the risks would be different in a country like Bangladesh?

Type of disaster	Number	Federal outlay ($'000 1982)
Ice and snow events	19	205 511
Hurricanes/tropical storms	39	1 947 939
Earthquakes	7	405 706
Dam and levée failures	7	80 806
Rains, storms and flooding*	337	2 439 852
High winds and waves	2	120 536
Coastal storms and flooding	7	205 357
Tornadoes	109	648 352
Drought/water shortage	4	5 344
Totals	531	6 059 403

Note: *Includes land, mud and debris flows and slides*

Involuntary risk	Risk of death/person/year
Lightning (UK)	1 in 10 million
Bites of venomous creatures (UK)	1 in 5 million
Leukaemia	1 in 12 500
Influenza	1 in 5 000
Struck by automobile (USA)	1 in 20 000
Struck by automobile (UK)	1 in 16 600
Floods (USA)	1 in 455 000
Earthquake (California)	1 in 588 000
Tornadoes (Mid-west USA)	1 in 455 000

FIGURE 1.13 The risk of death due to various hazards

FIGURE 1.14 12 factors influencing public risk perception with some examples of relative safety judgements

Factors tending to decrease risk perception

Voluntary hazard (mountaineering)
Delayed impact (drought)
Indirect impact (drought)
Common hazard (road accident)
Few fatalities per event (car crash)
Deaths random in space/time (drought)
Statistical victims (cigarette smokers)
Processes well understood (snowstorm)
Controllable hazard (ice on highways)
Familiar hazard (river flood)
Belief in authority (university scientist)
Little media attention (chemical plant)

Factors tending to increase risk perception

Involuntary hazard (radioactive fallout)
Immediate impact (wildfire)
Direct impact (earthquake)
Dreaded hazard (cancer)
Many fatalities per event (air crash)
Deaths grouped in space/time (avalanche)
Identifiable victims (chemical plant workers)
Processes not well understood (nuclear accident)
Uncontrollable hazard (tropical cyclone)
Unfamiliar hazard (tsunami)
Lack of belief in authority (private industrialist)
Much media attention (nuclear plant)

Hazard management decisions cannot be based entirely on objective statistical assessments of risk, as an individual responds to a hazard only after a threat has been perceived. Individual hazard perception will be influenced by direct or indirect past experiences, as well as present attitudes, personality, values and expectations. Risks are taken more seriously if they have concentrated life-threatening potential or if children or another specific victim group is identified.

STUDENT ACTIVITY 1.5

Risk perception
1 Study Figure 1.14 and try to explain the factors that increase and decrease risk perception.
2 What other factors would influence your own personal risk perception?

Logically people should avoid living in perceived and actual high-risk areas, and abandon sites which are prone to hazard. However, there are many complex reasons why people stay and become risk-takers. Hazards by their very definition are unpredictable. We do not know and cannot predict their frequency and magnitude, and often even their exact spatial occurrence. Most of the global population in Less Economically Developed Countries (LEDCs) lack alternatives, due to social, economic, political and cultural factors. Families and communities cannot simply uproot and leave homes, jobs and land. Finally we must concede that there are some perceived and actual advantages associated with some hazardous environments, with river floodplains and volcanic areas offering rich soils. Yet floods are the world's most common hazard accounting for 32 per cent of the world's disaster events, excluding tropical cyclones. They also cause the most damage. This is a very high-risk cost-benefit analysis strategy but does help explain the apparent illogical human persistence in proven hazard-prone zones.

Integrated Risk Management

Integrated risk management has been defined by Dr N Britton (1998) as:
'The process of considering the social, economic and political factors involved in risk analysis; determining the acceptability of damage/disruption; deciding on the actions to be taken to minimise damage/disruption.'
This risk management approach is therefore based on two critical elements:
1 Risk assessment: the scientific methods to define likelihood of harm (probability × consequence).
2 Risk communication: a two-way process between population-at-risk, risk assessors and policy makers to reach an acceptable level of choice. Several clear stages can be seen in the formulation of an effective integrated risk management strategy (see Figure 1.15):
1 Establish the context and develop the criteria.
2 Identification of the hazard risks (what? how?).
3 Analyse the risks – determine existing controls, likelihood(s), consequences and levels of risk.
4 Assess the risk and establish priorities.
5 Treat the risk – identify, evaluate, and prepare treatment plans and implement a risk reduction plan.
6 Monitor and review.
7 Risk communication – identify stakeholders, acknowledge concerns, develop a communication strategy.
8 Risk acceptance – develop public awareness programme(s).

FIGURE 1.15 The risk
management process

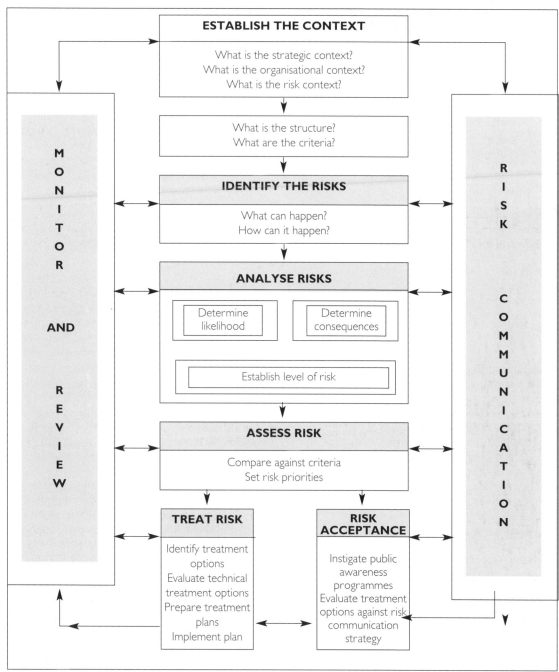

Source: *Britton, 1998*

Review of key ideas

■ The 1990s have been declared the International Decade for Natural Disaster Reduction (IDNDR).
■ Natural hazards are difficult to define. They can be regarded as perceived natural events that threaten life and property.
■ Natural hazards can be classified using a wide range of criteria.
■ There is a strong relationship between natural hazards and risk perception.
■ The impact of natural hazards may be related to levels of economic development.

References

IRC – World Disasters Report 1998

Emergency Management and Civil Defense in New Zealand, Dr N Britton, 1998, Govt. Publication

Glossary

Climatic hazards – caused by fluctuations in atmospheric processes.
Geological hazards – those that originate within the earth and are related to internal crustal processes.
Land instability hazards – those that relate to surface processes, e.g. landslides and avalanches.
Quasi-natural hazards – a predominantly artificial hazard due to the interaction of natural and human processes which is often the result of careless exploitation and non-sustainable use of the natural environment, e.g. smog, desertification.

2
CLIMATIC HAZARDS

This chapter outlines the importance of climatic hazards, their varied origins, their widespread impacts and the complexities of prediction and response. No other family of hazards is so universally present and, more worryingly, no other hazards are so easily triggered by human activities.

The nature of climatic hazards

Climatic hazards are amongst the most serious hazards affecting human populations. Compared to earthquakes or volcanoes, climatic hazards can appear unspectacular but they usually have an impact upon an enormous number of people. Between 1960 and 1980, droughts, floods and hurricanes accounted for 58.5 per cent of all deaths by natural disasters and 97 per cent of all people experiencing loss or damage by natural disasters. In addition to the substantial human cost, the financial costs can be astronomical. Between 1987 and 1993 there were 15 natural hazards that cost the insurance industry more than US $1 billion. Of these, ten were wind-related and accounted for 85 per cent of the US $53 billion total. The widespread impact of these hazards is due to several factors.

■ **Frequency**
Climatic hazards are frequent events. Floods are annual problems in many river basins. Snow is an annual event in high-latitude countries. Drought is very common in many subtropical regions. An average of eight Atlantic hurricanes occur every year. Tornadoes regularly occur in central southern USA from March to October.

■ **Size**
Climatic hazards can be very large in extent. Whilst earthquake damage is normally limited to a few hundred kilometres from the epicentre, a hurricane can cover 1 300 000km^2 and last three weeks. The China floods of 1998 affected 4.5 million people.

■ **Amplification**
Some climatic hazards (such as fog/smog and flood) are made worse by human activities or land use.

■ **Vulnerability**
Climatic hazards like flood and drought may be concentrated in particular regions, for example a flood is confined to a floodplain. These hazard-prone areas become 'marginal' lands that support the poorest and most vulnerable groups in a society. In Delhi, India, 500 000 of the city's poor live in shanty dwellings on the floodplain of the Yamuna River.

■ **Knock-on effects**
The problems do not stop when the hazard is over. Droughts may end, and flood waters may recede but the crop will still fail, the roads are washed away or the sewage system has broken down. The cost of coping with the aftermath of climatic hazards can represent an immense strain on the fragile economy of a Less Economically Developed Country (LEDC).

Classifying climatic hazards

Climatic hazards can be classified in a variety of ways which will influence the way you perceive and respond to them. The hazard equation has two distinct elements shown in Figure 2.1.

Some of the classifications in Figure 2.2 focus on the physical character of the hazard whilst others focus on the impacts of the hazard on human populations. If hazards are regarded primarily as physical events, then the reduction of hazard risk will tend to be seen in terms of technological responses – the so-called technological fix. Conversely, if hazards are seen to be problems of social and economic vulnerability, they will be tackled in entirely different ways that will involve attempting to change social and political structures to reduce the vulnerability of affected groups.

The simplest classification is by type of event. Using this classification we define each hazard according to its meteorological causes and character. Classifying by physical controls is an alternative approach. In this case drought and floods would be grouped together because they are hydrological in origin. Other climatic hazards could be considered aeolian (wind-related) or thermal (heat-related) depending on their physical controls. A further development of these ideas could consider the origins of the hazard. Some hazards are entirely natural in origin whilst others have distinctive human elements.

Another option would be classification by impact intensity as measured by the number of people affected. In many ways this is a more useful measure, but it suffers the problem that hazard impacts vary with culture, wealth, expectations etc.

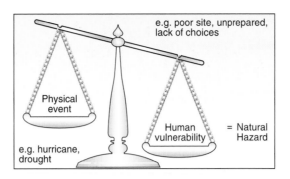

FIGURE 2.1 The hazard equation

For example, winter headlines like 'Blizzards sweep the South' are laughable for people in Scotland where far worse weather is experienced every year with scarcely a mention in the press. Nevertheless, broad generalisations can be made as to the impacts of the different climatic hazards.

Impact frequency is a useful classification for a given region because it helps emergency services to forward plan. However, there are two complications: firstly, accurate long-term records on the frequency of hazards do not exist for many areas of the world; and secondly, the more

FIGURE 2.2 Alternative classifications of climatic hazards

Classification 1: by hazard type

Flood	Drought	Hurricane	Tornado	Temperate storm	Snow	Fog/smog	Fire

Classification 2: by physical controls

Hydrological	**Aeolian** (wind)	**Thermal**
Flood, drought	Hurricane, tornado, temperate storm	Fire, snow/ice, fog/smog

Classification 3: by origin

Entirely natural	**Semi-natural** (some human influence)	**Anthropogenic** (major human influence)
Hurricane, tornado, temperate storm, snow/ice	Drought	Flood, fog/smog

Classification 4: by impact intensity

	Low impact (damage or death/injury)	**High impact** (damage or death/injury)
Localised	Fog/smog	Fire, tornado, flood, snow
Widespread	Temperate storm	Hurricane, drought

Classification 5: by impact frequency (UK example)

Low frequency (for UK)						**High frequency** (for UK)	
Hurricane,	tornado,	drought,	fire,	snow,	flood,	temperate storm,	fog

Classification 6: by geographical distribution

	Tropical	**Subtropical**	**Temperate**	**Polar**
Maritime	Flood, fog/smog	Fog/smog, flood, hurricane	Fog/smog, storm, flood	Snow
Continental		Drought, fire, tornado	Drought, fire, tornado, flood	Snow

Classification 7: by energy levels

Low			**High**
Tornado,	thunderstorm,	hurricane,	depression (temperate storm)

FIGURE 2.3 Hazard perception and frequency

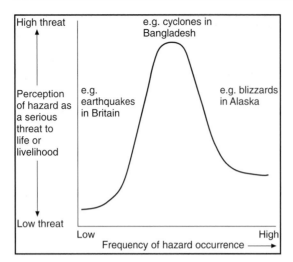

frequently a hazard occurs the better adapted the local population will be and it will be less likely to consider this as a hazard (see Figure 2.3).

Hazards can be classified on a geographical basis, e.g. temperate versus tropical climatic hazards. The problem here is that areas of similar climate may have entirely different hazards. Flood hazards in particular may depend more on human interference in the drainage basin than they do on high rainfalls.

Finally the least useful but possibly most intriguing classification might be by energy levels. It might be assumed that energy levels have a direct effect on hazard intensity but this is not always the case, as shown in Figure 2.2, classification 7.

STUDENT ACTIVITY 2.1

Classifying hazards
1 Which classifications would you find most useful if:
a) you were a County Councillor responsible for planning emergency services;
b) you were a risk assessor for an insurance company;
c) you were a Government adviser on Hazard Reduction Planning?
In each case give reasoned arguments for your choices.

The mechanisms of climate

The earth's atmosphere is unique in the solar system and comparatively eco-friendly. Venus has acid rain storms, fierce temperatures and 320km per hour (kph) winds. Mars is a drought-ridden desert. Jupiter's atmosphere contains an earth-sized hurricane that has raged for nearly 200 years. But none of these are hazards as no life exists to be affected. In contrast, the earth's atmosphere is extremely unusual, being quite high in oxygen and low in CO_2. Living organisms have successfully locked up excess CO_2 in coal, chalk, limestone and living tissue, whilst green plants have pumped oxygen into the atmosphere. Strangely, life has created an atmosphere suitable for life. The ingredients of the atmosphere are shown in Figure 2.4.

The atmosphere is over 80km thick but most weather and climate is found in the lowest 8–12km. This layer of turbulent air is known as the **troposphere** (Latin *tropos* = turning). Its temperature decreases as you go higher into the atmosphere. This is because the main source of heat for the troposphere is the warm ground, heated by the sun's rays. At the **tropopause** this pattern ceases and temperature remains stable or slowly increases with increased altitude. The tropopause, with its reversing temperature pattern, acts like a lid on the weather systems in the lower atmosphere. Without it, climatic hazards might be far more powerful – and damaging.

The ingredients of weather and climate

Climate has three main ingredients: temperature, **pressure** and **humidity**. These act together to produce a wide range of weather systems. Temperature is the driving force for the atmospheric engine. It acts on every scale from global to local. Different temperatures cause different air pressures in the various regions on the earth's surface. These pressure changes cause the great global wind patterns. Moisture levels in the air, humidity, influence the stability of air masses, controlling rainfall patterns and transferring heat from ground level into the atmosphere. Each of these ingredients has its own controlling factors, as outlined below:

Temperature – the source of the atmosphere's heat is, surprisingly, the ground. Incoming energy from the sun is in the form of shortwave radiation. The atmosphere is fairly transparent to shortwave **radiation** so that only a small percentage (see Figure 2.6a) of the incoming radiation is absorbed by the atmosphere and turns into heat. The ground, however, absorbs much more radiation, and so heats up more effectively. The heated ground then re-radiates its heat into the atmosphere, but in the form of longwave radiation (Figure 2.6b).

This re-radiation of heat into the atmosphere is the basis of **the greenhouse effect**. The greenhouse effect – caused by atmospheric carbon dioxide and water vapour – is essential to life. Without this

In terms of world climate, the three most significant gases in the atmosphere are water vapour, carbon dioxide and ozone. Together they account for less than 4.04 per cent of the atmospheric volume and yet their importance is disproportionately large.

Water vapour is variable in occurrence. At most it will form a few per cent of atmospheric composition in rainy areas but it is virtually absent from the upper regions of the troposphere. Water vapour plays a key role in redistributing energy around the globe; heat is used up in evaporating water and then

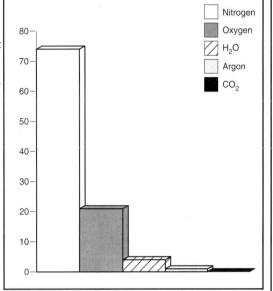

Figure 2.4 Atmospheric composition

	%
Nitrogen	74.00
Oxygen	20.94
H_2O	4.00
Argon	0.98
CO_2	0.08

released when the evaporated water re-condenses. In this way heat energy is transferred both across the surface by weather systems and into the atmosphere from ground level. The clouds that result from water vapour activity play an important role in influencing sunshine as well as temperature and moisture levels. The dynamic and variable nature of water vapour accounts for much of the changeability in weather.

Carbon dioxide (CO_2) is essential in maintaining global temperatures at levels suitable to life. A worrying trend is the increase in carbon dioxide as a result of human activity this century. Between 1870 and 1980, global CO_2 levels increased by 30 per cent due to the burning of fossil fuels. Fortunately land and ocean biospheres seem to have 'mopped up' about 50 per cent of the increase so the net gain is closer to 15 per cent. Nonetheless, CO_2 levels continue to increase at alarming rates with an ever-increasing population requiring fuel for heating, cooking, industry and transport. Whilst the details are argued over, there is little doubt that increasing CO_2 levels will cause changes to the earth's climates.

Ozone is present in minute amounts in the atmosphere. Whilst ozone excess from car exhaust reactions may cause ground-level problems, the ozone layer (concentrated between 15–35km up in the atmosphere) is a vital shield absorbing harmful ultra violet radiation from the sun. Its fragility can be appreciated when we consider that if all the ozone in the atmosphere were compressed to sea level pressures, the ozone layer would be only 3 mm thick!

Methane – natural methane exists only in trace amounts in the atmosphere but it is an extremely effective greenhouse gas. Over a ten-year period, methane's greenhouse effect would be more than 50 times as effective as a similar volume of CO_2. Humans have influenced methane levels in the atmosphere by agriculture. Both rice-growing and cattle-rearing produce large quantities of methane gas.

Particulates – the air naturally contains many particulates. These include dust, salt and smoke particles from forest fires. Human activities presently account for about 30 per cent of all particulates. The overall effect of increasing particulates is unclear but they are likely to influence both temperatures and moisture levels.

Particulates less than 10 microns in diameter (PM10's) are common products in vehicle exhausts. Recent research has linked PM10 levels in cities to deaths through respiratory disorders, although continuing studies suggest even finer particles (PM2.5's) might be more dangerous.

effect, the whole planet would experience severe arctic conditions and life on earth would be very unlikely. In addition to the longwave radiation warming the atmosphere from below, evaporation of surface water removes energy from the ground and transfers it to the atmosphere when the water re-condenses as clouds. The atmosphere is thus heated from below, but its heating and cooling is very uneven (Figure 1.5) causing irregular patterns of pressure to develop across the earth's surface.

Where air masses of different character meet, **fronts** may form. Strong temperature gradients exist across these fronts and these give rise to strong pressure gradients with the potential for high windspeeds to form. The Polar Front lies between the cold outflowing polar air and the warm, moist, air flowing polewards from the subtropics. The clash of these two very different air masses explains a good deal of the variability, wind power and excitement(!) of temperate weather conditions. The

FIGURE 2.5 Global
patterns of temperature,
pressure and wind

FIGURE 2.5 Global
patterns of temperature,
pressure and wind

The excess heat at the equator warms a belt of air that rises. As it rises to higher altitudes the air cools and condenses to form clouds and encourage heavy tropical rainfalls. This way a large proportion of the moisture in the air returns to the ground, leaving the rising air drier.

Tropic of Cancer

Equator

Tropic of Capricorn

Once it has reached the troposphere the risen air is now cold and dry. This cold dry air begins to sink either side of the rising plume of equatorial air. As it sinks, the air begins to warm again by compression. The warming effect means the air can effectively evaporate any moisture remaining. These descending belts of air are therefore very dry and cloudless, giving rise to arid and semi-arid conditions either side of the equator. These areas are known as the Subtropical Highs and more or less coincide with the tropics. The high pressure is caused because the air is moving downwards, exerting a pushing force on the lower atmosphere.

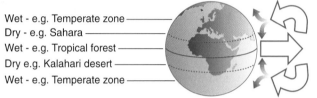

Wet - e.g. Temperate zone
Dry - e.g. Sahara
Wet - e.g. Tropical forest
Dry e.g. Kalahari desert
Wet - e.g. Temperate zone

Once landed the descending air splits into two flows, one poleward and one equatorward. The equatorward flow completes a circular flow known as the **Hadley Cell**.

In the polar regions, the cold dense air flows out towards the equator, pushed by its own weight. As this air moves towards the equator it meets the flow of warm air moving polewards from the tropics. The warm air has often had a chance to pick up moisture as it travelled out from the tropics, particularly if it moved over ocean areas. In the collision zone (the front between the polar and tropical air), the warm tropical air rises over the cold polar air and produces a region of generally high rainfall. This rain is caused by the renewed moisture in the tropical air cooling and condensing as it rises over the polar air.

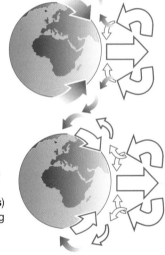

The final circuit is completed by the air that rose over the polar front descending into the polar regions. This maintains the high pressure of the polar regions. This final cell, the Polar Cell, also helps to explain why the upper air movements sweep pollutants such as chloroflurocarbons (**CFCs**) into the polar regions where they can do so much damage to the overlying ozone layer.

FIGURE 2.6 The
atmospheric heat budget
a) incoming and
b) outgoing radiation

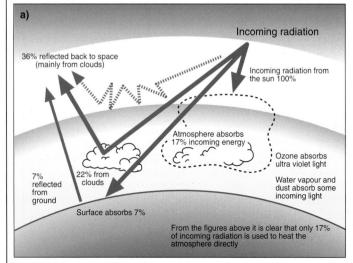

a)

Incoming radiation

36% reflected back to space (mainly from clouds)

Incoming radiation from the sun 100%

Atmosphere absorbs 17% incoming energy

Ozone absorbs ultra violet light

Water vapour and dust absorb some incoming light

7% reflected from ground

22% from clouds

Surface absorbs 7%

From the figures above it is clear that only 17% of incoming radiation is used to heat the atmosphere directly

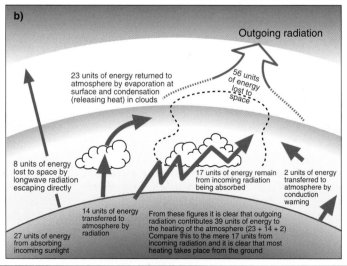

b)

Outgoing radiation

23 units of energy returned to atmosphere by evaporation at surface and condensation (releasing heat) in clouds

56 units of energy lost to space

8 units of energy lost to space by longwave radiation escaping directly

17 units of energy remain from incoming radiation being absorbed

2 units of energy transferred to atmosphere by conduction warning

14 units of energy transferred to atmosphere by radiation

27 units of energy from absorbing incoming sunlight

From these figures it is clear that outgoing radiation contributes 39 units of energy to the heating of the atmosphere (23 + 14 + 2) Compare this to the mere 17 units from incoming radiation and it is clear that most heating takes place from the ground

FIGURE 2.7 Satellite image of 6 August 1987. A severe storm system covers most of the British Isles

FIGURE 2.8 Influences on temperature

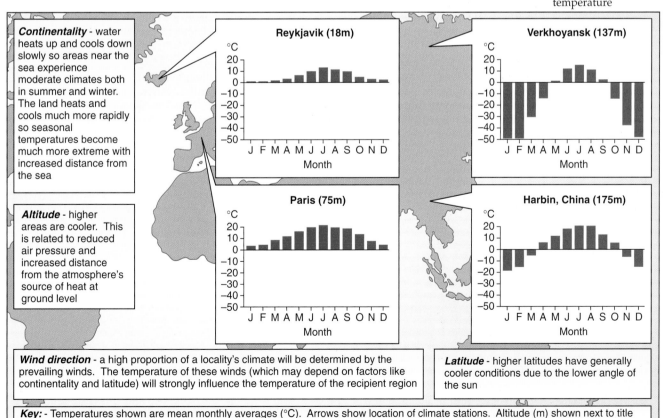

Continentality - water heats up and cools down slowly so areas near the sea experience moderate climates both in summer and winter. The land heats and cools much more rapidly so seasonal temperatures become much more extreme with increased distance from the sea

Altitude - higher areas are cooler. This is related to reduced air pressure and increased distance from the atmosphere's source of heat at ground level

Wind direction - a high proportion of a locality's climate will be determined by the prevailing winds. The temperature of these winds (which may depend on factors like continentality and latitude) will strongly influence the temperature of the recipient region

Latitude - higher latitudes have generally cooler conditions due to the lower angle of the sun

Key: - Temperatures shown are mean monthly averages (°C). Arrows show location of climate stations. Altitude (m) shown next to title satellite image (Figure 2.7) shows a typical **depression** moving across Britain. The streaming cloud spirals reflect high wind speeds formed as the cold air in the north and warm air in the south try to even out their pressures in a whirlpool motion of mixing.

In practice, temperatures are influenced by regional and global factors. These are summarised in Figure 2.8.

STUDENT ACTIVITY 2.2

Interpreting temperature patterns
1   Referring to Figure 2.8, explain the differences between each pair of climate graphs using the ideas given in the text (there are six possible pairings to explain). You may want to refer to an atlas to locate the places more precisely.

Pressure – the pressure exerted by the air resting on the ground is enormous. The atmosphere pushes down on the earth's surface with a weight of about 10 tonnes per m^2. This weight is affected by the temperature of the air. Warm air expands and so becomes less dense exerting a lower pressure on the ground beneath it. Cold air weighs more per unit volume and so exerts a higher pressure on the ground. Temperature differences cause pressure differences and these then cause winds to flow as air moves from a high pressure to a low pressure region. Pressure is also affected by the rising and falling of air masses (see Figure 2.5). Where air descends from the upper atmosphere (e.g. in the **Subtropical Highs**) the descending air weighs more heavily on the ground, raising the air pressure. At other locations fast winds in the upper troposphere suck up air from the lower atmosphere causing reduced air pressure. Droughts are associated with high pressure systems because the descending warm air evaporates moisture and clouds. The satellite image (Figure 2.7) shows the barren expanses of the northern Sahara – a region of persistent high pressure. By contrast, heavy rainfalls and flooding are associated with low pressure systems which produce rising air, condensation and clouds. Low pressure systems have well-developed boundaries where the low pressure air comes into contact with neighbouring air of a higher pressure. This pressure difference produces high windspeeds and may cause storm hazards. A final threat posed by low pressure systems like depressions and hurricanes is that of **storm surge**. The reduced weight of air over the low pressure in the storm centre allows the sea level nearby to rise, often up to several metres above normal. This can cause severe coastal flooding.

Humidity – moisture in the air controls how stable the air will be. Dry air is more stable than moist air. As air rises, the water vapour in the air will cool and then condense. As condensation takes place, heat is released. Air with a high water content (e.g. air masses over oceans) will experience much condensation. This will release more heat. The heat will encourage further convection with further condensation, further heat release and yet more convection. This may create large-scale convectional storms. So long as moist air continues to flow into the system, the storm will continue to grow, but as soon as it moves over land there is a tendency for the storm intensity to subside. This is noticeable with hurricanes. Consequently air masses with a high moisture content are associated with **tropical cyclones**, thunderstorms and flash flooding. Figure 2.7 shows a series of intense thunderstorms along the south western coast of Italy. Notice how localised each storm is, each capable of delivering damaging hailstorms, lightning or flash floods. Equally hazardous are air masses with a very low moisture content since these may result in droughts. Of all the climatic hazards it is probably drought, and the associated threats of famine and malnutrition, that cause most concern in developing nations. In the More Economically Developed Countries (MEDCs) the threat of windstorms undermines a $1 000 000 000 industry – the world insurance markets.

Wind hazards

Disasters caused by wind hazards are increasing. There may be a number of reasons for this but the bare facts are indisputable. Figure 2.9 shows the figures for windstorm disasters on a decade by decade basis from 1960 to 1990. The insurance industry is worried by the figures; in real terms (after adjusting for inflation etc) windstorms are costing the industry over 3.5 times more than in the 1960s. And the situation is worsening. In 1992 (after the table had been compiled) Hurricane Andrew cost the insurance industry $16 billion in one single storm and put nine insurance companies out of business. This cost was nearly as much as all of the storms in the 1980s added together!

The reasons for this increase in windstorm hazards are varied but undoubtedly involve the following considerations.
■ *Physical factors* may account for occasional periods of extreme climate. The **El Niño** event (a warm ocean current that regularly replaces the cold Peru Current off western South America) is linked

FIGURE 2.9 How real are the changes

Any three decades could be expected to have different values for storm damage, number of storms etc. Just because the figures in the table show a steady increase, we cannot conclude that the increase is significant or meaningful. To test for the significance of the trend we must employ an objective statistical technique. A suitable one in this case is the Chi- (pronounced kye) Squared Test.

First start with the *observed* values for the three decades. Using the figures for the number of storms we get three observed values – 8, 13 and 29 for the 1960s, 70s and 80s respectively. We then compare the observed values with the *expected* values we might get if there was no difference between the number of storms in each decade. In this case the total number of storms was 50 for the three decades, so the expected value would be 16.6 per decade (i.e. 50 ÷ 3).

For each cell in the table we can compare the expected value with the observed value. The more different these values are, the more likely it is that the differences in the table are *not* simply variations around a random figure but a genuine trend that needs explaining. The way we measure the size of these differences is by calculating a figure known as the Chi-squared value. This is shown by the Greek letter χ. The Chi-squared value is worked out from the following formula:

This symbol (sigma) means add together the results of the individual calculations for each cell in the table.

'O' is the observed value for the decade. 'E' is the expected value if each decade had exactly the same number of windstorms.

$$\chi = \sum \frac{(O - E)^2}{E}$$

Worked example using the figures below.

Decade	1960s	1970s	1980s	Total
Observed storms	8	13	29	50
Expected	16.6	16.6	16.6	50
$\frac{(O - E)^2}{E}$	4.45	0.78	9.26	

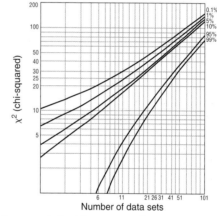

Chi-squared significance graph

$$\sum \frac{(O - E)^2}{E} = 4.45 + 0.78 + 9.26 = 14.49$$

The Chi-squared value is now plotted on a graph that shows the percentage likelihood of the Chi-squared result arising purely by chance. The Chi-squared value is read along the side of the graph. Along the bottom of the graph read off the number of data groups used – in this case three (one for each decade). The lines across the graph represent the probability of your result springing from an equal set of data groups. If there is less than 5 per cent chance of the Chi-squared value arising from an equal set of figures we can confidently assume that our figures are *not* equal and that there are significant differences between the data sets examined. In the context examined above we would conclude that *'There is a statistically significant difference between the storm frequency in each decade. Storms are definitely on the increase.'*

to extreme weather conditions in the Pacific but a notable reduction in North Atlantic hurricanes.
■ *Demographic factors* such as increased population totals and densities mean that more people exist in more vulnerable concentrations. This is worsened because some high-risk areas, such as coastlines, are being developed.
■ *Economic factors* such as increased standards of living make the cost of a windstorm higher than ever before.
■ *Technological factors* increase vulnerability because increased technology encourages higher levels of risk taking. For example, North Sea oil and

gas platforms in the 1990s are exposed to levels of windstorm risk that would have been unthinkable in the 1950s. Structures such as bridges, pylons, high-rise blocks and so on can be built to more ambitious limits with lighter modern materials but there are bigger risks if they fail.

Windstorm hazards include tropical cyclones (hurricanes), **extratropical storms** and tornadoes. Wind hazards are arguably more widespread than any other hazard. There is no country in the world that does not experience strong winds from time to time. Wind hazards have accounted for some 50 per cent of the 114 largest natural hazards between 1960

FIGURE 2.10 The effect of wind on structures

and 1989. The effects of wind hazard are very varied but Figure 2.10 summarises some of the effects of wind on structures. Because these effects are so varied, assessment of damage potential is difficult and the problem of prediction and preparation is increased. Some structures are more vulnerable than others because of age or design, but it is the insurers who are most economically vulnerable in a windstorm.

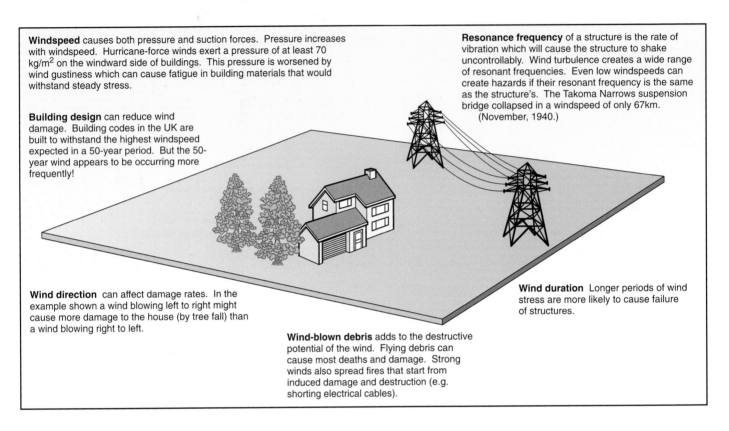

Windspeed causes both pressure and suction forces. Pressure increases with windspeed. Hurricane-force winds exert a pressure of at least 70 kg/m^2 on the windward side of buildings. This pressure is worsened by wind gustiness which can cause fatigue in building materials that would withstand steady stress.

Building design can reduce wind damage. Building codes in the UK are built to withstand the highest windspeed expected in a 50-year period. But the 50-year wind appears to be occurring more frequently!

Resonance frequency of a structure is the rate of vibration which will cause the structure to shake uncontrollably. Wind turbulence creates a wide range of resonant frequencies. Even low windspeeds can create hazards if their resonant frequency is the same as the structure's. The Takoma Narrows suspension bridge collapsed in a windspeed of only 67km. (November, 1940.)

Wind direction can affect damage rates. In the example shown a wind blowing left to right might cause more damage to the house (by tree fall) than a wind blowing right to left.

Wind-blown debris adds to the destructive potential of the wind. Flying debris can cause most deaths and damage. Strong winds also spread fires that start from induced damage and destruction (e.g. shorting electrical cables).

Wind duration Longer periods of wind stress are more likely to cause failure of structures.

Tropical storms and hurricanes

Different names, same creature:

A tropical cyclone with hurricane force winds is called a 'hurricane' in the Atlantic, a 'typhoon' in the Pacific and a 'tropical cyclone' in the Indian Ocean.

Significance of the hazard

There is a spectrum of tropical weather events that runs from the harmless to the full fury of a hurricane. Hurricanes (also known as typhoons or cyclones) are defined as rotating **tropical storms** with windspeeds in excess of 118kph. Although the havoc caused by hurricanes can be enormous they do have the advantage of predictability. There are 'hurricane seasons' within which more precautions can be taken. In the short term, **satellite imagery** usually provides several days' warning of a hurricane – time enough for lives to be saved even if property is lost. However, as we shall see below, advance warning may not benefit every community.

Origin of the hazard

The hurricane, or tropical cyclone, is the end product of a range of weather systems that can develop in the tropics. They all involve an area of low pressure into which warm moist air is drawn. Hurricanes are relatively small (average 650km diameter) but they are more intense than their temperate cousins – the familiar winter depression of the higher latitudes.

Small-scale weather disturbances (known as wave disturbances) may enlarge into rotating wind systems called tropical depressions. These in turn may grow into rapidly rotating wind systems called tropical cyclones. A tropical cyclone with windspeeds in the region of 63–120kph is known as a tropical storm whilst a tropical cyclone with speeds in excess of 120kph is a fully-fledged hurricane. On average, about 70 tropical storms will develop in a year. Just over 50 of these will become a full hurricane. The exact cause of hurricanes is uncertain but the following factors are important.

■ A location over the sea with sea surface temperatures above 27°C. This provides three things:

a) the initial heat energy;

b) the moisture that will power intense condensation and convection;

c) a friction-free surface that allows a rapid, continuous supply of warm moist air into the vortex.

■ A location at least 5° north or south of the equator. The coriolis effect (caused by the earth's rotation underneath the air movements of the atmosphere) causes maximum twisting of air movement near the poles but minimum near the equator. If the storm develops too close to the equator the weak coriolis effect will stop a circular air flow developing so that the low pressure disturbance will rapidly fill.

■ A location on the western side of oceans where the descending air from the Subtropical High pressure systems is weaker. This allows large-scale upward convection to occur.

■ The presence of an upper atmosphere air rotation which spreads air outwards (anticyclone). This ensures air sucked into the hurricane can spray out into the upper atmosphere. Without this the in-rushing air at ground level would simply fill the low pressure and the system would die.

Hazard vulnerability: physical factors

The effect of a hurricane on a community depends on physical, economic and political factors. Physically, damage will depend on several things. The intensity of the hurricane (measured from 1 to 5 on the Saffir Simpson Hurricane scale – see Figure 2.12) will be a major influence. The highest steady windspeeds ever recorded were 317kph in Hurricane Inez, 1976. The highest recorded gusts were in excess of 360kph. The hurricane intensity will be modified by the distance to the path of the hurricane – the 'storm corridor'. When Hurricane Hugo hit South Carolina in 1989, the destruction was significantly higher along the storm corridor. There is also a relationship between distance from the sea and amount of damage because the hurricane dies as it moves inland. Finally, whether a settlement lies to the right or left of a hurricane's path can influence the destruction caused. In the northern hemisphere, the hurricane rotates anticlockwise. The hurricane's travel speed (perhaps 50kph) is therefore added to the windspeeds on the right of its path but subtracted from those on its left. This can result in a 96kph difference in windspeed depending on which side

FIGURE 2.11 An insurer's nightmare

of the storm centre you lie! The travel speed also determines how long the hurricane takes to leave a location. Hurricanes usually nudge their vicious wind circulations along at a leisurely 6–50kph. Slower moving hurricane systems can cause more damage because the destructive winds take longer to move on. Hurricane Hugo caused more damage in the Virgin Islands than the Leeward Islands because it slowed from 32kph to a mere 14kph.

High relief will exaggerate already high hurricane rainfalls. Cyclone Hyacinthe (1980) dumped an incredible 2200mm of rain in two days on the 3000m high mountain peak on the island of Reunion. Flooding, arising from these high rainfalls, is often a major component of hurricane deaths and damage. Typhoon Thelma (November 1991) claimed 3000 lives in the Philippines. Most drowned in flash floods triggered by the torrential rain.

STUDENT ACTIVITY 2.3

Summarising hurricane hazards

1 Sketch a large version of Figure 2.13. Using examples in the text, annotate the sketch with a range of hurricane effects.

FIGURE 2.12 Saffir Simpson (SS) hurricane scale

SS	Description	Mean wind velocity		
		Metres per second (m/s)	Kph	Knots
1	Weak	32.7–42.6	118–153	64–82
2	Moderate	42.7–49.5	154–177	83–96
3	Strong	49.6–58.5	178–209	97–113
4	Very strong	58.6–69.4	210–249	114–134
5	Devastating	69.5–	250–	135–

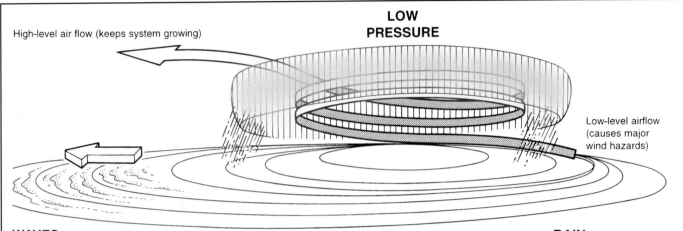

LOW PRESSURE

High-level air flow (keeps system growing)

Low-level airflow (causes major wind hazards)

WAVES

High winds spiralling out in front of the hurricane pile up the ocean into powerful waves that arrive ashore hours – even days – before the hurricane

SURGE

Atmospheric pressure beneath the hurricane eye falls by about 5% – equivalent to removing half a tonne of air per m^2 of ocean. The ocean heaves upwards under the reduced pressure to create a **storm surge**

WIND

Rising air currents suck in moist air from the surrounding ocean. This inflowing air rises, cools and condenses. Condensation releases more heat which draws in more air – a vicious circle of high windspeeds

RAIN

Intense condensation results in clouds up to heights of 12km. Such giant clouds produce enormous quantities of intense rain

FIGURE 2.13 Hurricanes – a multiple hazard

Landslides are equally dangerous in areas of high relief. Tropical storm Bret (August 1993) had a death toll of 150, many of whom were buried in their hillside shanties by mudflows triggered by the torrential rain. On the other hand, low relief will make a region more vulnerable to storm surges. Hurricane Audrey (1957) sent a 3.7m storm surge up to 40km inland through low-lying Louisiana in the USA. Tide timings may avert or create catastrophes by reducing or increasing storm surges. Hurricane Hugo hit South Carolina at high tide, increasing flood levels by 6m. These surges are worsened by wind-whipped waves up to 10m high. Coastal flooding can be the main killer in a hurricane. In 1970 a 6m storm tide killed 300 000 people in the Ganges delta region of Bangladesh. Hurricanes, therefore, represent a mixture of hazards. Figure 2.13 summarises these component problems. Once the hurricane strikes, damage, death and destruction may depend more on economic and political factors than anything else.

Hazard vulnerability: human factors

A wide range of economic and political factors contribute to a community's resistance to hazards. Economically the patterns of death and damage are related to the stage of development of the affected

nation. Poorer countries suffer because building codes, warning systems, defences, emergency service and communications **infrastructure** may be inadequate, resulting in high death tolls. Wealthier countries stand a better chance of evacuating people in time but have more to lose in simple material terms. Figure 2.14 illustrates the point.

The death tolls illustrate the huge differences between the vulnerability of American and Bangladeshi citizens but the damage totals can be misleading. The raw figures suggest that the USA suffered more damage because of the higher costs incurred but this is not true. The USA suffered a higher monetary cost because the buildings, contents and infrastructure had a higher monetary value. However, money is not necessarily a reliable measure since the loss of a home has a big impact on a family whatever it cost. Indeed the loss of an American home worth $150 000 (and covered by insurance) may be less significant than a tin and wood shack on the Ganges delta that represents years of irreplaceable (and uninsured) savings. A study of death tolls in the 1977 cyclone in Andhra Pradesh showed that a range of factors varying from wealth to local ecology had a marked influence on death rates (see Figure 2.15). Political factors influence the underlying causes of poverty and vulnerability,

FIGURE 2.14 Hazard resistance

Event	Date	Windspeed	Death toll	Damage ($US)
Cyclone Gorky (Bangladesh)	May 1991	232kph	131 000	1700 M
Hurricane Andrew (USA)	August 1992	264kph	60	20 000 M

but it is not simply national politics and priorities which are to blame. International relationships are also responsible as shown in the 1988 Hurricane Gilbert in Jamaica.

Prior to Hurricane Gilbert, Jamaica was already in debt – partly as a result of previous hurricane damage. The high interest repayments on the debts saw the Jamaican Government attempting to improve their economy by reducing inflation (by raising interest rates) and cutting public spending. The increased interest rates reduced profits in the construction industry and houses were built cheaply and shoddily. Cutbacks in health budgets reduced nutritional levels in a country where more than 30 per cent of the population live in poverty, more than 50 per cent of women of childbearing age are anaemic and 50 000 children under five are malnourished. The combination of declining building standards and decreasing healthcare served to increase Jamaica's vulnerability. Hurricane Gilbert caused huge losses to Jamaica's economy, estimated at some US $7 billion. This further increased Jamaica's debt, so the Government is now looking at the possibility of mining peat from Jamaica's coastal wetlands to provide a cheap fuel source. This will help the balance of payments and, economically, makes sense. Unfortunately, it would also remove the first line of defence against hurricane surges. To pay for the repairs from the last hurricane it seems Jamaica has to increase its vulnerability to the next – a very vicious 'vicious circle'.

If the burden of Third World debt could be reduced, LEDCs could increase their 'disaster resistance' by focusing investment on development schemes aimed to improve the welfare of the rural poor.

The politics of war can have positive and negative effects on hurricane vulnerability. Hurricane Joan hit Nicaragua in 1988. The economy was already weakened by a long-running war of attrition with the US-backed Contras and an economic embargo imposed by the US. A combination of guerrilla warfare and US economic policy meant that the hurricane damage gave a significant shock to the economy. War reduced the country's ability to cope. By complete contrast North Vietnam suffered a cyclone storm surge in 1971 on the Red River delta but the existence of efficient wartime communication and organisation networks at village level reduced a potential multi-thousand death toll to a few hundred.

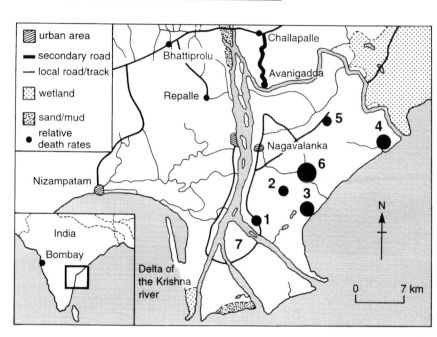

FIGURE 2.15 Patterns of vulnerability: the distribution of deaths in the 1977 Andrha Pradesh cyclone

---

STUDENT ACTIVITY 2.4

Flow diagram for hurricane vulnerability
1 Construct a flow diagram based on the Jamaican case study to illustrate the cycle of vulnerability that can trap a developing country.

STUDENT ACTIVITY 2.5

Summary sketch map of the Andhra Pradesh Cyclone, India
1 Using the information in Figure 2.15, produce an annotated sketch map to highlight the key points of this case study with colour coding. Use two colours for vulnerability during and after the hazard.
2 From the above it is clear that the disaster was: a) waiting to happen; and b) is likely to be repeated. The following responses would all contribute to reducing the impacts of the next cyclone.

Better warning and evacuation procedures; Build embankments around settlements; Grants for storm-proofing houses; Better road/transport infrastructure to aid evacuation; Construct elevated community buildings to double as cyclone shelters; Construct bridge to link islands; Set up community groups to strengthen political voice of landless classes; Improve sanitation to reduce disease risk after flooding; Set up co-operative bank schemes with emphasis on low-interest, high-access credit; Plant shelter belts along coastal margins; Protect existing mangrove swamps from felling; Upgrade meteorological stations with weather radar; Education programmes aimed at preparing communities for storm hazard; Literacy programmes to increase local skills base; Primary healthcare programmes to improve post-flood disease resistance; Land redistribution and zoning to enable village resettlement; Set up relief camps.
Group the responses above into a table as shown below.

Tackling the cause Tackling the effects	Politically likely	Politically unlikely

3 The main response after the 1977 Andhra Pradesh cyclone was to improve the warning system and improve evacuation procedures. In 1990 this area was again hit by a cyclone but 650 000 people were evacuated by 2000 teams and 1000 temporary relief camps were set up. The casualties were only 5–10 per cent of the 1977 figures. Suggest reasons why: a) these responses were chosen; and b) the other available responses were ignored.

FIGURE 2.16 Windstorm deaths and damage totals

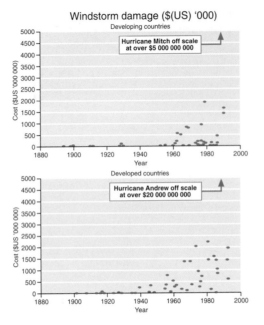

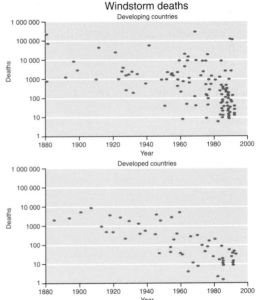

Extratropical storms

From the point of view of insurance, the biggest increase in risk is not the increase in hurricane incidence but the increase in temperate storms. As can be seen from the graph of wind disasters (Figure 2.16), the majority of hurricane deaths occur in LEDCs. By contrast, MEDCs appear to suffer more damage. The 1990 winter storms in Europe caused more than $10 billion damage to the insurance industry. The chief causes of these storms are the depressions that track from west to east across the temperate latitudes. Extratropical storms have some similarities to hurricanes – they form over the sea where friction is low, develop into rotating wind systems and are refuelled by heat released from condensing air – but there are also big differences. Hurricanes depend on convection over a warm sea but temperate depressions are more dependent on interactions between contrasting air masses. Depressions cover bigger areas than hurricanes (2000km compared to 1000km) but generate lower windspeeds, rarely exceeding 200kph in the most exposed coastal locations. The origin of the depression is complex but the key ideas are summarised in Figure 2.17. These storms are most common in winter because the extremely low temperatures of the arctic winter increase the contrast in air mass temperatures at the polar front, the conflict zone where the depressions form.

Although extratropical storms have lower windspeeds than hurricanes they cause far more problems for the insurance industry. The reasons for this include:
■ the large number of storms produced (between January and February 1990 eight storms crossed Europe);
■ the concentration of insured wealth in densely populated industrialised countries;
■ the larger size of the storm affecting a greater area – several million km²;

■ the variety of effects produced. These include the 'hurricane' suite (wind, rain, flood, wave damage and storm surge) but may also include snow with devastating impacts on transport and commerce.

Some parts of Europe are more susceptible to storm damage than others, as can be seen in the case study of the 1990 European storms shown in Figure 2.18.

STUDENT ACTIVITY 2.6

Windstorm deaths and damage in MEDCs and LEDCs
1   Referring to the graphs in Figure 2.16, comment on:
a) the differences between MEDCs and LEDCs in terms of death and damage patterns;
b) the similarities between the patterns.
Try to explain your observations.

STUDENT ACTIVITY 2.7

Impact of the European storms, 1990
Refer to Figures 2.18 and 2.19 and an atlas map of population densities.
1   On an outline map of Europe, plot a bar chart for each country to show the total loss and shade in the percentage of the bar that represents the insured losses.
2   Describe the pattern of total losses, relating them to geographical location (coastal areas and wind exposure, low-lying areas and flood risk), storm tracks and population densities.
3   Comment on the degree of insurance cover and how it varied from country to country (why might some countries be better covered?).
4   Comment on the impacts of these storms on the insurance industry.

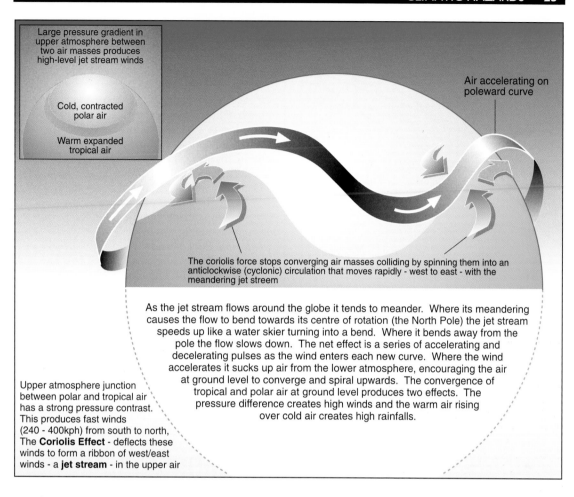

FIGURE 2.17 The origin of extratropical storms

Large pressure gradient in upper atmosphere between two air masses produces high-level jet stream winds

Cold, contracted polar air

Warm expanded tropical air

Air accelerating on poleward curve

The coriolis force stops converging air masses colliding by spinning them into an anticlockwise (cyclonic) circulation that moves rapidly - west to east - with the meandering jet streem

As the jet stream flows around the globe it tends to meander. Where its meandering causes the flow to bend towards its centre of rotation (the North Pole) the jet stream speeds up like a water skier turning into a bend. Where it bends away from the pole the flow slows down. The net effect is a series of accelerating and decelerating pulses as the wind enters each new curve. Where the wind accelerates it sucks up air from the lower atmosphere, encouraging the air at ground level to converge and spiral upwards. The convergence of tropical and polar air at ground level produces two effects. The pressure difference creates high winds and the warm air rising over cold air creates high rainfalls.

Upper atmosphere junction between polar and tropical air has a strong pressure contrast. This produces fast winds (240 - 400kph) from south to north, The **Coriolis Effect** - deflects these winds to form a ribbon of west/east winds - a **jet stream** - in the upper air

Adjusting to wind hazards

The normal hazard responses include: avoid the hazard; modify the hazard causes; reduce the hazard effects; or do nothing. In the case of wind hazard there is little that can be done to modify the gigantic weather systems that pose threats to human activities so the key responses are avoidance or reduction of vulnerability. Hazard prediction is a useful tool by which avoidance and vulnerability reduction can be achieved. In the long term, maps showing storm probability help to pin-point areas where future developments may need to be minimised or existing settlements protected. Figure 2.20 shows how hurricane probabilities vary for the western Pacific. By combining these probabilities with information on population densities, indications of risk and vulnerability can be obtained.

Country	Total losses (million Deutschmark)	Insured losses (million Deutschmark)
Austria	400	260
Belgium	1 800	1 100
Denmark	300	150
France	3 400	2 300
Germany	7 100	3 550
Great Britain	8 200	7 240
Luxembourg	600	400
Netherlands	3 000	1 950
Scandinavia	200	100
Switzerland	300	200
Total	**25 300**	**17 250**

FIGURE 2.18 Case study of 1990 European storms

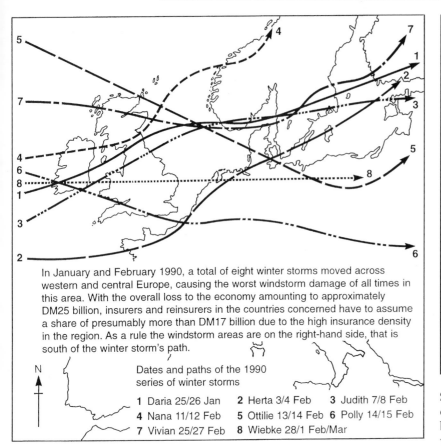

In January and February 1990, a total of eight winter storms moved across western and central Europe, causing the worst windstorm damage of all times in this area. With the overall loss to the economy amounting to approximately DM25 billion, insurers and reinsurers in the countries concerned have to assume a share of presumably more than DM17 billion due to the high insurance density in the region. As a rule the windstorm areas are on the right-hand side, that is south of the winter storm's path.

N

Dates and paths of the 1990 series of winter storms

1 Daria 25/26 Jan	**2** Herta 3/4 Feb	**3** Judith 7/8 Feb
4 Nana 11/12 Feb	**5** Ottilie 13/14 Feb	**6** Polly 14/15 Feb
7 Vivian 25/27 Feb	**8** Wiebke 28/1 Feb/Mar	

FIGURE 2.19 Windstorm tracks over Europe, 1990

From this exercise it is clear that long-term planning could be based on such records. Shorter-term predictions of hurricane landfalls are reasonably accurate within a 24-hour period but – to avoid overwarning – evacuation orders are not usually given until 10 hours before landfall. Longer than this and the accuracy declines and with it the credibility of the warning system. A 10-hour forecast can be vital in saving lives by evacuating areas at risk. There are potential difficulties, however, on densely urbanised coastlines. A hurricane tracking across Florida from Miami to Tampa could have 1 million people living in the storm corridor. How do you evacuate 1 million people in 10 hours? Where do they go to? And is it safer facing a hurricane in a boarded-up house or in a car on a 15km traffic tailback in torrential wind and rain? And should people evacuate?

Studies show that houses experience lower levels of damage if occupied during a hurricane. This is because small problems (like corrugated tin roofs working loose) can be repaired rapidly before they develop into large-scale structural failures. But whether evacuation is desirable or not, it is certainly not easy. If it is difficult to evacuate Florida in the face of a hurricane, how easy is it to evacuate Bangladesh where there is little transport infrastructure, few bridges and few boats? Although weather satellites enable us to predict the storm path more accurately than ever before there are still false warnings because hurricanes possess an eerie instinct for survival which includes last-minute course changes. Passage over land weakens the storm by increasing wind friction and reducing the essential moist air flow which fuels the whole system, so hurricanes avoid land for as long as possible, even diverting their courses to miss islands (Figure 2.21). This response is due in part to the frictional slowing that the spinning winds 'feel' as they approach land. The slower winds on one side of the system upset the equilibrium,

FIGURE 2.20 Western Pacific hurricane patterns, 1940–80

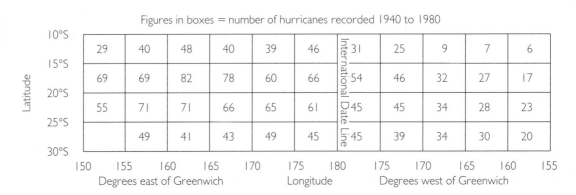

Figures in boxes = number of hurricanes recorded 1940 to 1980

Latitude											
10°S	29	40	48	40	39	46	31	25	9	7	6
15°S	69	69	82	78	60	66	54	46	32	27	17
20°S	55	71	71	66	65	61	45	45	34	28	23
25°S	49	41	43	49	45	45	39	34	30	20
30°S											

150	155	160	165	170	175	180	175	170	165	160	155

Degrees east of Greenwich   Longitude   Degrees west of Greenwich

(International Date Line)

diverting the system in the way a spinning top might change course if it made temporary contact with a wall.

If prediction and avoidance of hurricanes is difficult, prediction and avoidance of extratropical storms is far more difficult. They are harder to predict because their courses depend not only on the character of the surface over which they pass but also the invisible character of the jet stream movements in the upper atmosphere. Avoidance by evacuation is normally inappropriate because the windspeeds are lower than in a hurricane and the area of the storm is too big to easily avoid. Nonetheless, evacuation warnings are important parts of hazard response in the low-lying areas of eastern England and along the coast of Holland. Wind hazards in urban areas can be reduced by good planning and building design. Figure 2.22 shows how urban structures can produce very high windspeeds. The effects of high winds around large structures can vary from nuisance value (hats blown off pedestrians) to structural damage or collapse. Three cooling towers over 100m high

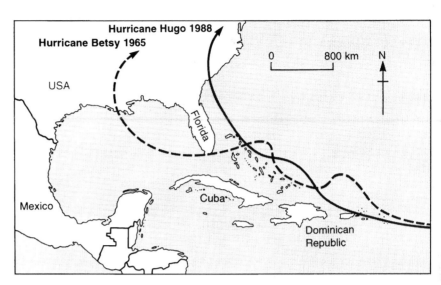

FIGURE 2.21 Selected hurricane tracks showing 'avoidance' behaviour

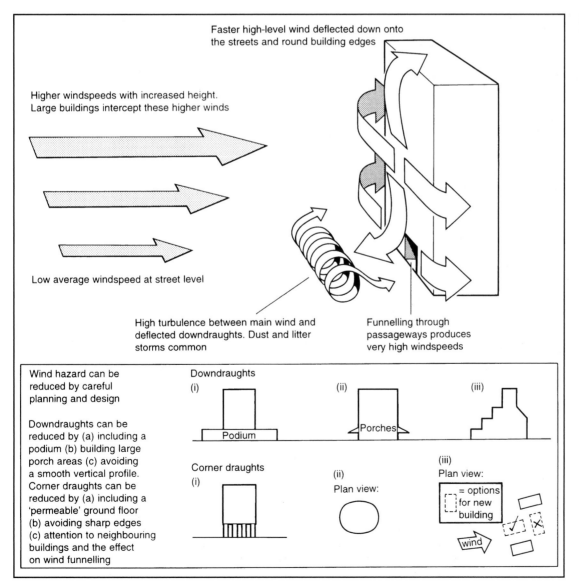

FIGURE 2.22 Building design and wind hazard

FIGURE 2.23 Responding to wind hazard: there are a variety of responses to wind hazard. Priorities depend on stage of development shown

LEDCS

■ Reduce the debt burden so that countries are not forced to exploit the natural defences offered by intact ecosystems such as forests, wetlands and mangrove swamps.

■ Encourage development policies that diversify the economy so that the poor do not need to live near flood-prone land for a livelihood.

■ Encourage rural development so that high vulnerability urban areas grow more slowly.

■ Improve primary healthcare so that the population is more resistant to disease in the aftermath of a disaster.

■ Improve warning systems and organisational structures for evacuation.

■ Improve communications infrastructure to enable more rapid evacuation.

■ Increase the access of the poor to low-interest loans to increase their recovery prospects after a disaster.

■ Use planning controls to prevent building in vulnerable areas.

■ Use traditional house designs to reduce wind impact (e.g. thick, low walls and shallow angle roofs of Scottish crofts).

MEDCS

■ Improve land-use planning to discourage housing in high-risk areas, e.g. barrier islands.

■ Promote education on 'hurricane drill' in affected regions.

■ Tighten building regulations in high-risk areas.

■ Invest in protective structures, e.g. flood barriers, dykes, etc.

■ Continue to develop the science of prediction by investing in appropriate technology and research.

■ Improve modelling of wind vulnerability on large-scale structures such as high-rise buildings and bridges.

■ Design urban areas with 'wind abatement' structures, e.g. porches, podiums, 'soft' storeys.

■ Relate insurance premiums to wind hazard potential to discourage poor siting.

collapsed at Ferry Bridge power station in England as a result of wind flows around the neighbouring towers.

The alternative to avoiding storm damage is to reduce the vulnerability of a population to storm effects. Some of these ideas have been discussed above (see Figure 2.15) but the options can be summarised as in Figure 2.23 going from the large-scale to the smaller-scale solution. From the two lists it is clear that the responses to wind hazard are

very different according to degree of development. This reflects the fact that wind hazard is mainly an inconvenience in developed countries (even if a very expensive one) whilst it is still a matter of life or death in the developing world. This contrast in the effects of a particular hazard is seen even more clearly in the next section covering the hazard of drought.

Drought hazard

Drought is often quoted as one of the major natural hazards of the developing world. This reputation is not without foundation. The worst storms may kill a few hundred thousand but drought killed tens of thousands in India in 1770 and just under 10 million in China in 1878. Drought is different from other climatic hazards and unlike hurricanes or floods, never directly kills people but people die of the consequent hunger.

Drought may cause lower crop yields but access to food depends on more than this. Political, social and economic factors all have a major part to play and the climatology of the region is only one factor among many. Nevertheless, locations prone to drought can be identified and understanding the nature of dry areas is an important starting point.

Arid and semi-arid areas are defined by the variability of their rainfall as much as its scarcity. Rainfall may be non-existent for months, then a

single storm delivers the equivalent of a year's average rainfall. Productivity varies with the rainfall and can be quite high given suitable conditions. The photographs in Figure 2.28 show a range of semi-arid landscapes. Most plants in such areas are adapted to drought and have deep roots, small leaves (reduced evapotranspiration), thorns (protection against hungry predators) or a rapid life cycle that capitalises on the short wet spells. The intense but short-lived nature of tropical rain storms encourages rapid runoff. In order to store this water, soils need to be reasonably thick and protected by a vegetation layer. Where overgrazing has removed this, rain may be as much a problem as a solution and rapid erosion may result. There are also longer-term trends in the climates of these areas.

The desert climate varies over a period of decades. In the 1950s and 1960s, rainfall in the Sahel region (south of the Sahara) was higher than the long-term average. During the 1970s and 1980s rainfall was lower than average. Successive years of lower than average rainfalls are difficult to cope with if the economy is based on agriculture.

Distribution of drought hazard

On a global scale, drought-prone areas can be predicted with reasonable accuracy:

- Tropical high-pressure zones (near the tropics of Cancer and Capricorn) will have low rainfalls since the air warms as it descends (Figure 2.13). This results in atmospheric moisture evaporating, leaving few clouds and little rain. Examples include the Sahara and Arabian deserts.
- Mid-continental areas (e.g. the Gobi desert) have low rainfalls due to their distance from the moist oceanic air.
- Lee coast deserts (e.g. the Kalahari desert) form where the prevailing winds across a continent bring the dry interior air over the coast. This means that the coastal areas are less moist than expected since the air is blowing offshore from the dry interior rather than onshore from the sea. They can occur on the east coast of continental regions (if the prevailing winds are westerly) such as the Patagonian desert but are more commonly found on the west coasts of continental areas where the easterly prevailing winds of the tropics blow dry air out across the western coasts.
- Rainshadow deserts are found where dry air descends in the lee of a mountain range (e.g. the Atacama desert in South America). Much of the air's moisture is rained out on the windward slopes so the remaining air is dry as it descends on the lee slopes of the mountains.

Whilst these areas are all drought-prone, their lack of rainfall is seldom considered a natural hazard since the populations that live in these desert areas are generally small, dispersed and well-adapted to drought. The greater threat is found in the semi-arid regions adjacent to the desert areas. Here seasonal rainfall often maintains relatively high agricultural populations in monsoon or savannah climates. In this context, any change in the patterns of rainfall can increase the vulnerability of millions of people. As Figure 2.24 shows, drought may be only one factor among many, but because of its unpredictability, it may be the one to trigger a host of other changes.

Drought in the western Pacific – 1997–8

The El Niño effect is second only to the seasons in terms of its impact on global weather and climate. These case studies look at two contrasting impacts of a recent El Niño in the western Pacific. The impacts differed largely as a result of human influences. It is important to recognise that any hazard is a mixture of physical processes and human vulnerability. Human vulnerability is often more complex and difficult to remedy than the physical event itself.

A strong El Niño effect in 1997–8 caused a reversal in the normal ocean-current patterns in the Pacific Ocean. The normal situation has very warm water in the western Pacific near Papua New Guinea and Indonesia and cooler water in the East near Peru and Chile. The steady trade winds blow from east to west and help maintain the piling of warm water downwind in the western Pacific. This warm water encourages active convection in the air above. This convection results in thunderstorms and heavy reliable rainfall. As a result of the steady trade winds blowing towards the west, the sea level

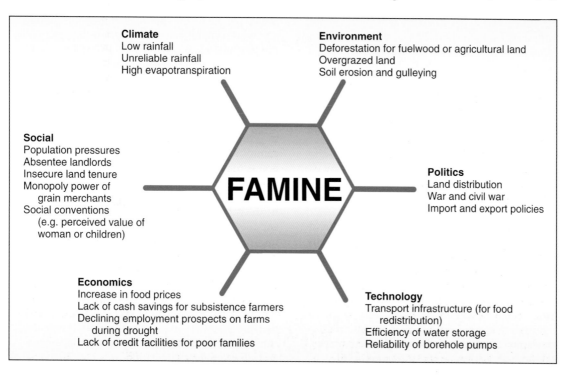

FIGURE 2.24 Factors influencing famine

Climate
Low rainfall
Unreliable rainfall
High evapotranspiration

Environment
Deforestation for fuelwood or agricultural land
Overgrazed land
Soil erosion and gulleying

Social
Population pressures
Absentee landlords
Insecure land tenure
Monopoly power of
    grain merchants
Social conventions
    (e.g. perceived value of
    woman or children)

FAMINE

Politics
Land distribution
War and civil war
Import and export policies

Economics
Increase in food prices
Lack of cash savings for subsistence farmers
Declining employment prospects on farms
    during drought
Lack of credit facilities for poor families

Technology
Transport infrastructure (for food
    redistribution)
Efficiency of water storage
Reliability of borehole pumps

FIGURE 2.25 Normal year/E1 Niño year

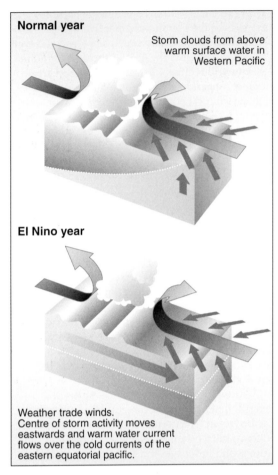

Normal year

Storm clouds from above warm surface water in Western Pacific

El Nino year

Weather trade winds.
Centre of storm activity moves eastwards and warm water current flows over the cold currents of the eastern equatorial pacific.

is actually higher in the western Pacific than the east. Occasionally, for reasons that are not understood, the trade winds weaken and the pile of the warm water in the west slides out towards the eastern Pacific. As the warm water pile slips across the breadth of the Pacific it takes with it the convectional rainfall. Suddenly the warmest (and therefore wettest) parts of the Pacific have moved from the west to the east. The west then experiences drought conditions while the normally dry east experiences record rainfall, flash floods and mudflows. In the El Niño of 1997–8, Indonesia and Papua New Guinea were both badly hit by drought.

Drought case study 1: Papua New Guinea – drought, agriculture, health and political conflict

Papua New Guinea is a mineral rich country with enormous economic potential but a poor infrastructure in this land of high mountains and steep-sided valleys. Papua New Guinea normally has an abundant rainfall but in 1997 had no significant rain from May until December. By September food was running out in many remote provinces where drought destroyed village crops. Around eighty people were dead, with up to seven hundred thousand facing starvation. Although some rain fell in mid-December '97 and January 1998 and allowed some replanting there was still

the problem of survival until the new crops were ready for harvest. In January 60 000 people faced life-threatening food shortages, 260 000 people found themselves with no food other than what they could collect from the wild and 980 000 with 'inadequate food supply'. Forty per cent of the rural dwellers in PNG were suffering severe food shortage. In terms of water, 47 000 people had extremely limited and contaminated water available to them and another 363 000 were carrying water of poor quality for excessive distances.

Drought is a slow-onset hazard and a slow killer. There were many reports of people dying from the complications of eating 'bush' food in the wild. The incidence of severe malaria increased in at least three provinces as higher temperatures helped mosquitoes complete their life cycles more quickly. Figures are difficult to get but it seems 500–700 died directly from drought-related causes – mainly the very old and the very young.

The impact of the drought was worsened by poverty. The World Bank estimates that 80 per cent of the population earn less than $350 a year. This poverty is in spite of the huge mineral wealth of the region. In a land of tribal diversity, the obligation to support one's kin through jobs, money and gifts is very strong – a system of patronage and favours known as Wantok. Unfortunately the Wantok system can create corruption and favouritism. Elections are often fought on the basis of tribal priorities and the high turnover among M.P.s – up to 60 per cent at each election – gives them little opportunity to pursue long-term policies. The absence of consistent and objective long-term planning means that an estimated 77 per cent of the population have no access to regular long-term water supplies and basic health and education have been underfunded for years.

More than 1740 MT of food aid was delivered to 60 000 people facing life-threatening food shortages and who were only accessible by air. In April 1998 the World Bank approved a US $5 million loan for Papua New Guinea to help finance an El Niño Drought Response Project. The project will help rural Papua New Guineans cope with drought and other natural disasters. The project is made up of three complementary parts:
■ a rural works program – involving local communities in 'public works projects' to maintain access roads, drains, erodible sites, schools, health facilities, sewerage systems, airstrips, and foot bridges;
■ the provision and maintenance of rural water supplies – by constructing new wells and improving existing water supply systems at strategic locations (e.g. schools, hospitals, health posts);
■ agricultural research into the selection and breeding of drought- and frost-tolerant varieties of PNG's major staple food crops (sweet potato, taro, banana, cassava, yam, and sago palm). It will also support research into soil moisture management and supplementary irrigation.

Drought Case Study 2: Indonesia – fires and regional air pollution

In the dry season in Indonesia, small-scale farmers clear their land using fire. In drought years these fires can get out of control as in the previous big El Niño event in 1982 where an area bigger than Belgium burned out of control. But the 1997 fires were different in many ways. They were smaller than the terrible fires of 1982 but they caused far greater problems and their causes were less excusable. The 1997 Indonesian fires spread rapidly because of the El Niño drought conditions in the western Pacific. But there were many additional human elements:

■ deforestation had already opened up large areas of the canopy, allowing the forest to dry more effectively;

■ government policies in Indonesia include extending oil plantations, converting swamp land to rice production and maintaining position as a leading wood exporter – both of these involve clearance of forest areas by fire;

■ unjust land deals take place where the government allow plantation companies to clear and plant land that has been traditionally used by tribal groups. Fires are sometimes used to try to drive the protesting tribes away from the area;

■ much of the area being burned consisted of peaty swamp forest. Peat fires burn with a huge release of smoke and they can burn for over a year.

In the summer of 1997 smoke from the fires became so dense and widespread that an estimated 20 million people in the SE Asia region suffered respiratory problems. 300 died as a result of aircraft and shipping accidents. On the islands of Borneo and Sumatra where the fires were worst people were evacuated because the fires were completely out of control. In Indonesia, 8 000 firefighters were called in to tackle the fires. Neighbouring Malaysia sent another 1 200 but it is not easy fighting fires in an area which has had no rain for 6 months and has little water available!

The Indonesian government is – directly or indirectly – responsible for much of the fire damage. They have the means to reduce the problem through legislation – Indonesian law allows up to 10 years in jail or a $33 000 fine for deliberately setting fire to land. But this law has not been enforced to date. The costs of the smog are difficult to accurately measure but – in simple economic terms – tourist bookings for South-east Asia fell by a third – a cost of nearly 20 million US dollars to the Indonesian National Airline alone. In addition to economic costs are the environmental costs to wildlife. Orangutan, the Sumatran rhino, tigers and other endangered species live in these forests. The combination of reduced habitat and the stresses of thick smog will do little for their chances of survival.

The fires of Indonesia are a classic case of natural hazards being less an 'Act of God' and more an act of human foolishness, ignorance or both. El Niño-induced drought is semi-predictable in that El Niño

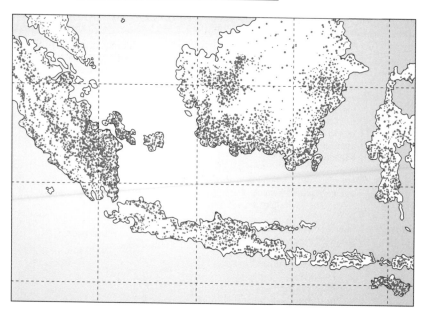

FIGURE 2.26 Location of fires in SE Asia during 1997, based on NASA/ NOAA satellite imagery

events build up gradually and so there is usually a few months warning. There are few excuses for drought-induced fires when policies encourage forest clearance during El Niño conditions. The subcontinental scale of the smog impacts suggests a need for international co-operation when responding to hazards.

Responding to drought hazard: the Indian Famine Codes

Traditional responses to drought have gradually become eroded over the last 30–50 years and yet no other responses have been effectively organised to replace them. The first recorded attempt to organise against drought is recorded in the Bible where Pharaoh dreams of seven 'years of plenty' followed by seven 'lean years' (Genesis, chapter 41). Joseph both interprets the meaning of the dream and organises effective storage of surplus grain during the years of plenty. His successes (both economically and politically) were due to the accuracy of the forecasts. Unfortunately most present governments cannot rely on the same sources that Joseph used, so preparation needs to be more systematised. A successful system used by the British Government in India from 1883 onwards was known as the Famine Codes. These were a series of staged responses to increasing drought stress and relief was organised so 'as not to check the growth of thrift and self-reliance among the people or to impair the structure of society …'. Whilst the success of the Codes relied in part on the strong centralised authority of an Imperial power there were many insights that could usefully be adopted today. The basic principles are outlined below:

■ labour-intensive public works schemes (e.g. building dams, reservoirs etc) to be set up to create employment;

■ relief in the form of raw grain or money to be distributed on a local basis by local officials;

TECHNOLOGICAL RESPONSES TO DROUGHT

Method	Examples
Improved forecasting	Monitoring of El Niño and other **Sea Surface Temperature** anomalies (**SSTs**) may give advance warning of droughts caused by complex atmospheric **teleconnections**. Examples include droughts in Australia during El Niño years and droughts in the Sahel following large spring temperature differences between the southern and northern oceans. In 1988 the British Meteorological Office predicted a Sahel drought but noticed a sudden alteration in ocean currents during May. This led them to revise their predictions from drought to higher than average rain. Within a few months the Sahel had experienced its wettest rainy season for 20 years.
Ecosystem monitoring	Using satellite monitoring to spot early stages of degradation allows rapid responses. Unfortunately knowing the problem doesn't necessarily make it easier to know how to respond!
Improved water conservation and agriculture	Improvements can be either *low tech* or *high tech*. Low-tech improvements include: • stone bunds across fields to reduce overland flow; • use of mulches to retain rainfall and soil moisture; • creating miniature basins for tree planting; • use of small earth dams to store water; • use of stone piles to increase fog interception; • use of agroforestry, (combine low-density forestry with traditional agriculture). High-tech improvements include: • drip and sprinkle irrigation; • increased use of fertiliser; • increased mechanisation of farming; • use of genetically engineered drought-resistant crop varieties; • use of steel or concrete storage silos to protect harvest from pest damage.

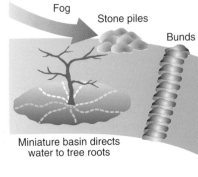

Miniature basin directs water to tree roots

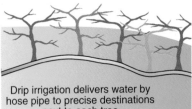

Drip irrigation delivers water by hose pipe to precise destinations next to each tree

FIGURE 2.27
Technological responses to drought

were cultivators and labourers who were thrown out of employment, traders deprived of profits derived from the poorer classes, aged or weakly dependants and public beggars. By recognising with surprising clarity the human and economic dimensions of drought and famine, the Famine Codes were able to target appropriate help.

The Codes included detailed instructions on the organisation of famine preparedness. Districts would declare '*Scarcity*' at an early stage of drought, later moving up to '*Famine*' if conditions worsened. Relief was organised by a chain of responsibilities starting with the District Commissioner who liaised with the District Officer who in turn received information from Inspectors of Village Records (Kanungos) who looked after the work of Village Accountants (Patwaris). The latter worked with the Village Headmen in preparing lists of the infirm and needy. Much emphasis was placed on the importance of saving the cattle so that ploughing could continue when the drought eventually broke.

In addition to the organisational responses to drought there are technological responses which could prove promising under certain circumstances. These range from long-term drought forecasting based on ocean current changes to improved ecosystem monitoring, water conservation, agricultural techniques or even genetically improved plants. These responses are shown in Figure 2.27. One of the choices facing LEDCs is whether to opt for a hi-tech or low-tech response. Low-tech responses are often the cheapest and easiest to implement but it is significant that most are labour intensive and need high rural populations. This provides an important counterbalance to the current emphasis on population control in developing countries. High populations may – with the right type of agricultural policies – be part of the solution rather than part of the problem. In the Yanchi area of China's Gobi desert, reclamation schemes involve a variety of approaches such as tree planting, digging and removal of salt crusts, digging up and mixing in soils buried by sand encroachment and the 'planting' of straw blocks to reduce wind erosion. Without abundant cheap labour, such reclamation schemes would be impossible.

■ private trade and local markets were encouraged to distribute food, and government interference in local markets was kept to a minimum;
■ local landowners to be given access to easy loans to encourage them to open work schemes on their estates to provide employment for labourers and tenants;
■ land rents to be suspended during the drought period;
■ easy credit was to be made available to small farmers for purchasing seeds and bullocks;
■ the cost of relief was to be mainly met by local taxation and the organisation of relief was to be locally administered. Central Government would provide a safety net in case of excess tax burden;
■ arrangements to be made to allow the migration of cattle to forested areas during drought;
■ an annual 'Famine Relief and Insurance' component was built in to the state budget.

The Famine Codes were based on the assumption that the largest population likely to be affected by drought at any one time was about 30 million people and that the main victims of famine

FIGURE 2.28 Responding to arid landscapes

STUDENT ACTIVITY 2.10

Technological responses to drought
1 Refer to Figures 2.27 and 2.28. Sketch each photo in Figure 2.28 in turn and use annotations to include the technological responses that you would feel appropriate for the context shown.

Drought in the developed world

Drought in wealthy countries disrupts lifestyle and economic activity but access to capital makes drought problems little more than an inconvenience compared to the very real problems in the developing world. Nevertheless there are serious impacts for MEDCs whose long-term effects have yet to be realised. These impacts often show that the use of water by developed countries is less intelligent and sustainable than that by developing countries. The only difference being that wealthier countries can afford to buy their way out of the consequences of poor water conservation at the moment.

The western United States is a semi-arid region with frequent droughts. As long ago as 1878, John Wesley Powell conducted the first survey of the western USA and noted that 'land as mere land has no value. What is really valuable is the water privilege'. His remarks were prompted by the settlement of western USA by white settlers taking water-hungry agriculture into drought zones. Powell proposed the following:
a) The government should not sell land that had no access to water;
b) Property boundaries should not be arbitrarily straight but based on natural watersheds and drainage basins to avoid conflict over access to water;
c) Irrigation systems should be built co-operatively by farmers to avoid exploitation by water supply companies.
Powell's approach was extremely foresighted but it was also extremely unpopular with land speculators and big business interests who quickly controlled the best streams in the region (and stood to make a lot of money by selling water to those who had none). It was decades later that publicly funded irrigation schemes would attempt to share water equitably amongst the farmers and settlers of the west. By then much of the damage had been done. Cities and farms sited in deserts and semi-deserts had already begun to make their insatiable demands on the region's least reliable resource – water.

More recently, between 1986 and 1993, California has experienced significant drought conditions (see Figure 2.29). Growing at more than twice the national average and containing over 14 million people in Los Angeles alone, California is not a suitable climate for providing reliable water

supplies. The natural vegetation in the region consists of **xerophytic** (drought-tolerant) scrub with small leaf areas, deep roots and a rapidly completed life cycle (see Figure 2.28). If the vegetation is adapted to expect drought, there is no reason for humans to expect otherwise.

The stress caused by the Californian drought has highlighted tensions between conflicting water demands including conservation, agriculture and urban land use.

Low river flows (worsened by water abstraction) have reduced salmon catches by over 60 per cent since 1988. Typical of ecosystem complexities, the drought has influenced a whole range of plants and animals up and down the food chain. Waterfowl populations have declined, ten species of wildflower and nine species of butterfly are endangered. Forestry has been hit with an estimated 10 per cent of trees dying.

Two-thirds of California's water is supplied from the rural areas north of the Sacramento Delta yet two-thirds is consumed by the population south of the delta. Farmers in rural areas resent this massive transfer of water to the cities of the south,

FIGURE 2.29 Aspects of
the US drought

Drought statistics	Drought responses
■ Precipitation in California declined to between 55 and 75 per cent of normal rainfalls. ■ Surface runoff declined to 50 per cent of normal. ■ 155 major reservoirs held 60 per cent of long-term average.	■ Water rates increased dramatically. ■ Water authorities ordered 25 per cent reduction in water use in San Francisco, and 45 per cent reduction in Santa Barbara. ■ Some cities (e.g. Pasadena) offered free installation of water saving devices. ■ Some districts refused permission for new water services to be installed – thus crippling new developments. ■ Rules introduced to prevent water wastage on 'non-essential' uses. ■ Farmers switched to higher value, less thirsty crops, e.g. fruit and vegetables rather than corn and cotton. ■ Santa Barbara approved plans for a coastal desalination plant. ■ New sewage recycling plant planned for the Upper San Gabriel Valley. This will reclaim water from a sewage treatment plant and save about 10 billion gallons of water a year (about 30 per cent of the valley's imported water).

particularly when much is destined for swimming pools or dishwashers. City dwellers respond by pointing out that farmers pay less than $10 per 1 000m^3 for water whilst they can pay up to $200. Furthermore, farmers use 80 per cent of California's water to contribute less than 5 per cent to the state's economic productivity. To reduce some of these conflicts, George Bush passed new water legislation in 1992 to encourage more 'water trading' between farmers, the cities and the Central Valley Project (a major water supply project delivering 20 per cent of California's water). By giving water enhanced economic value it is hoped that it will be used and reused more effectively. Ultimately it is likely that unrestricted urban demands will outstrip any political or economic tricks to make the water last longer. Californians may need to adjust their lifestyle to their environment and not vice versa.

Flood hazards

Floods are normal parts of a river's life cycle. Regular flooding offers many benefits such as replenishing soil nutrients, recharging soil moisture and encouraging high agricultural productivity. Regular flooding produces a wide variety of habitat niches which encourage a diverse ecosystem. Floods also build up the height of the river floodplain, reducing the vulnerability of the floodplain to future floods. On the other hand, floods can wash away whole harvests, destroy property and infrastructure and threaten lives. Stagnant pools left after flooding can breed diseases. Humans have always had an ambiguous relationship with rivers, using them for water, fishing, waste disposal, energy, irrigation, recreation and transport routeways, yet fearing the power unleashed by a river in flood. We need to live near rivers and so since earliest times have sought to manage them for our benefit. It is only in recent decades that we have begun to understand rivers sufficiently enough to realise that our management sometimes makes matters worse rather than better.

Rivers behave like living creatures, responding in logical ways to changes in their environments. These changes might be to do with their water inputs, sediment inputs or channel shapes and gradients which the river is always trying to balance. Any change made as a result of human interference will have knock-on effects as the river tries to get back to an equilibrium. Since rivers live on a time scale much slower than humans, the rivers responses to our changes may not be apparent for some years. When the responses eventually emerge they may well take a form that is unexpected and sometimes unpleasantly so.

Flood origins

Figure 2.30 shows that channel flow in a river is just one part of the hydrological cycle. Floods can be caused by climatic factors, drainage basin factors or both. Even without human interference flooding occurs regularly because hydrological stores experience annual changes. For instance, vegetation storage decreases in temperate climates in the winter since there is less vegetation around. Soil storage decreases because winter rains fill up much of the storage potential. In most climates there is a certain predictability regarding floods – they tend to be found in one particular season.

In Britain two different types of flooding occur at two different times of the year. In the winter time 'slow onset' floods occur when river levels gradually rise with increased winter rainfalls and low evaporation rates. Periods of prolonged rainfall fill all the other soil stores so a point is reached when any increase in rain can only be accommodated over the bank as a flood. These floods are relatively easy to predict. Rivers like the Severn have a whole network of monitoring stations measuring river flow and rainfall volumes in the upper catchment. When the monitoring stations measure unusually high rainfalls or river levels, flood alerts are issued for vulnerable areas downstream. Flood warnings are regular parts of winter life in towns like Shrewsbury or Gloucester. By contrast, summer is a time where many soil stores are relatively empty – vegetation is lush (giving large leaf areas for storage), and soils are dry but the warm summer air can hold huge volumes of water and the intensity of summer cloudbursts can be such that the precipitation input is greater than the capacity of the stores to absorb the rain. This is most likely to be the case in urbanised catchments. These floods are known as flash floods and often cause more severe damage due to their unpredictability and ferocity. In addition to natural storage changes, human activities in drainage basins can have profound effects on storage capacities and rates of processes (Figure 2.32).

The complexity of drainage basin hydrological cycles and river systems is such that predictions become difficult. Models must not only take account of static factors such as geology, basin shape etc (Figure 2.30) but also account for a number of very dynamic factors. These include land use and vegetation – both of which can change in the short term (seasonal) and long term (as a basin is urbanised or farmed more intensively). They also include the dynamics of the storm itself as seen in the South China floods of 1994.

The 1994 floods on the Pearl River in China (see Figure 2.31) were intensified by a tropical storm moving downstream from source to mouth. Had the storm moved upstream the flood peak would have been much lower because the downstream water would have passed away by the time the upstream water moved to the lower reaches. This movement of the storm centre made the flood pattern more difficult to predict but prediction was made worse by the uneven distribution of high rainfalls. The western tributary of the Pearl River (the Xi Jiang – pronounced Shee zhaung) experienced an average of 302mm of rain in 10 days; but within the huge catchment area, 32 000km^2 received more than 500mm of rain and one small region had over 900mm. The Northern tributary (the Bei Jiang – pronounced Bay zhaung) averaged only 201mm over its catchment area in the same period, but more than 50 per cent of the drainage basin had over 400mm and a small region had over 780mm.

The effect of multiple 'pulses' of rain from different locations, each a different volume, all moving down different tributaries and combining at confluences makes prediction difficult in the best of circumstances. The Chinese flood prediction was severely hampered by a lack of accurate gauging data on the vast network of the Pearl River drainage basin. As a result, 200 million people were affected by the flood and damage totals were estimated at 300 billion yuan (£21 billion).

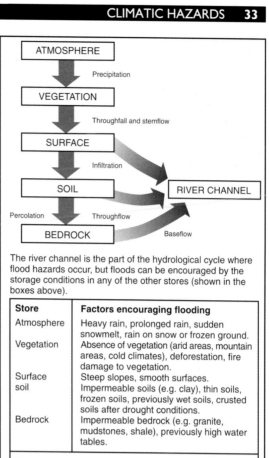

FIGURE 2.30 Floods and the natural hydrological cycle

Acute flooding v Chronic flooding

Just as there are different flood origins, we can also distinguish different styles of flood impacts. Acute floods are high-magnitude events with a long return period (the period between one event and the next). Chronic floods are lower-magnitude events but much more frequent and persistent in their impacts. Examples of acute floods include the China floods of 1998 which submerged more than 25 million hectares of crops and nearly 5 million homes for more than two months.

Hurricane Mitch in Central America was another example of an acute weather-related hazard. In contrast, Bangladesh had three major floods during July and August, leaving about 50 per cent of the country under water, up to 3m deep, for periods of

FIGURE 2.31 The catchment of the Pearl River, South China

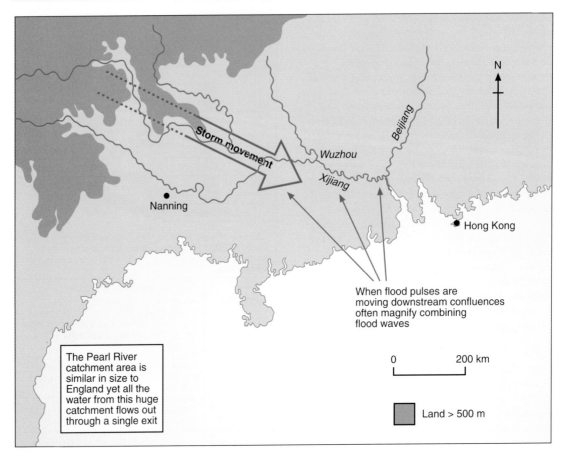

The Pearl River catchment area is similar in size to England yet all the water from this huge catchment flows out through a single exit

When flood pulses are moving downstream confluences often magnify combining flood waves

Land > 500 m

up to 67 days. This was an acute flood by most measurements but a quick glance at the recent history of Bangladesh shows that the country experiences regular large-scale flooding. In other words floods in Bangladesh are not a 'once in 200 years disaster' as Mitch was estimated to be. Bangladesh has chronic flood problems with large floods many times per decade.

The two types of flood have different management implications. Acute flooding may cause loss of life and enormous damage bills but chronic flood hazards – with their persistent regularity – may permanently disable a country's economic development. The case studies below consider Bangladesh as an example of chronic flooding and Hurricane Mitch as an example of acute flooding.

STUDENT ACTIVITY 2.11

The hydrology of towns
1 Produce a cartoon diagram of a city with annotations taken from Figure 2.32 to show the effects of urbanisation on the character of the river and its hydrograph.

Flood problems in Bangladesh

Bangladesh was created by floods. Over millions of years the erosion of the rising Himalayas has dumped silt at the mouths of the major rivers in the region – the Ganges, Brahmaputra and Meghna. These rivers converge in Bangladesh. Most of Bangladesh lies less than 6m above sea level. Large floods can regularly leave over 25 per cent of the country under water. Flooding on this level has created one of the most fertile lands in the world supporting population densities of 800 people per km^2. How then, can flooding be considered a problem?

In August/September 1988 over 60 per cent of Bangladesh was flooded by record river flows. The country was brought to a virtual standstill for more than a month with communications disrupted and agriculture and industry virtually shut down. Such floods have a significant death toll (see Figure 2.33) and a marked impact on housing and cattle – both of which influence recovery rates after flooding. In addition the 1988 floods caused damage estimated at $US 2 billion and destroyed 900 bridges and culverts. 15 000km of road was affected by the floods. From Figure 2.33 it is evident that this scale of flooding is not uncommon and that it wreaks havoc with the economy of such a poor country. The obvious question is 'What can be done to reduce the flooding?' This may be the wrong question pointing to the wrong solutions. The other question which may be more significant in the long term is 'What can be done to reduce the vulnerability?'

There are five effects that urbanisation has on rivers:

I Vegetation and soils are replaced by impermeable tarmac, tiles and concrete. In city centres over 90 per cent of the original surface may be covered. This causes:

a) reduced storage on surface and in soil; **b)** faster rates of overland flow; **c)** decreased evapotranspiration; **d)** reduced percolation to groundwater.

2 Small networks of natural streams are replaced by large networks of artificial streams (gutters, drains and storm sewers). This causes:

a) overland flow to reach channels (normally artificial ones) more quickly; **b)** channel flow to take place more rapidly because the artificial channels are smooth in cross-section.

3 Building activity is commonplace and causes:

a) erosion of bare soils when building takes place; **b)** high volumes of eroded sediment to be deposited in streams and channels during the building phase, reducing the size of the channel floods more likely.

4 The river channel usually has roads or buildings built alongside which means:

a) floods flow more quickly and rise faster (since the water can't spread sideways). Areas downstream may receive more water more quickly; **b)** bridges across the river may restrict the flow of water, causing river levels to rise more rapidly upstream.

5 The local climate of the city is dustier and warmer than the surrounding rural areas. This encourages:

a) more rainfall (especially in summer); **b)** more thunderstorms with intensive rain bursts.

As a result of these changes, a graph of stream flow after a storm (the hydrograph) shows a distinctly quicker rise to a higher peak after an area has been urbanised. This makes the river hydrograph more 'flashy' – i.e. more prone to both floods and drought – with a higher peak flow and a shorter lag time (i.e. time between height of storm and height of flood).

FIGURE 2.32 The hydrology of towns

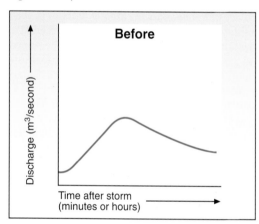

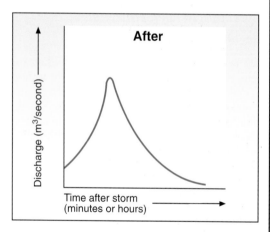

FIGURE 2.33 Impacts of abnormal river flooding in Bangladesh

Year	Death toll	Loss of livestock ('000s)	Houses damaged/ destroyed ('000s)	Rice yields (thousand tonnes) Wet season	Dry season
1971	120	2	229	Whilst Bangladeshi farmers have cultivated a wide	
1974	1 987	46	6 165	variety of rice strains they fall into two basic	
1975	15	n/a	19	categories – wet-season rice, and dry-season rice	
1976	54	n/a	89	that grows in the months after the monsoon.	
1984	553	76	536	Typical yields for a non-flood year comparison would be as follows (1986 figures): wet season = 11.4; dry season = 4.0.	
1987	1 657	65	2 536	10.7	4.7
1988	2 379	172	7 179	9.7	5.8
1991	370	n/a	1 000	n/a	n/a
1993	592	n/a	n/a	n/a	n/a

n/a not available

Approaches to flood protection in Bangladesh

Structural responses to floods involve building engineering structures to store, divert or restrain the river. Storage of water behind dams would involve a co-operative project with Nepal whereby Nepal would gain irrigation water and HEP from dam projects while Bangladesh would gain protection from floods. The main problem is that the basic requirement of flood protection would be to have empty reservoirs (to give maximum water storage) but the requirements of irrigation and HEP need fairly full reservoirs. These contradictory needs mean that co-operation between the countries would be unlikely.

Diverting the waters within Bangladesh has been suggested by US and Japanese consultants. Using barriers and sluice gates to divert water away from high-value to lower-value areas could achieve a saving of life and property at a relatively modest cost. A similar technique is used in China. The problem is who defines the low-value areas? Are they the areas where poor people live? Are they the rural areas?

Restraining the waters by means of large embankments is the final structural option and one that is being seriously pursued as a key part of the Bangladesh Flood Action Plan. This proposal will cost up to $10 billion, take 30 years to complete and have maintenance costs of about $500 million per year. It will attempt to embank the major rivers in order to constrain their flood waters. If this succeeds in reducing major flooding it will allow Bangladesh agriculture and industry to develop rapidly. At present the threat of flood damage is a major disincentive to investment or entrepreneurial activity but embankments are not without problems as shown in Figure 2.34. There are fundamental questions to ask about the feasibility of the project and the social impacts. Many critics have expressed doubts that these rivers can be tamed. The Ganges, for instance, can move its channel 500m during a flood and erode channels up to 45m deep. The biggest doubts are whether this type of hazard response is appropriate for the poor in Bangladesh. Existing river control schemes have not always proved adequate for such a monster of a river. The

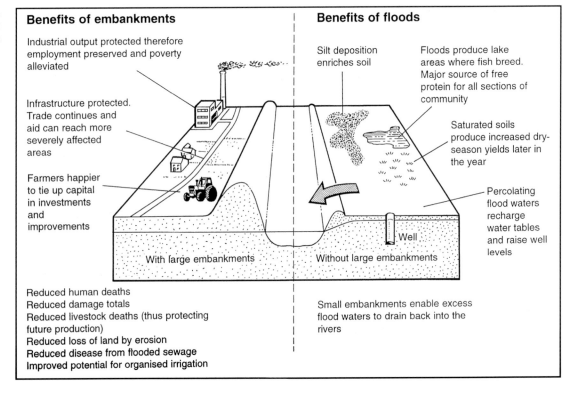

FIGURE 2.34 Floods versus embankments: weighing the benefits

Benefits of embankments

Industrial output protected therefore employment preserved and poverty alleviated

Infrastructure protected. Trade continues and aid can reach more severely affected areas

Farmers happier to tie up capital in investments and improvements

With large embankments

Reduced human deaths
Reduced damage totals
Reduced livestock deaths (thus protecting future production)
Reduced loss of land by erosion
Reduced disease from flooded sewage
Improved potential for organised irrigation

Benefits of floods

Silt deposition enriches soil

Floods produce lake areas where fish breed. Major source of free protein for all sections of community

Saturated soils produce increased dry-season yields later in the year

Percolating flood waters recharge water tables and raise well levels

Well

Without large embankments

Small embankments enable excess flood waters to drain back into the rivers

Meghna-Dhanagoda Irrigation Project had 200m of banks swept away in the 1988 floods. Even when the structures survive, their value in aiding the poorest 30 per cent of the community are open to question. Studies in the Chandpur Irrigation Project area (Varley 1994) show that whilst average incomes and yields improved within the project area the distribution of benefits was uneven. Large landowners with other sources of income had significant benefits but the smaller farmers and the landless labourers were no better off than outside the project area.

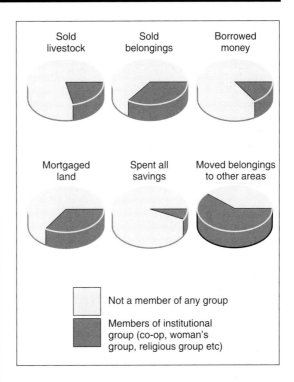

FIGURE 2.35 The role of grass roots organisation in reducing flood vulnerability in Bangladesh

---

STUDENT ACTIVITY 2.13

Flood embankments in Bangladesh
Refer to Figure 2.34 and the examples above.
1 Which section of society benefits most from flood protection?
2 Which section of society pays the cost of flood protection (through reduced government spending on health, education, and social protection) due to the increase in national debt?
3 Embankments shift large volumes of water downstream more quickly. What problems might result from this for areas nearer the river mouth?

Other approaches

A final option is to examine the underlying causes of vulnerability and tackle the root causes of the hazard. The problems of flooding are as much to do with economics and politics as with rainfall. Many households have limited access to good water or regular food supplies and they are vulnerable to disease. Many make their living as landless labourers and are vulnerable to flood-induced unemployment. Many homes are illegal squats in low-demand flood-prone land and are vulnerable to flood loss. Many incomes are very low with negligible savings or capital and are vulnerable to becoming trapped in a cycle of debt and poverty. Yet simple responses like co-operative organisations can make significant differences. A survey after the 1988 floods compared the coping ability of those villagers belonging to organised groups (e.g. women's groups, religious groups, agricultural co-operatives etc) with those coping on their own. Some of the study results are shown in Figure 2.35. The pie charts show the different responses villagers made to the flood in order to solve the immediate problems of lack of food or shelter. From Student Activity 2.14 it is clear that those belonging to organised groupings were less often forced to compromise their livelihood in order to survive. One of the key reasons for this was that the groups acted as focal points through which aid was organised and directed. The number of group members receiving help from relief agencies was

---

STUDENT ACTIVITY 2.14

Group responses to flooding
Refer to Figure 2.35.
1 What is the favoured coping strategy for members of groups?
2 How does belonging to a group enable such a strategy to take place?
3 Using your own value judgements and intuition rank the six coping strategies in order from: a) least damaging in the long term; to f) most damaging. Justify your choices.
4 When group membership is so helpful, why do so many not belong to such a group? (Your answer should include social/economic factors as well as personal factors.)

---

four times more than amongst non-group members. In addition, organised groups often act as a centre for day-to-day development. They organised cheap loans, bulk purchase, and mutual assistance. The real hazard in Bangladesh is not the occasional flood but the daily struggle with malnutrition and poverty. River floods kill an average of 500 people a year in Bangladesh. Yet if the national death rate in Bangladesh (due to malnutrition, disease etc) was to improve to that of neighbouring India, 500 000 people a year would be saved. Compared to that the Flood Action Plan seems merely a drop in the ocean.

The year of the storms – climatic hazards in 1998

Global overview

In 1998 Munich Re – a leading insurance company – warned that certain areas of the world might become 'uninsurable' for climate-related hazards if the global trends were to continue. Their evidence of increasing risks to insurers was brought home by a depressing series of climatic disasters through the year.

The Worldwatch Institute estimated that global economic loss due to weather-related disasters was at least $89 000 million for the first 11 months of 1998. This represented an increase of 48 per cent over the $60 000 million in losses for 1996. The 'costliest' disaster of 1998 was the flooding of China's Yangtze River which resulted in 3700 deaths, 223 million evacuees, and 25 million hectares of cropland flooded. Its economic impact was estimated at $30 000 million.

Bangladesh had its most extensive biggest flood of the century causing over $3.4 million in damage and leaving 30 million homeless. The Atlantic had a vigorous hurricane season with 14 tropical storms and hurricanes. In September there were four Atlantic hurricanes on the go at the same time and, in late October, Hurricane Mitch became the most powerful Atlantic storm for 200 years. This hurricane brought devastation to Central America, particularly Honduras and Nicaragua. The case studies below outline the impact of Mitch on both a regional, national and local scale. In each case the role of physical and human processes are inextricably linked.

Central America overview

On 22nd October 1998 a tropical storm formed in the Atlantic. Within 4 days the storm had grown to a category 5 hurricane (Saffir Simpson scale) gusting at over 200mph (320kph). It remained a category 5 hurricane for 33 hours then the windspeeds began to fall as Mitch drifted towards Honduras. But wind was not the problem with this monster storm. Mitch made landfall on the Honduras coast on 30th October and an unexpected twist of fate set the scene for terrible devastation. Mitch stalled in the worst possible

FIGURE 2.36 1998 was a vigorous Atlantic storm season – this illustration of a NOAA image shows Hurricane Mitch over Central America

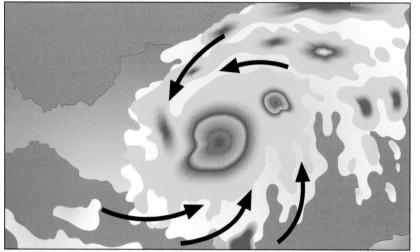

FIGURE 2.37 Summary of impacts of Hurricane Mitch on Central America

	Honduras	**Nicaragua**	**El Salvador**	**Guatemala**
Deaths/ missing	6 500 dead with up to 11 000 still missing, presumed dead	3 800 dead and 7 000 missing, presumed dead	230 deaths	200+ deaths
Homes damaged or destroyed	1.5 million (20% of country's population) had to evacuate their homes	750 000 evacuated homes	500 000 evacuated homes	80 000 evacuated homes
Infrastructure damage	Estimated 70–80 per cent of transportation infrastructure destroyed. One-third of all buildings in the capital damaged by the floods	71 bridges destroyed – many on the few arterial roads in the country	Not known	Not known
Crop damage	70 per cent of crops destroyed – losses estimated at $(US) 900 million	30% coffee crop lost. Beans, sugar and banana crops devastated	80% of maize crops lost. Coffee plantations and sugar cane lost	Extensive damage to coffee and banana plantations
Total cost	$(US) 4 billion	$(US) 1 billion	Not known	Not known

place. Normally when a hurricane hits land it begins to die. The warm, moist oceanic air which drives the hurricane's energy is replaced by dry continental air. Lack of moisture means lack of condensation – so no more release of latent heat to drive the hurricane. Unfortunately, Central America is a thin landmass and the swirling 'feeder bands' were reaching out beyond the land, drawing in moist oceanic air from both the Atlantic and the Pacific at the same time. As the air spiralled into the hurricane centre it encountered the high relief landscapes of Honduras, Nicaragua, and Guatemala. The combined effect of hurricane rainfall, relief rainfall and a stalled system (keeping the rain in one small region) meant record rainfalls were produced. Worse was to come. The rain fell into a region of easily eroded volcanic rock where many hillsides consist of a friable fertile soil of weathered ash and lava – easily eroded under the best of management, but the landscape is not well managed. Tropical rain forest on the Caribbean coast of Honduras is disappearing at a rate of 80 000 hectares a year, caused mostly by farmers burning trees to create arable land. However, once they cut down trees on the steep slopes the fragile soil is quickly washed away and the farmers move on to clear more land, spreading the problem further. A year's worth of rain fell in four days. Deforested slopes contributed to massive floods

and mudslides that swept away people, farms and homes. Rivers protected by trees, such as the Rio Danto had visibly less damage than along other rivers in the area.

STUDENT ACTIVITY 2.15

1 Refer to the table opposite.
a) On an outline map of Central America annotate the different impacts shown in the table.
b) Create a simple model to show the contributions of climatic processes, geology, relief and land use to the damage caused by Hurricane Mitch.
c) Use the information on the *Further Information – Mitch* section of the accompanying website to explain why the damage varied from country to country.

STUDENT ACTIVITY 2.16

1 Plot a graph to show
(i) changes in damage totals through time
(ii) changes in numbers affected through time for the hurricanes in the table below.
Describe and suggest reasons for your findings.

Nicaragua case study

Nicaragua is no stranger to hurricane damage. The table below summarises Nicaragua's hurricane experience in the last 20 years:

FIGURE 2.38 Nicaragua's hurricane experience in the last 20 years

Year	Event	Impacts
1982	Hurricane Alleta	480 million US dollars damage
1988	Hurricane Joan	840 million US dollars damage
1991	Floods	20 000 people affected
1993	Tropical storms Gert and Bret	120 000 people affected
1995	Floods	17 million US dollars damage
1998	Hurricane Mitch	1 360 million US dollars damage, 3 863 deaths, 867 000 affected (20% of population); 7 000 missing

Through most of Central America, wind was not the main problem with Hurricane Mitch. The greatest damage was caused by the extensive flooding and landslides. By November, the Nicaraguan National Emergency Commission estimated that 2863 people had died and 867 752 were affected by the disaster. A major headache for the relief operations was trying to assess priorities. How are conflicting needs resolved when so many different impacts occur in different places with different long-term and short-term impacts? Some of the key issues are covered in the next few pages.

Intensity of the event

The map in Figure 2.39 (showing areas of highest flood threat) demonstrates that the most vulnerable areas were in the lowland plains downstream of major river basins. Nicaragua's population has a different pattern with the majority living on the coastal plains of the west. Nearly 20 per cent of Nicaragua's 4.5 million people live in Managua. Other urban centres in the west include Leon, Granada and Masaya. Outside of the western coastal zone there are few settlements larger than 30 000 people. As a result of these differing

FIGURE 2.39 Areas of highest flood risk

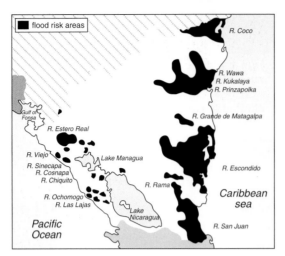

settlement patterns, impacts were not necessarily worst where flooding was worst, but where people were most vulnerable to flood threats.

Intensity of the impacts

The map (Figure 2.40) shows the percentage of the population affected by Hurricane Mitch. The effects show the worst hit areas were in the north and north-western regions where high intensity of rain coincided with reasonably high population densities.

The high rates of impact in Chinandega were due to a specific event – a giant mudflow triggered on the slopes of Casita Volcano. Here meteorology, geology and poor siting conspired to create a tragedy. In this region, Mitch brought 5 months rainfall in 5 days. As a result, rain-sodden fault-lines on the top of the volcano were lubricated, allowing a 200 000 cubic metre rock pile to move off the crated rim, tumbling into the steep gullies of the valley side.

Range of impacts

Figure 2.41 shows the lahar (a volcanic mudslide) which resulted from the avalanche on Casita Volcano

FIGURE 2.40 Percentage of the population affected by Hurricane Mitch

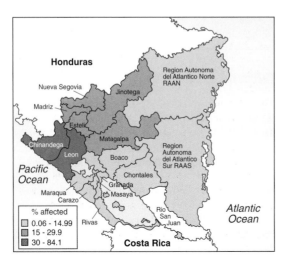

near Posoltega in the north-western province of Chinandega. This event was the single biggest cause of death in Nicaragua but the aid operations to the area were greatly hindered by the hundreds of 'minor' flood and landslip events set off by Hurricane Mitch. Seventy per cent of all roads were impassable immediately after the storm. Over 70 bridges had been destroyed. In many cases, restoration of bridges and roads had to come before the immediate needs of people because it was impossible to meet needs without a transport system.

Timing of events

The hurricane struck shortly before the coffee harvests were due to start. Mitch had already caused direct damage to the coffee harvest but lack of transport infrastructure could prove equally damaging for the economy if the surviving crop was unable to be taken to market in time.

Secondary impacts

Cholera increased in the unsanitary conditions. From a weekly average of 16 cases before the hurricane, weekly totals rose to 170, 87, and 39 respectively for the three weeks after. Contaminated food was suspected as the main cause. Likewise, there were no known reports of Leptospirosis ('mud fever' or 'infectious jaundice') in the pre-Mitch period but epidemics were reported in several regions after the hurricane. The week after, Mitch saw 1 reported incident. The next week had 56, by the last week in November there were 232 recorded incidences. If not treated quickly this disease leads to heart and kidney failure. In addition to these outbreaks, diarrhoea, dengue fever, malaria and respiratory disorders all increased as a result of the hurricane disrupting normal health and hygiene. In Posoltega – devastated by the lahar from the Casitas Volcano – villagers were desperate for water. Mitch destroyed the town's water treatment facilities. People were now relying on the river for water but nobody knew how safe it was. There were unburied bodies – human and animal – in all the riverbeds. Risks were very high but alternatives very few.

Politics

In the aftermath of grief and suffering feelings ran high. There was already widespread frustration because government policies had created an increasing gap between rich and poor. In addition, there were many accusations of government corruption. There were also deep-seated divisions from Nicaragua's turbulent recent history. The northern areas were politically sympathetic to the Sandinistas – Nicaragua's left wing party who were defeated by US-backed groups in a recent civil war. Since the north was worst affected by Mitch, and the government seemed slow and unresponsive, northerners regarded the government's inaction as politically motivated. Local officials at Posoltega accused president Aleman of withholding aid to the area. The president claimed the Sandinistas were trying to exploit the tragedy of the hurricane for political purposes. When the president visited the city of Leon a few days after the hurricane, he was met by rock-throwing crowds. The Anti-American feelings of the Sandinista north spilled over the northern town of Esteli when villagers met US doctors (part of a relief party) yelling 'Yankees out of Nicaragua', a slogan of the former Sandinista government. In December 1998, Washington announced it would forgive 90 per cent of the bilateral debt owed by Nicaragua and make a 'significant donation' in cash to help Central American countries recover.

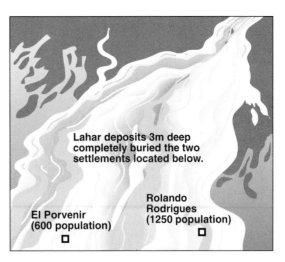

Lahar deposits 3m deep completely buried the two settlements located below.

El Porvenir (600 population)

Rolando Rodrigues (1250 population)

FIGURE 2.41 Lahar resulting from the avalanche on Casita Volcano near Posoltega in the northwestern province of Chinandega (Nicaragua)

STUDENT ACTIVITY 2.17

1 Summarise the impacts of Hurricane Mitch in Nicaragua under two headings:
(i) Physical factors
(ii) Human factors.
Which column is largest and what does this suggest about natural hazards?

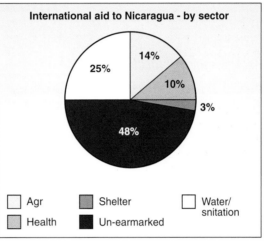

FIGURE 2.42 International aid to Nicaragua by sector

International responses

Hurricane Mitch made international news and there were generous responses from a number of nations. The reasons why some events are perceived as more tragic than others can be difficult to understand. Both China and Bangladesh had had severe flooding (affecting far more people) in the months prior to Hurricane Mitch yet they had attracted little media attention. Possible reasons for Mitch attracting more attention include:
■ A new location – not Africa or Asia;
■ A location closer to USA and more accessible to media coverage;
■ A sense of guilt – Central America is heavily indebted, providing tidy incomes to wealthy nations through debt repayments. Further, many Americans have a conscience about recent US interference in Nicaragua's independence.

By March 1999 the UN Office for the Coordination of Humanitarian Affairs (OCHA) estimated that 58 per cent of the immediate needs of the affected Central American countries had been met by international donations. The pattern of donations is shown in Figure 2.42. Many donations are earmarked for particular projects – agriculture, health etc. There is enormous benefit to the recipient country if donations are 'unearmarked' – it gives them flexibility in spending the money. Donor countries are often less happy with unearmarked donations because it is harder to track the way the money was used. In addition to intergovernmental aid, much of the relief effort depended on the work of non-governmental organisations such as the Red Cross and a range of church groups. These groups often have people already involved in the community and can respond rapidly with local

knowledge. For example, Catholic Relief Services distributed food to 27 000 people in the Department of Matagalpa in the early months of 1999 and involved 3632 families in 'Food for Work' activities. The Food for Work programme resulted in 235km of roads being cleaned and rehabilitated. Other organisations used Food for Work to plant trees, start soil conservation programmes and generally rehabilitate community infrastructure.

Monitoring and evaluation

In order to evaluate the impact of food aid on beneficiaries, the World Food Programme (WFP) organised a 'post-distribution' survey. The objective was to interview 800 beneficiaries across different regions of the country to ensure donations were reaching the right people and Food for Work was achieving the right ends. This is particularly important because Food for Work programmes can go wrong – for example, drought in North East Brazil resulted in Food for Work programmes where farmers were given food in exchange for labour to build earth dams across streams on the land of wealthy landowners. This ensured the landowners would have a reservoir of water on their land whilst the poor farmers had an even more depleted water supply!

Tipitapa – a small-scale study of disaster management

Background and location

Tipitapa is a satellite town about 14 miles (22km) from the capital Managua. It is a town of about 100 000 with a mixed economy including metal working, agriculture, tourism (related to medicinal springs) and fishing but many rely on the excellent road link to Managua for their livelihood. The Pan American Highway clips the western edge of Tipitapa, as shown in Figure 2.43. Built about 30 years ago this is the major north/south artery linking Managua to the rest of the country. Ironically the road that has brought so much to the economy of Tipitapa played a part in amplifying the effect of the floods. Tipitapa was an obvious route for the Pan American Highway. As Figure 2.43 illustrates, there is a relatively narrow tongue of land between the lakes and hills. Tipitapa is sited on this tongue at the crossing point of the Tipitapa river. The construction of the road hindered the outflow of water from Lake Managua southwards to Lake Nicaragua. This restricted the outflow of water from Lake Managua. This never normally presents a problem, but Hurricane Mitch created unprecedented water levels in the lake and the

water ponded against parts of the highway, unable to escape quickly.

Figure 2.44 shows the location of Lake Managua in relation to the rest of Nicaragua. Lake Managua drains a vast area of high land to the north and west – the very areas experiencing record rainfalls. The normal level of Lake Managua is 37m above sea level. Mitch raised the water level to about 41.5m – a rise of 4.5 metres or nearly fifteen feet. Since the gradients at the edge of the lake are shallow, a rise of this size causes the shoreline to move a long way inland.

Impacts

There were three main effects in Tipitapa:
1 first, the lakeside residences began to flood. It was the residents themselves who alerted the town's Mayor of the problem and he ordered the evacuation of the lakeside communities into local schools, halls and cinemas;
2 secondly, the river level backed up against the road embankment, eventually overflowing the Pan American Highway and washing out part of the road in the process;
3 finally, the immense flows of water down the Tipitapa river washed out the bridges on the only other crossing points in the area. Suddenly Managua was cut off from the north of the country.

Responses – local and national

There were three distinctly different response levels to this hazard – local people, the Nicaraguan government and outside agencies like the Red Cross and CARITAS. The government concentrated solely on repairing the road network. The government paid little attention to the local people's plight until over a month after they had lost their homes. In fairness to the government, there were other problems to attend to – 70 major bridges destroyed, 1600 people buried by landslips near Posoltega and

FIGURE 2.43 The location of Tipitapa

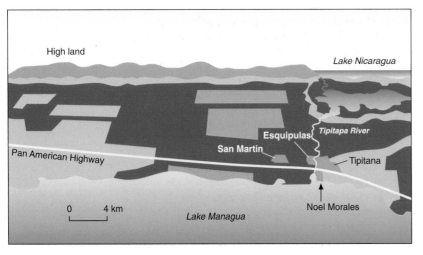

High land

Lake Nicaragua

Pan American Highway

Esquipulas *Tipitapa River*

San Martin

Tipitana

Noel Morales

0   4 km

Lake Managua

70 per cent of the road network inoperable. Communications had to be a priority. It was the Non Governmental Organisations (NGOs) and the people themselves who took responsibility for the short-term problem solving. Whilst the hurricane was still dying out, some of the refugees from Tipitapa saw trucks from a relief organisation and approached them for help. Within 5 days the Costa Rican Red Cross and other aid agencies were providing staple foods (rice, beans, oil and milk) to the 220 families (over 1000 people) who had been forced from their homes.

A month after Mitch it was clear the people would not be able to return for a long time. The refugees would need a permanent home and land of their own on which they could begin the slow process leading back to self-reliance. Two areas of land were set aside – (a) at San Martin on the outskirts of an existing settlement about 3km NNE of Tipitapa where there was suitable land already in community ownership (b) at Esquipulas on what was previously private land on the outskirts of Tipitapa. At both locations the Government provided each family with:

- A plot of land 25m × 8m;
- 14 sheets of corrugated iron;
- A latrine;
- 12-metre length of black polythene sheeting.

Figure 2.46 shows a typical home built in this style. Note the barren surroundings compared to the tree-lined, brick-walled properties that were evacuated (Figure 2.45).

STUDENT ACTIVITY 2.19

1 Use the images above and the additional images on the website *Further Information – Mitch* to contrast the likely standard of living for the refugees before and after the flood.

Recovery prospects

Whilst the government's responses improved the recovery prospects for these people, significant problems remained. First, many of the families affected were among the poorer people since they have fewer resources to fall back on and less reliable incomes. Furthermore, the land they received is smaller than the land area they previously owned and far less fertile. Secondly, the refugees included many fishing families. The relocated settlements are about a mile by road from the lakeside – the family's source of livelihood. Some fishers have to pay to transport their boats twice a week to the water's edge. The obvious answer would be to form co-operatives, pooling resources and purchasing power for transport and equipment. Co-operatives are encouraged by the government but they are closely regulated and registration is expensive. Monthly membership costs are equivalent to about a week's income for a poor family. In the long run the benefits (cheaper purchases, grants, access to

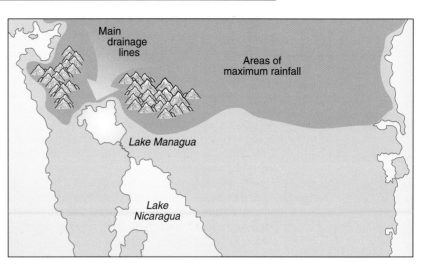

FIGURE 2.44 The location of Lake Managua in Nicaragua

credit etc) would outweigh the costs but the problem of start-up costs is a real barrier to impoverished people.

The impacts of politics on recovery

In many respects refugees resettled at Esquipulas could be regarded as more fortunate than those at San Martin – they are much closer to the town and its markets. There is, however, an underlying complication which has hindered recovery at Esquipulas. It is a problem which plagues development projects in many developing countries – the issue of land tenure. If you own the land on which you live it is worth your while investing your time and energy to make it as productive as possible. It is also worth others helping you because their help will have a long-term benefit.

San Martin has no problems of land security. The local Alcadia (council) already owned the land at San Martin so were able to donate it to the refugees. In time they will receive their legal deeds proving ownership. Since there is no doubt on the long-term future of San Martin's refugee settlement the council has planned a programme of works to include water supply, electrical connection, medical post and a 6-class primary school.

The situation at Esquipulas is very different. The Central Government made an agreement with an indebted landowner for the settlement to be located on his land. The landowner is reputed to be on friendly terms with the president. His land is valued at $27 500 (about 20 per cent of the value of his debt). As a result of the agreement, the Central Government instructed the Alcadia of Tipitapa to locate some of the refugees on the land, which they did. The government then washed its hands of the agreement and effectively passed over responsibility to the Alcadia.

The Alcadia wanted nothing to do with the $27 500 required to pay for the land. For five and a half months there was a legal stalemate: central government no longer interested, local government not willing to pick up the bill for central government decisions and an indebted landowner wanting payment. Refugees had to get on and rebuild their lives but they knew (i) they might be evicted through no fault of their own and (ii) no aid agency or local government help would be available until their tenure was secure. Even the most basic of needs – water – was only granted after the community hand-dug a 300m trench to the nearest water main and insisted on connection.

In May 1999 the original owner promised to write a legal document stating that he will not evict any of the new residents but the legal quagmire remains unresolved. Whilst the Alcadia and aid agencies are now reassured and ready to start putting resources into the settlement, 200 families (already disadvantaged by poverty) are six months further behind through reasons of politics.

STUDENT ACTIVITY 2.20

1 Using Esquipulas and San Martin as contrasting case studies, list the different factors that influence recovery rates for a displaced community.

River responses to structural control

Every dam, channelised section, embankment, bridge or drain alters the energy conditions in the channel. The river then adjusts to the new energy conditions by changing its gradient (by erosion, deposition or both) and/or by changing its channel plan (altering the meander pattern, switching from meanders to braiding or vice versa). The changes caused by engineering works may not be apparent at the site of work but will operate either upstream or downstream of the site. These changes are sometimes significant enough to cause problems at other locations.

Hamburg (120km from the North Sea on the River Elbe) demonstrates problems upstream of an engineering site. In the 1980s, the Lower Elbe (below Hamburg) was upgraded for shipping. The river was widened and deepened and the flood-prone regions surrounding this section of the river were protected by raising the embankments. Unfortunately the combined effect has been to make the city of Hamburg far more vulnerable to flooding. Now the tidal surge up the Elbe can move faster (up a larger more efficient channel) and the new embankments keep the enlarged flow from spilling over onto the lower floodplain. Coastal surges now travel unhindered up 120km of the Elbe to threaten Hamburg. The rising high tide levels on the Elbe now threaten 320 000 people and more than £5 billion of potential property damage.

The River Blackwater (Missouri, USA) demonstrates problems propagated downstream. Channelisation of the stream in 1910 shortened the stream. In doing so, the stream's velocity was increased. This led to an increased erosive capacity. The river has now increased its cross-section area by a factor of ten, causing bank erosion and bridge undermining. The rapid evacuation of water in floods now threatens areas downstream by passing flood waves much more rapidly.

Dams, however, may threaten areas upstream. In the 1991 floods in eastern China, flood levels on the Huaihe and Chuhe Rivers were rising too rapidly because the dams downstream were holding back too much water. The rising water was putting increasing strain on the river levées and there were fears of a catastrophic failure. In order to reduce pressure on the levées, three dams were deliberately destroyed to release flood water downstream. This caused severe flooding in the farming areas below the dams but at least it was pre-planned and therefore successfully evacuated. There are also important lessons in perception here. In Chinese culture the individual is seen as less important than the requirements of the state. Large areas of land can be deliberately flooded if required. There is no debate on the ethics of the decision or the appropriateness of the action. The media will report on the 'loyal sacrifices of the Chinese workers' rather than criticise or question the actions of the Government. This disregard for the rights of the individual may seem alien to Western minds but it does give the Government the option of some rather radical responses to flooding without the fear of political backlash that so often compromises Western responses.

The lesson to be learned is humbling. We rarely understand the systems we study well enough to attempt to control them. Rather than trying to adjust dynamic river systems to static urban structures we need to be more intelligent about our siting. We can use land zoning to ensure flood-prone land is used for less vulnerable land uses – recreation, grazing, conservation. We can learn to live with river seasons (as our ancestors did) and where necessary relocate. The settlement of Valmeyer, Illinois, on the Mississippi is re-siting on higher land rather than risk a repeat of the 1993 floods. The decision to relocate was based on more than a simple cost-benefit analysis. The psychological impacts of the flood played a significant part in the decision.

FIGURE 2.45 Flooded house at Noel Morales, Tipitapa

The psychological effects of flooding: the 1993 Mississippi floods

The effects of a natural disaster go beyond material damage and reduced levels of income. The psychological impacts affect both individuals and whole regions. The Mississippi floods of July 1993 had a profound effect on the American people. In material terms alone it was the worst recorded flood in America – an area the size of England was laid waste, 50 000 people made homeless, and at least 32 people died and damage totalled around $10 billion. The effects went deeper. Many farmers in the devastated floodplain areas suffered post-traumatic stress syndrome, a psychological disorder that is most commonly seen in soldiers returning from violent conflicts. A stress counsellor reported 'The flood reminds them how they lack power over nature. And many can lash out at what they do still control, beating their families, their farm animals.'

For a nation used to a high standard of living and level of control in their lives, the stench of raw sewage, clinics offering free tetanus shots, communal shelters, and queuing for water and chemical lavatories on street corners were all extremely difficult to come to terms with. The scale of the floods rekindled an awe and respect for the forces of nature and a new recognition of the impotence of human societies. During a period of 49 days it rained every day, sometimes as much as 12.5cm in a few hours. This was during a season often associated with drought.

Flood impacts are more localised than other disasters. Part of a community may be wiped out whilst 20m away shops and services on higher ground carry on as normal. But the 1993 floods had a much wider effect by undermining the entire transport infrastructure of the region. Eleven Mid-west airports closed; six key bridges across the Mississippi and Missouri Rivers closed, cutting east–west links for 400km; and cross-country goods trains were rerouted, adding greatly to journey times. North–south river traffic stopped along a 950km stretch of the two great rivers, leaving 2000 barges stranded.

Whilst the flooding was a source of great trauma to many communities, there were some positive aspects perceived in the responsiveness of volunteers. After it was broadcast that Sainte Genevieve was under threat, volunteers came from all over the country to help build a 5m-high levée, 10km long to protect the town. Along the length of the threatened Mississippi, thousands of volunteers filled sandbags, some working 15–20 hours a day. There were virtually no reports of looting or stealing from abandoned houses. Communities experienced a rare bonding together in facing a common enemy. The real tensions came later; and from outside the affected communities.

Does state aid discourage farmers from taking out private flood insurance? Should the farmers be bailed out or should they pay out or move out?

FIGURE 2.46 New dwelling at Esquipulas

Many small farmers argued that they couldn't afford the high premiums on flood insurance. Neither could they sell their wrecked farms now, even if they wanted to. Is it cheaper for the state to intervene through aid or allow bankruptcy – only to pick up the costs through welfare and unemployment benefits instead?

The debate continues and in its complexity of social, economic and political issues wrapped around an unpredictable event it neatly epitomises the whole question of human responses to climatic hazards. There are plenty of easy questions to ask. But no easy answers.

Review of key ideas

■ Climatic hazards can be perceived and classified in a variety of ways.

■ An increase in hazards is due to an increase of people in more vulnerable areas.

■ Human activity can significantly worsen floods and droughts. It is possible that the greenhouse effect may be worsening windstorm hazards.

■ Hurricanes are a 'bundle' of multiple hazards – wind, rain, surge, waves.

■ Hurricane (cyclone) impacts differ depending on the stage of development of a country and the distribution of wealth within a country.

■ Extratropical storms cause fewer deaths but are more worrying to the insurance industry because of concentrations of wealth and insurance risk.

■ Wind hazards are predictable on different scales but prediction does not always help nor is it always reliable.

■ There are a range of responses to wind hazard, depending on stage of development. The most successful responses may be related less to tackling wind and more to tackling vulnerability of individuals or nations.

■ Drought hazard is more problematical in semi-arid areas than in deserts.

■ Droughts operate on a variety of time scales. They can be influenced by human activity – often in ways that are less than obvious.

■ Droughts related to El Niño are semi-predictable.

■ Political factors influence the variety of drought responses available.

- Some drought problems in developed countries are related to inappropriate water demands in poorly sited areas.
- Clay shrinkage may cause additional problems.
- Floods are normal and natural parts of river systems and have benefited humans in many ways.
- Floods bring secondary impacts that last longer than the flood.
- Flooding is worsened by human impacts on the drainage basin.
- Political factors influence flood hazards at all scales.
- Flood control measures may shift the problem to a different place or social group rather than solve it.
- Floods have social and psychological effects as well as physical effects.
- There are no easy answers.

Glossary

CFC – chlorofluorocarbons. Artificial gases which destroy the ozone layer in the upper atmosphere.

Continentality – the climatic conditions of hot summers, very cold winters and low rainfalls found in mid-continental areas.

Coriolis effect – the influence of the spinning earth on the air resting on its surface. This effect deflects most air movements from straight paths to curving paths.

Depression – a storm system, usually applied to storms in the temperate regions. Air sucked into the upper atmosphere jet stream causes low pressure at the surface and colliding air masses that produce rain.

Dry farming – agriculture that relies on simple adjustments to low rainfall, including specialised crops, use of bunds etc.

Ecosystem – a natural plant/animal community.

El Niño – a warm current flowing off the coast of Peru where cold currents normally flow. This current reversal has significant effects on distant weather and climate by teleconnections in the atmosphere.

Extratropical storm – a major storm outside the tropics. Usually associated with a well-developed depression.

Fluvial – to do with river systems.

Front – a boundary between two contrasting air masses, usually associated with rain and wind.

Greenhouse effect – the heating effect caused because outgoing radiation (longwave) is blocked more easily than incoming radiation (shortwave).

Hadley Cell – an air circulation caused by heated air rising at the equator and descending at the subtropical highs.

Humidity – moisture content of the air. This influences air stability and rainfall.

Humus – the decomposing organic material in soils. Humus is important in maintaining soil moisture during dry conditions.

Hurricane – a rotating tropical weather system with windspeeds over 118kph.

Infrastructure – the main communications structures and networks that a community depends on. These include roads, railways, bridges, gas, electricity, mains water and sewage, administration networks and telephone connections etc.

Intertropical Convergence Zone (ITCZ) – final section of the Hadley Cell where air returns from the subtropical highs to meet over the equatorial regions and rise again, producing heavy rain in the process.

Jet stream – a ribbon of high-velocity wind in the upper troposphere. Common in temperate regions where the polar and tropical air masses meet.

Pastoral farming – raising livestock.

Peds – lumps of soil held together by humus and natural glues. Well-developed peds make a soil more resistant to being eroded away.

Pressure – the weight of air pressing down on the earth's surface. Can be influenced by air temperature and air movement (e.g. rising or sinking air masses).

Radiation – energy transmitted in electromagnetic waves. May include visible light bands, shortwave (ultraviolet) bands and longwave (infra-red) bands.

Resonant frequency – the vibration frequency at which a structure will experience uncontrolled shaking.

Satellite imagery – images obtained from satellites circling above the atmosphere. These can view the earth in a variety of ways (visible light, infra-red, radar etc) and can be particularly helpful in monitoring weather systems and their impacts on vegetation (e.g. drought).

Storm surge – the tendency for ocean waters to rise above their normal level when air pressure is reduced under a depression or hurricane.

Sea Surface Temperature Anomaly (SST) – unusually warm (or cool) patches of ocean have significant effects in determining regional climates, e.g. Sahel rainfalls.

Subtropical High – a belt of high-pressure air cells encircling the earth, north and south of the equator. Represents the descent of previously heated equatorial air and is associated with drought areas.

Teleconnections – links between weather conditions in different parts of the globe, e.g. wet summers in the Sahel produce Atlantic Hurricanes in August/September.

Tropical cyclone – see Hurricane.

Tropical storm – a tropical weather system with lower windspeeds than a hurricane. Given the right conditions these may develop into hurricanes.

Tropopause – the upper limit of the lower atmosphere.

Troposphere – the lower layer of the atmosphere where most weather systems form.

Typhoon – see Hurricane. A hurricane in the Pacific Ocean.

Vortex – a spinning system of air.

Xerophytes – plants adapted to drought conditions with small, fleshy or waxy leaves and/or deep root systems.

3
GEOLOGICAL HAZARDS

'... *puis ce fut le silence*'
(and then there was silence): the sole survivor of the Mont Pelée eruption in Martinique, 8 May 1902.

This chapter outlines the different causes of geological hazards and explores their varying and widespread impacts on both Less Economically Developed Countries (LEDCs) and More Economically Developed Countries (MEDCs).

Eyewitness accounts

'Hey, boy-oh-weee, that's a good one! Hey, boy, oh boy oh boy! Man, that's an earthquake! Hey, that's an earthquake for sure! – Wheeee boy oh boy – this is something you'd read – doesn't come up very often up here, but I'm going through it right now! Man – everything's moving – you know everything in the cabinets have come up loose ... Whoooeee! Scared the hell out of me man! I wish this house would quit shaking! That damn bird cage too – ooooo-oh, man! I've never lived through anything like this before in my life, and it hasn't even shown signs of stopping yet, either – ooooeeee – the whole place is shaking – like someone was holding – Hold it, I'd better put the television on the floor. Just a minute, boy! Let me tell you that sure scared the hell out of me, and it's still shaking. I'm telling you! I wonder if I should get outside? Oh boy! Man, I'm telling you that's the worst thing I've ever lived through! ...'
R Pate, radio station announcer, KHAR, Anchorage, 27 March 1964

'It was eight o'clock, and my daily ration had not yet been brought to me, when suddenly a terrible noise was heard. Everyone was shouting "Help! I'm burning, I'm dying." After a few minutes, I was the only one left shouting. Then smoke and fumes began to pour in through the window in my door. These fumes were so scorchingly hot that for a quarter of an hour, I leapt into the air from right to left to avoid them. Afterwards there was a frightening silence. I listened, shouting for someone to come and rescue me, but no-one answered ...'
Louis Sybaris, prison inmate in St Pierre, Martinique, 8 May 1902

Islam threat cuts quake aid to Algeria

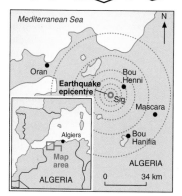

An earthquake ripped through northwest Algeria early yesterday, destroying thousands of homes and killing at least 150 people. Rescuers said at least 289 people were injured and 8,000 to 10,000 left without shelter by the quake in the Mascara region 250 miles west of Algiers.

The disaster increased the suffering of a country where more than 4,000 people have been killed in two and a half years of Islamic revolt. Western agencies considering whether to send aid have had to consider extremist threats to kill foreigners.

The quake, measuring 5.6 on the Richter scale, hit hardest in rural areas, causing thousands of straw-and-mud dwellings to collapse on their sleeping occupants. Several aftershocks followed, the strongest measuring 5.1.

"I lost my wife, my children, my house, everything," said an elderly man at Hassine, a village almost razed by the quake.

Officials appealed for blood donations, food, milk for children and blankets, and gave warning that drinking water could soon be in short supply. But no international request for aid has been launched.

The French aid agency Secours Populaire Français has sent a small team to assess needs and to work with local relief organisations. M Joel Bedos, a member of its emergency co-ordination unit, expressed the hope that Islamic gunmen who have killed 58 foreigners in the past year would take a different view towards aid workers.

"I don't think the fundamentalists would be hostile to aid coming in, even from France, but that needs to be verified," M Bedos said.

However, France's two main medical relief agencies, Medecins Sans Frontières and Medecins du Monde, had no immediate plans to send aid workers.

"If there's no international aid appeal we're not going to break down doors," said M Alain Fredaigue, a spokesman for Medecins Sans Frontières. "We're already overwhelmed with Rwanda."

If the government did request outside help, "we'd have to have very strong security guarantees for our teams," he added.

The Daily Telegraph, 19 August 1994

FIGURE 3.1 Islam – threat cuts quake aid to Algeria

STUDENT ACTIVITY 3.1

Hazard reporting styles
1 Summarise the differences in style of reporting of the two events in Figures 3.1 and 3.2. Attempt to explain the differences in style.
2 The two accounts differ in substance as well as in style. Prepare an A4 page-sized matrix to show how coverage of:
a) causes;
b) consequences;
c) hazard management;
receive varying emphasis within the two accounts. Briefly try to explain why you think these variations in treatment exist.

FIGURE 3.2 Emission of carbon dioxide from Lake Nyos, Cameroon, 21 August 1986

On 21 August 1986 a cloud of dense gas was emitted from Lake Nyos in Cameroon causing death, by asphixiation, of over 1700 people in the nearby villages. An international relief effort was initiated and scientific teams from a number of countries were sent to Lake Nyos in order to determine the cause of the gas release. It was agreed that the carbon dioxide, which was the predominant gas in the cloud, had a deep-seated magmatic origin and that the lake was charged with it to near-saturation levels prior to the gas outburst. Uncertainty remained, however, about the mechanism of its eruption from the lake; in particular, whether the lake overturned in response to a small external trigger or whether a **phreatic** volcanic eruption occurred.

In an attempt to resolve this problem, and following the report of a second 'eruptive event' on 30 December 1986, the British Geological Survey installed a network of hydrophones and geophones in and around the lake during February 1987. During the following six months, regional earthquakes and small local seismic events, interpreted as rockfalls, were detected but no significant crustal earthquakes were found beneath or close to the lake. No clear evidence of magma movement or other signs of volcanic activity were found, suggesting that direct volcanic activity was not involved. Noise outbursts detected, mainly at night, may have been due to gas emissions from rock fissures.

The lack of tectonic seismicity at the lake during the monitoring period argues against an earthquake trigger for the gas release. In the wider volcanic province, however, many earthquakes were detected and such a trigger cannot be completely ruled out.

The future safety of people who live around the

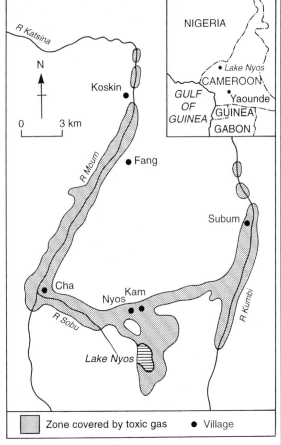

lake depends either on controlled degassing or lowering of the lake level with monitoring of CO_2 levels in the lake on a continuous basis. The data-recording techniques used in this study could readily be applied to such a broadly based monitoring system.

Two case studies: earthquake in north-west Algeria, 1994 and gas eruption at Lake Nyos in Cameroon, 1986

Two contrasting accounts of geological hazards appear in Figures 3.1 and 3.2. Figure 3.1 is a report on the earthquake in north-west Algeria and Figure 3.2 summarises an abstract from a report made by three British geologists on the Lake Nyos disaster.

The causes of geological hazards

The three main geological hazards are earthquakes, volcanoes and **tsunamis**. Both earthquakes and volcanoes release enormous amounts of energy in a relatively short space of time. Their impact is often sudden, and they can occur with very little warning. Earthquakes generally occur more frequently than volcanic eruptions; over 3000 recorded earthquakes occur each year, although only about ten of these are likely to result in serious damage to property and loss of life. By way of comparison only about half of the 1300 volcanoes that have erupted in the last 10 000 years can be considered active, and about 50 are likely to erupt in any one year. In terms of loss of life, the death toll from earthquakes in the last 500 years is estimated to be as many as 3 million people, whilst those dying directly or indirectly as a result of volcanic eruptions is significantly less at 200 000. Tsunamis, or seismic sea waves result from earthquakes under the oceans, or volcanic eruptions near, or under the sea. Loss of life from tsunamis is not always well documented, but 30 000 people were drowned by tsunamis after the eruption of Krakatoa in 1883, and 26 000 perished in Japan in the Sanriku event of 1896.

It is the surface manifestations of geological hazards that clearly have the greatest impact, in terms of loss of life and damage to property. If such consequences of these hazards are to be reduced and minimised, then an appropriate level of management is necessary. Ultimately, development of accurate prediction techniques for seismic and volcanic events, and the establishment of a range of precautionary procedures depend on an understanding of the physical processes that are responsible for the eruptions. It is in the uppermost layers of the interior of the earth that the causes of seismic activity and volcanicity have to be sought.

Earthquake waves

Most earthquakes are caused by sudden movement along a **fault plane** within the interior of the earth. The movement is the result of the release of strain in the rocks that builds up over a period of time. Figure 3.3 illustrates the build up of strain in the rocks and its subsequent release. The diagram shows a road with a thin white line at its centre, running at right angles to a fault. The tectonic forces active in this fault zone are shown by thick black and white arrows. The white line bends in response to these forces, which cause a few metres of deformation in 50 or so years. Eventually the rocks break under the strain, and the rocks on both sides of the fault at **A** rebound to their positions **A1** and **A2**. It is this **elastic rebound** that is the basic cause of earthquakes.

The point of fracture is known as the **focus** of the earthquake, and the point vertically above the focus on the surface of the earth is known as the **epicentre**. Foci of earthquakes are broadly grouped into three zones:

■ shallow focus: 0–70km deep;
■ intermediate focus: 70–300km deep;
■ deep focus: 300–700km deep.

Shallow focus earthquakes tend to cause the greatest damage, and they are responsible for 75 per cent of the total release of earthquake energy in the world.

Three main types of shock wave are released by the rupture of rocks at the focus:

1 P- or primary waves: these travel fastest (about 8km sec^{-1}), and therefore arrive first at a recording station. These are compressional waves that vibrate in the direction in which the wave is travelling. P-waves can travel through both solids and liquids.

2 S- or secondary waves travel at about half the speed of P-waves. These waves shear the rock by vibrating at right angles to the direction of travel. S-waves are unable to travel through liquids.

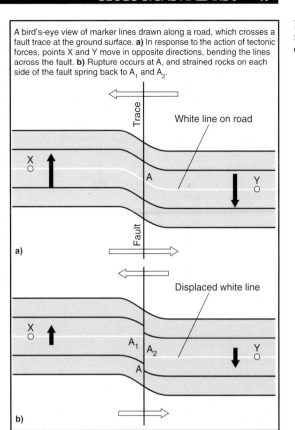

A bird's-eye view of marker lines drawn along a road, which crosses a fault trace at the ground surface. **a)** In response to the action of tectonic forces, points X and Y move in opposite directions, bending the lines across the fault. **b)** Rupture occurs at A, and strained rocks on each side of the fault spring back to A$_1$ and A$_2$.

FIGURE 3.3 The elastic rebound theory of earthquakes

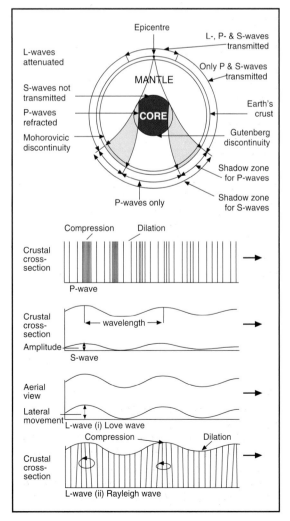

FIGURE 3.4 Seismic waves and their travel through the interior of the earth

FIGURE 3.5 Seismogram trace of shallow focus earthquake

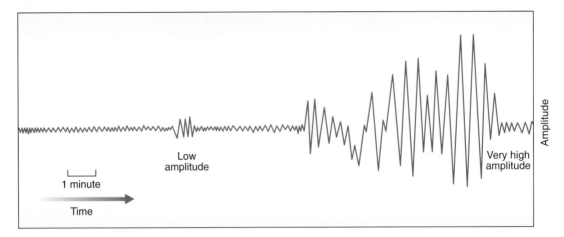

3 L-waves are surface waves whose motion is restricted to near the ground surface. These travel more slowly than S-waves, and are thus the last to arrive at a recording station. There are two types of L-waves: Love waves vibrate at right angles to the direction of propagation, but have no vertical displacement; Rayleigh waves have both horizontal and vertical movement in a vertical plane pointing in the direction of propagation of the wave.

The mode of travel of the different types of earthquake waves is shown in Figure 3.4.

STUDENT ACTIVITY 3.2

Seismograms and building damage
1 Make a copy of Figure 3.5, which shows a seismogram of a distant shallow focus earthquake. Annotate the diagram to identify three different types of earthquake wave.
2 Assess the varying degrees of damage to buildings likely to be caused by the four different types of earthquake wave.

Earthquake waves and the interior of the earth

Both P- and S-earthquake waves travel through the interior of the earth and are recorded on **seismographs**. Within the interior, P- and S-waves travel at different rates according to the density of the material through which they are travelling (it will be recalled that S-waves are not able to travel through liquids). Using data from seismographs, geologists have been able to calculate speeds of travel of P- and S-waves through the different layers of the interior, and build up a picture of their thickness and composition. This is summarised in Figure 3.4 which shows the conventional division of the interior into crust, mantle and core. The surfaces separating the different layers are known as discontinuities: the Mohorovicic discontinuity separating the crust from the mantle; and the Gutenberg discontinuity separating the mantle from the core.

Important subdivisions exist within each of these

three layers, but from the standpoint of geological hazards, recent advances in the study of the first 250km depth of the earth are the most important. Old ideas of the division of the earth's crust into an upper division (sial, having the average composition of granite) and a lower layer (sima, having an overall composition of basalt), though still valid, have had to take account of the discovery of an important low-velocity zone (LVZ) within the uppermost part of the underlying mantle (between 100–250km). Velocities of both P- and S-waves are reduced when they pass through this layer. This reduction in velocity is probably explained by the fact that this layer is partially molten (up to 10 per cent liquid).

This low-velocity layer is known as the **asthenosphere**, and it is now convenient to refer to all of the layer above the LVZ as the lithosphere. On average the **lithosphere** is about 100km thick, although geologists think that it is thinner beneath the oceans. The relative positions of the lithosphere and asthenosphere are shown in Figure 3.6. The recognition of the existence of these two layers has been fundamental in the development of understanding geological processes in the uppermost layers of the earth. The lithosphere is seen as a relatively rigid layer, whilst the asthenosphere is plastic. All of the shallow focus earthquakes occur within the lithosphere, and it is within the lithosphere and asthenosphere that most volcanicity has its origins.

Lithospheric plates and plate tectonics

Geologists now believe that the earth's lithosphere is made up of a number of rigid **plates**. These plates vary considerably in size (see Figure 3.7). Some, such as the Pacific Plate, and the smaller Nazca Plate, are made up entirely of oceanic lithosphere. Most of the other plates consist partly of continental lithosphere, and partly of oceanic lithosphere, such as the Eurasian Plate. Plates move relative to one another over the plastic asthenosphere below. The causes of this motion are deep-seated within the earth, and are likely to result from convection currents operating within the mantle.

The majority of important geological

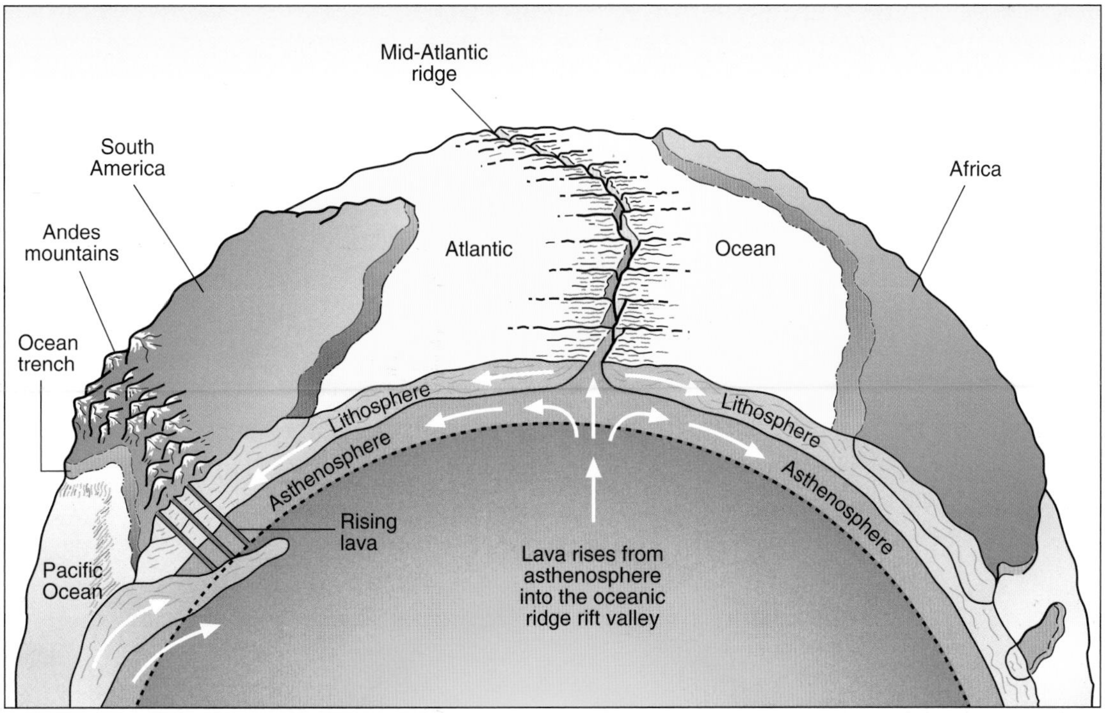
Mid-Atlantic ridge
South America
Africa
Andes mountains
Atlantic
Ocean
Ocean trench
Lithosphere
Lithosphere
Asthenosphere
Asthenosphere
Rising lava
Lava rises from asthenosphere into the oceanic ridge rift valley
Pacific Ocean

FIGURE 3.6 Location of lithosphere and asthenosphere

processes occur at **plate boundaries**. There appear to be three main types of plate boundaries or margins:

1 Constructive margins: these are found principally at the mid-oceanic ridges; an unusual example is the Red Sea. It is at these margins that new lithospheric material is being formed (see Figure 3.6), e.g. the Mid-Atlantic ridge on which Iceland is situated;

2 Destructive margins: these are found at deep **ocean trenches** and **island arcs**. They are well displayed around the margins of the Pacific Ocean (see Figure 3.7), e.g. Japan and New Zealand (see Figure 3.8). Here oceanic lithosphere is being destroyed in **subduction** zones.

Where two plates which are made up of continental lithosphere collide (e.g. the Indian and Eurasian Plates), thickening of the continental

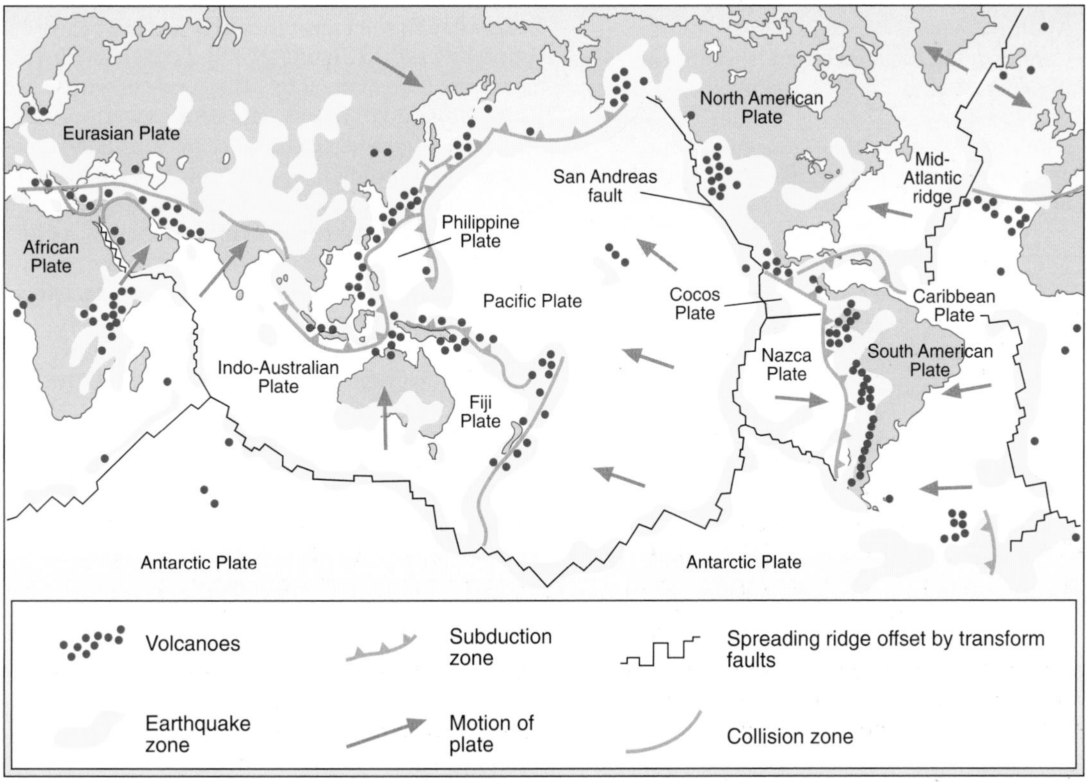
Eurasian Plate
North American Plate
Mid-Atlantic ridge
San Andreas fault
African Plate
Philippine Plate
Pacific Plate
Cocos Plate
Caribbean Plate
Indo-Australian Plate
Nazca Plate
South American Plate
Fiji Plate
Antarctic Plate
Antarctic Plate
Volcanoes
Subduction zone
Spreading ridge offset by transform faults
Earthquake zone
Motion of plate
Collision zone

FIGURE 3.7 The relationship between the major tectonic plates, distribution of recent earthquakes and volcanoes

FIGURE 3.8 a) Hekla: Iceland volcano
b) Ruapehu (North Island, New Zealand): volcano
c) Himalayas: fold mountains
d) San Andreas Fault

a)

b)

c)

d)

lithosphere occurs with the development of fold mountains, e.g. the Himalayas (Figure 3.8c).

3 Conservative margins: at these margins lithosphere is neither being created nor destroyed, plates merely slide past one another. The best-known example of this type of margin is the San Andreas fault in California (see Figure 3.8d).

With some notable exceptions (the mid-plate volcanoes of the Hawaiian Islands) central areas of plates are relatively inactive, lacking in **seismicity** and volcanicity.

The study of plates, their movements and the processes operating at their margins is known as plate tectonics.

STUDENT ACTIVITY 3.3

Plate boundaries and geological hazards
Figure 3.7 shows the earth's plates, the different types of plate margin, the distribution of recent earthquakes, and volcanoes.
1 What appears to be the broad general relationship between the distribution of earthquakes, and the location of plate boundaries?
2 To what extent does the distribution of volcanoes show a similar relationship?
3 Discuss any differences between the two distributions.

Geological processes at constructive plate margins

Mid-oceanic ridges are one of the most important features of the ocean basins. Commonly they are between 1000 to 1500km wide, and individual peaks may rise some 3000m from the ocean floor. The ridges have a somewhat irregular pattern, being offset by a series of faults, running at right angles to the main trend of the ridge. These are known as **transform faults**. These faults ensure even spreading from the ridge when it changes direction. Sometimes a deep rift runs down the centre of these ridges. An examination of the global distribution of earthquakes shows a clear linear concentration of shallow focus earthquakes along the line of the mid-oceanic ridges. The ridges are also an important site of volcanicity.

Geological research in the second half of the twentieth century has been able to provide an explanation of the relationships between the mid-oceanic ridges and their seismic and volcanic patterns. Oceanic lithosphere is made up principally of **basalt**. Examination of the ocean floor on either side of the central zone of the ridge has revealed a remarkable magnetic pattern preserved within these basalts. After basalt has been erupted, any iron minerals present align themselves to the current pattern of the earth's magnetic field. Periodically the magnetic field of the earth undergoes reversal, and such a change will be recorded in the iron minerals within the basalt.

The pattern on either side of the central zone shows a series of 'strips' of normal and reversed polarity, each side being a mirror image of the other (see Figure 3.9). Geologists also discovered that these strips increased in age away from the central zone, and, again, the pattern of ages of the strips on each side, coincided exactly with that on the other. Thus patterns of age and magnetism are symmetrical about the central zone of the ridge.

Based on these discoveries the concept of **sea-floor spreading** has been established. Basalt is erupted at the mid-oceanic ridges, cools, and its iron minerals take on the current polarity of the earth's **magnetic field**. Subsequent eruptions of basalt force existing basalt to one side. Thus the youngest oceanic lithosphere is at the centre of the mid-oceanic ridge, and the oldest is at the margins of the ocean basins.

The basalt that is erupted at mid-oceanic ridges appears to originate at depth (approximately 50km) within the asthenosphere, which is much closer to the surface beneath the mid-oceanic ridges, simply because the lithosphere is so thin there. Partial melting of asthenosphere material occurs, and since the molten material is lighter than the surrounding material it begins to rise to the surface. Some of this **magma** will solidify in the cracks that are formed as oceanic lithosphere is forced away from the central zone of the ridge. Some of the magma reaches the land surface as lava (as in Iceland, which is on the Mid-Atlantic Ridge), and is erupted to form central volcanoes such as Hekla (Figure 3.8a) or Askja, or reaches the surface through massive linear fissures and forms extensive basalt plateaux.

Earthquakes at the mid-oceanic ridges are always of shallow focus. They appear to have three main causes (see Figure 3.9):

■ earthquakes are associated with rising magma from the asthenosphere (these are sometimes known as harmonic tremors);

■ earthquakes are located along the faults associated with the fracturing of the lithosphere as it moves away from the ridge;

■ earthquakes also occur along the transform faults that offset the ridge, and produce its characteristic irregular pattern. Although the two sections of lithosphere are pulling away from the ridge as a result of sea-floor spreading, they will actually be sliding past one another along the transform faults. The friction caused by the movement will cause shallow focus earthquakes.

STUDENT ACTIVITY 3.4

Sea-floor spreading and earthquakes
Figure 3.10 shows some geological data for the ocean floor off the north-west coast of the USA and British Columbia.
1 Locate the position of the ridges from which the sea floor is spreading (N.B. these are not mid-oceanic ridges, but the principle is the same!). What is your evidence for this?
2 Locate the position of two transform faults and explain your choice.
3 Explain the distribution of earthquakes shown.

FIGURE 3.9 Seismic and volcanic patterns at mid-oceanic ridges

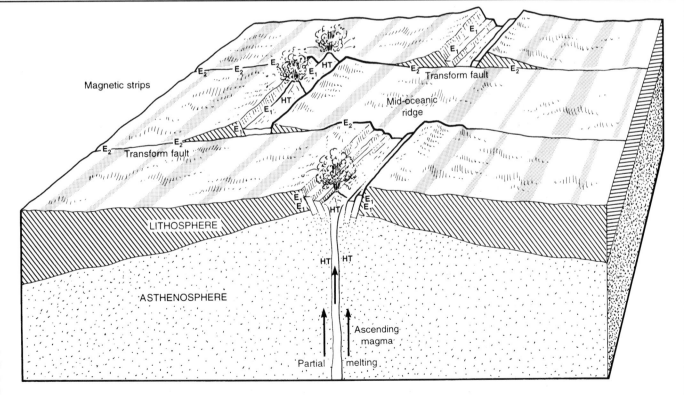

Earthquakes
1 Harmonic tremors from rising magma **HT**
2 Earthquakes on faults of fractured lithosphere **E₁**
3 Earthquakes on transform faults **E₂**

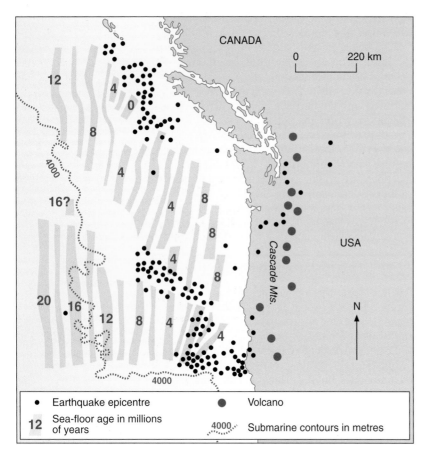

FIGURE 3.10 Tectonic features off the coast of north-west USA and British Columbia

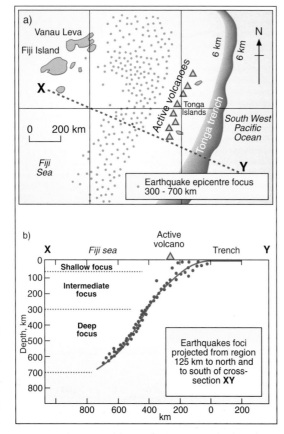

FIGURE 3.11a Distribution of earthquakes to the west of Tonga Islands

FIGURE 3.11b Vertical distribution of earthquakes west of Tonga Islands

STUDENT ACTIVITY 3.5

Earthquakes and subduction zones
Figure 3.11a shows a surface plot of earthquake epicentres associated with the subduction zone beneath the Tonga Islands in the South West Pacific. Figure 3.11b shows a three-dimensional view of the foci of these earthquakes.
1 Describe the distribution of earthquakes as indicated in the two diagrams.

Geological processes at destructive plate margins

Destructive plate margins are found around the edges of oceans, but more particularly around the Pacific Ocean. With the exception of the Caribbean they are not found in the Atlantic Ocean. This is because the Atlantic is a 'young' ocean, and the process of destruction of oceanic lithosphere has yet to commence. It is at the destructive plate margins that the process of subduction occurs. Oceanic lithosphere is denser than continental lithosphere, and thus at destructive plate margins it plunges down (or is subducted) beneath the continental crust (see Figure 3.6). In one case the Pacific actually subducts beneath another smaller oceanic plate, the Philippine Plate.

Earthquakes have a more complex pattern at destructive plate margins, than the simple shallow earthquake phenomena at the constructive plate margins. The oceanic lithosphere is subducted at varying angles. Beneath Peru it descends at a mere 10–15°, below Japan the Pacific Plate subducts at 40–45°, whilst in the New Hebrides there is a much steeper descent at 65–70°.

The inclined zone in which shallow, intermediate and deep earthquakes are recorded in a subduction zone is known as a **Benioff zone**. The earthquakes in this zone appear to be due to different causes.

■ Shallow earthquakes in the descending slab result from fracturing in the outer part of the downward-bending cold oceanic lithosphere.

■ Shallow earthquakes in the overlying slab of continental lithosphere result from block uplift and subsidence as the slab is disturbed by the subducting oceanic lithosphere beneath.

■ Intermediate and deep earthquakes in the descending slab seem to be related to compression or extension, within the slab, but with the pressures experienced at these depths it is uncertain whether the oceanic lithosphere is capable of fracturing.

The origin of magma erupted at destructive plate margins is much more complex than that at constructive margins. The simplest view is that magma is derived from partial melting of the upper surfaces of the descending oceanic lithosphere in the subduction zone. It is now thought likely that partial melting in the asthenosphere in the wedge above the descending slab may make an important contribution to the genesis of magma. Figure 3.12 summarises the main factors involved in a volcanic

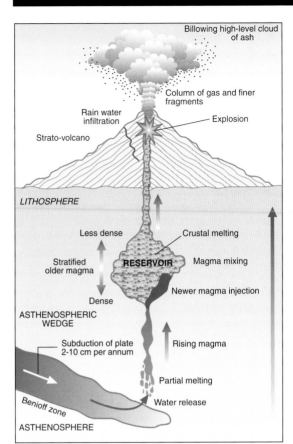

FIGURE 3.12 (*left*)
Eruption of volcano in a
subduction zone

FIGURE 3.13 (*right*)
Eruption of Mount
Merapi, Indonesia

eruption at a destructive plate margin. A much
wider variety of lavas is inevitable in such a
complex situation, but in general, they tend to have
higher silica content than those at constructive
margins, and are thus, geologically speaking, more
acid. Styles of eruption, which will be discussed
more fully later, are generally much more violent
and hazardous at destructive margins because the
lava is more viscous, contains more gases and
increases pressure within the conduit (the passage
leading to the surface) of the volcano (see Figure
3.13).

Geological processes at conservative plate margins

These margins are much less common than either
constructive or destructive plate examples. Apart
from the San Andreas Fault, other instances include
the Alpine Fault in New Zealand, and the Anatolian
Fault in Turkey. At these margins lithosphere is
neither being created nor destroyed, the plates
simply slip laterally past one another. The San
Andreas Fault (see Figure 3.14) separates the south-
western part of California from the rest of North
America. It forms the boundary between the North
American Plate and the Pacific Plate. The relative
motion between the North American Plate and the
Pacific Plate is probably about 6.3 cm per year, with
the Pacific Plate slipping to the north-west past the
North American Plate. As a result of this slippage,
in 10 million years time Los Angeles is likely to be
abreast of San Francisco! In 60 million years time it

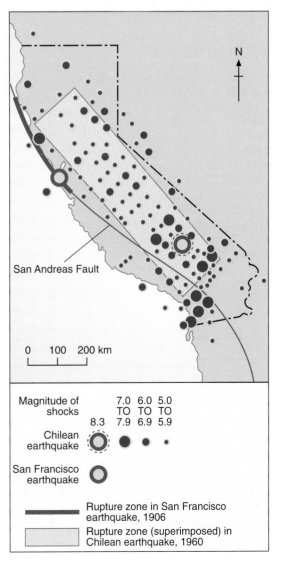

FIGURE 3.14 Rupture
zones: San Andreas
Fault, 1906 and Chilean
earthquake, 1960

will start sliding into the Aleutian Trench south of Alaska!

Earthquakes along the San Andreas Fault are almost always shallow in focus. The Loma Prieta earthquake of 1989 had unusually deep foci for earthquakes along the San Andreas Fault, at 15–18km. These earthquakes appear to be caused when some sections of the fault seem to lock, and the resultant tension is then suddenly released in a severe earthquake.

STUDENT ACTIVITY 3.6

Earthquakes and conservative plate margins
Figure 3.14 shows the San Andreas Fault, the epicentre of the 1906 earthquake, and the area that ruptured in this earthquake (15km deep, 400km long). Also shown, superimposed, for scale purposes, is the area that was ruptured in the Chilean earthquake of 1960, together with its epicentre, and the location of aftershocks. The Chilean earthquake occurred at a destructive plate margin.
1 Explain the spatial pattern of the aftershocks that occurred in the Chilean earthquake.
2 Both the 1906 and 1960 earthquakes were recorded at 8.3 on the Richter scale, and were therefore of similar magnitude. Explain why damage in a Chilean earthquake is likely to be more widespread than in an earthquake on the San Andreas Fault.

The consequences and impact of geological hazards

Earthquake hazards

Two main concepts are used for measuring the size of earthquakes – **magnitude** and **intensity**. The concept of magnitude was first developed by C F Richter for comparing earthquakes in California. Since there is such a huge size range in earthquakes, the Richter scale of magnitude is logarithmic, each unit measures a ten-fold increase in the amplitude of measured earthquake waves and a nearly 30-fold increase in energy. Earthquake intensity measures the degree of shaking, and records the level of damage and other consequences of the earthquake. In 1902 Guiseppe Mercalli developed a 12-point scale for measuring the intensity of earthquakes. Magnitude and intensity measure two different properties of earthquakes, but it is possible to establish an approximate correlation between the two as below.

Intensity	Magnitude
Level I (detected by seismometers but felt by very few people)	2
Level VIII (weak buildings, walls and chimneys fall)	6
Level XII (total destruction, ground seen to shake)	8.5

Lines of equal intensity (**isoseismal lines**) can be drawn for an earthquake, showing the decrease of intensity from the epicentre. Four main earthquake hazards exist and they can be classified into the following.

1 PRIMARY EARTHQUAKE HAZARDS	a Ground shaking
2 SECONDARY EARTHQUAKE HAZARDS	b Soil liquefaction c Landslides, rock and snow avalanches d Tsunamis

Ground shaking is the main hazard created by earthquakes. Its severity at any one point depends on a range of factors, including the magnitude of the earthquake, the distance from the epicentre, and local geological conditions.

Soil liquefication is a common secondary hazard: sediments that have a high water content lose their mechanical strength when violently shaken and behave like a fluid.

Landslides, rock and snow avalanches occur in mountainous areas when slopes respond to strong shaking by weakening and eventually failing.

Tsunamis are seismic sea waves resulting from earthquakes under the oceans, or submarine volcanic eruptions.

Case studies of earthquakes

The Good Friday earthquake, Alaska 1964

This earthquake appears to have occurred in the subduction zone where the Pacific Plate is being thrust down beneath the North American Plate, along the line of the parallel Aleutian Islands and the Aleutian Trench. This is one of the most powerful seismic zones in the world, with a recorded history of shocks of high magnitude, e.g. between 1899 and the 1964 earthquake there were 11 shocks greater than Richter 7.7 in this zone. Figure 3.15 shows the main regional effects of disturbance. Much of the coastal zone was uplifted by up to 11m. On the landward side a parallel zone of subsidence occurred where a huge tract of coastal mountains appears to have subsided by 2m. The death toll of 131 in the Good Friday earthquake was relatively low and many of these resulted from the ensuing tsunamis. It was the unprecedented degree of ground disturbance, and the consequent damage to buildings, public utilities and communications that make this earthquake of particular interest (see Figure 3.16).

The epicentre of the earthquake was close to College Fiord, an arm of Prince William Sound, and appears to have been of shallow focus at between 20–50km in depth. Shaking of the ground lasted for an unusually long time – up to 7 minutes in some areas. Surface movement took a variety of forms, including rockslide avalanches on the coastal glaciers, submarine slides from lake shores and coasts, horizontal slipping and sliding of soil and loosely consolidated sediments. One of the most documented and most studied events was the great landslide at Turnagain Heights, an affluent suburb of Anchorage overlooking the inlet of Knik Arm (Figure 3.17).

Robert Atwood later recalled the terrifying events of that Good Friday afternoon.

'I headed for the door. At the door I saw walls weaving. On the driveway I turned and watched my house squirm and groan. Tall trees were falling in our yard. I moved to a spot where I thought it would be safe, but, as I moved I saw cracks appear in the earth. Pieces of ground in jig-saw puzzle shapes moved up and down tilted at all angles. I tried to move away, but more appeared in every direction. I noticed that my house was moving away from me, fast ... deep chasms opened up. Table top pieces of earth moved upwards, standing like toadstools with great overhangs, some were turned at crazy angles. A chasm opened beneath me. I tumbled down. I was quickly on the verge of being buried ... Then my neighbour's house collapsed and slid into the chasm ...'

Figure 3.17 shows a cross-section through part of the Turnagain Heights area. It is underlain by a clay formation with lenses of sand, covered by glacial outwash material of sand and gravel. Under intense earthquake stress the sand lenses liquefied, and the clay lost much of its strength, and began to fracture and slide towards the inlet of Knik Arm. Similar slides devastated much of the central part of Anchorage.

The small town of Valdez lies on one of the inlets of Prince William Sound, about 70km from the epicentre of the Alaska Earthquake. It is built on a delta, made up of loosely consolidated sediments, mainly sands and gravels, which are inherently unstable, and liable to liquefy in an earthquake. Eyewitness accounts of the events at Valdez present a picture even more frightening than the landslides

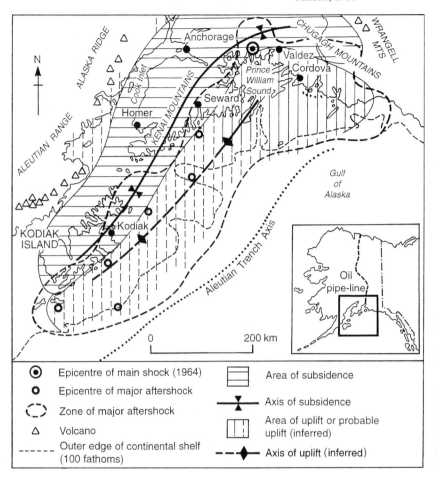

FIGURE 3.15 Regional effects of the Good Friday earthquake, Alaska, 1964

◉ Epicentre of main shock (1964)	▤ Area of subsidence
○ Epicentre of major aftershock	Axis of subsidence
⟋‾⟍ Zone of major aftershock	⊞ Area of uplift or probable uplift (inferred)
△ Volcano	Axis of uplift (inferred)
------ Outer edge of continental shelf (100 fathoms)	

FIGURE 3.16 Damage to Fourth Avenue, Anchorage in Alaska, 1964

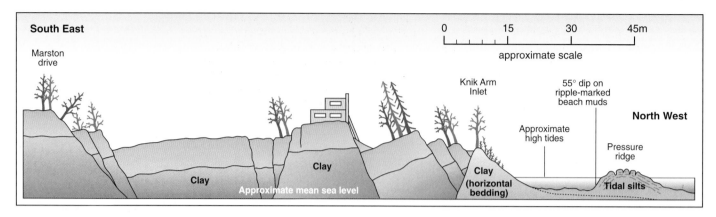

South East

Marston drive

0   15   30   45m

approximate scale

Knik Arm Inlet

55° dip on ripple-marked beach muds

North West

Approximate high tides

Pressure ridge

Clay

Clay

Approximate mean sea level

Clay (horizontal bedding)

Tidal silts

FIGURE 3.17 Section through the eastern part of Turnagain Heights

at Anchorage. A small freighter, the SS Chena was being unloaded at the piers running out from the shore. Captain Stewart, master of the Chena, recalls the events.

*'The Valdez piers began to collapse right away ...
The whole ship raised about 30 feet on an incoming wave. The whole ship lifted and heeled to port about 50°. Then it was slammed down heavily on the spot where the docks had disintegrated moments before. I saw people running – with no place to run to. It was just ghastly. They were just engulfed by buildings, water, mud and everything ...'*

Much of the front of the delta sheared off in a huge submarine landslide (see Figure 3.18), the result of intense liquefaction of the sandy sediments. As the material from the delta slumped out into the bay it generated a huge wave some 10m high that surged on to the devastated waterfront. This was followed later by a reflection of the first wave from the opposite side of the bay.

STUDENT ACTIVITY 3.7

Lessons from the Alaskan earthquake, 27 March 1964

1 In *The Alaska Earthquake, March 27, 1964: Lessons and Conclusions*, Edwin B Eckel wrote *'Every large earthquake, wherever located should be regarded as a full scale laboratory experiment whose study can give scientific and engineering information unobtainable from any other source.'*
a) What general points could be learnt from the Good Friday earthquake?
b) Why could the sites of Turnagain Heights, Valdez and Seward be shown on a post-earthquake risk map as being particularly hazardous?
c) Valdez was totally abandoned after the earthquake, and relocated elsewhere on Valdez Arm (see Figure 3.18), and subsequently chosen as the terminus for the Trans-Alaska Pipeline. What assurances concerning the new site would need to have been given before the new town and installations were built?

FIGURE 3.18 Submarine slide that destroyed the waterfront in Valdez

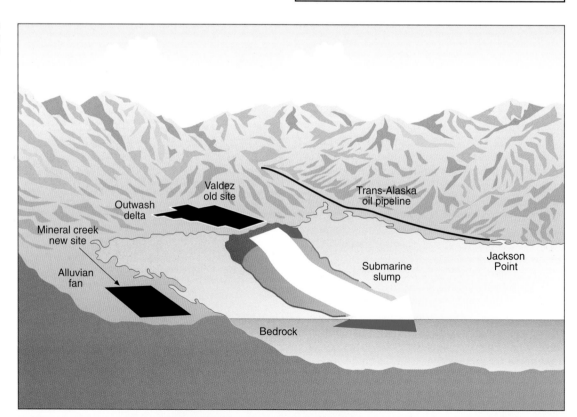

Outwash delta

Valdez old site

Trans-Alaska oil pipeline

Mineral creek new site

Alluvian fan

Submarine slump

Jackson Point

Bedrock

Seward is a small port, some 120km south of Anchorage, built on an alluvial fan. It is the southern terminus of the Alaska railroad, and, like Valdez, has the advantage of being ice-free throughout the year. It was some 150km from the epicentre, and the effects of the earthquake were remarkably similar to those at Valdez. Much of the waterfront was sheared off in a submarine landslide. Subsequent waves did enormous amounts of damage to the oil and railroad installations. Locally generated waves were followed by much larger tsunamis, which increased the damage. In addition much devastation was caused by shaking of the ground.

FIGURE 3.19 Factors controlling the degree of damage in Mexico City earthquake
(a) Influence of lake sediments
(b) Thickness of clay in the lake zone
(c) Building height
(d) Mode of construction

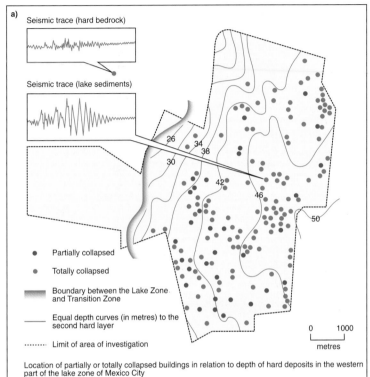

Location of partially or totally collapsed buildings in relation to depth of hard deposits in the western part of the lake zone of Mexico City

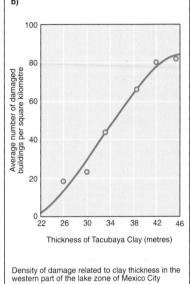

Density of damage related to clay thickness in the western part of the lake zone of Mexico City

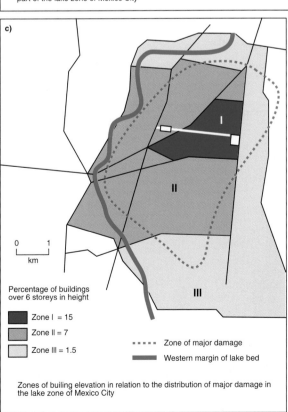

Zones of builing elevation in relation to the distribution of major damage in the lake zone of Mexico City

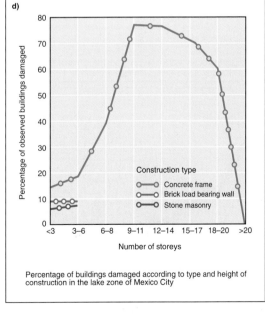

Percentage of buildings damaged according to type and height of construction in the lake zone of Mexico City

The Mexico City earthquake, 19 September 1985

Many people were very surprised when it was revealed that the epicentre of this earthquake, with a magnitude of Richter 8.1, was some 350km away from Mexico City in the trench that lies off the Pacific coast of Mexico. Evidence from records, however, indicates that the 1985 earthquake follows a pattern. In the twentieth century alone, 34 major earthquakes with magnitudes ranging from Richter 7.0 to 8.4, have occurred in the subduction zone where the Cocos Plate is being thrust beneath the North American Plate (Figure 3.7). The rupture causing the earthquake occurred in the Michoacan Gap (this is a seismic gap where no major earthquakes had occurred for some time, and therefore considerable stress had built up). It is likely that Mexico City is under even more threat from the Guerrero Gap to the north-west of Acapulco. Considerable damage was done in the coastal states adjacent to the epicentre, but by far the greatest devastation occurred in Mexico City.

After a transmission time of 1 minute, the earthquake waves arrived in Mexico City. Much of the city centre is built on the bed of an old lake, Lake Texcoco, and this helps to explain the notorious Mexico City effect. Soft, high-water-content sediments within the lake bed cause an intensification of the vibrations of earthquake waves as they pass through them (Figure 3.19a).

More than 10 000 people were killed, approximately 50 000 injured and 250 000 were made homeless. Out of 800 000 buildings in the city the relatively small number of 770 were totally destroyed, although the total number damaged was 7400. Mexico City has a population of approximately 20 million (over 20 per cent of the population of Mexico), and is growing at 2.56 per cent per annum. It is clearly one of the world's most hazard-prone cities.

FIGURE 3.20 Seismic gaps: San Andreas Fault

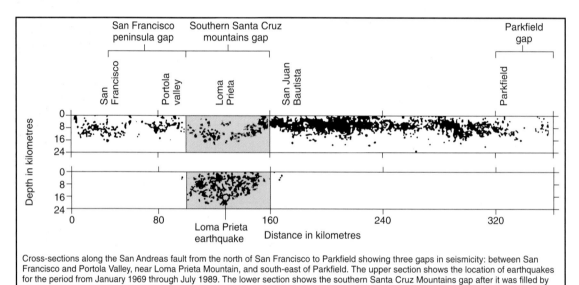

Cross-sections along the San Andreas fault from the north of San Francisco to Parkfield showing three gaps in seismicity: between San Francisco and Portola Valley, near Loma Prieta Mountain, and south-east of Parkfield. The upper section shows the location of earthquakes for the period from January 1969 through July 1989. The lower section shows the southern Santa Cruz Mountains gap after it was filled by the 17 October Loma Prieta earthquake (open circle) and its aftershocks.

FIGURE 3.21 Probability and magnitude of future earthquakes along the San Andreas Fault

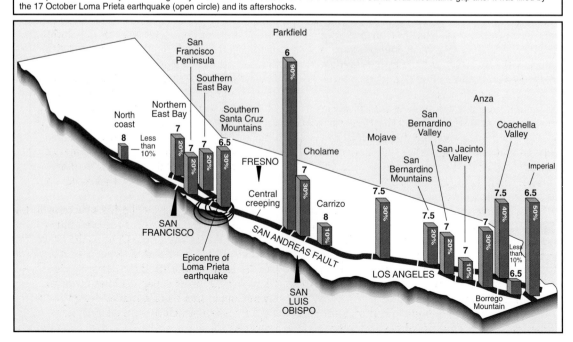

The Loma Prieta earthquake, California, 17 October 1989

This earthquake with a magnitude of Richter 7.1, occurred in the Santa Cruz mountains, some 96km south-east of San Francisco. It was the worst to hit the city and its surrounding area since the massive earthquake of 1906. The earthquake appears to have been caused by a slip along the San Andreas Fault. It was, as expected a shallow focus event, some 18km below the surface, with the rupture eventually spreading over 40km along the fault, and upwards to within 6km of the surface. Loma Prieta is located within one of the locked sections of the San Andreas Fault, which last had major movement in 1906. The Loma Prieta section had been almost aseismic for 20 years before the event, and a clear 'seismic gap' existed. The main shock and the ensuing aftershocks almost completely filled the gap (see Figure 3.20). Thus the event was not entirely unexpected, but, like all earthquakes, it was not possible to predict it precisely. Figure 3.21 shows the probability and likely magnitude of earthquakes along the San Andreas Fault for the next 30 years in densely populated areas. Fortunately the damage that occurred near the epicentre of the Loma Prieta earthquake was relatively small because of its low population. Figure 3.21 shows that with future earthquakes along the San Andreas Fault, much greater levels of damage might well occur.

As in both the previous case studies the role of loose saturated sands in promoting greater levels of vibration appears to have been crucial in determining which areas are likely to have suffered the most damage. In the rocky parts of the hills around San Francisco Bay intense vibrations lasted for two seconds or so whilst buildings on soft sands or filled ground saw more intense vibrations lasting for ten seconds. Areas that suffered from liquefaction in the 1906 earthquake saw a repetition of the process, with the same devastating results. Some of the most serious damage resulting from liquefaction was in the Marina district (Figure 3.22).

Awareness of the earthquake hazard is probably higher in California than in almost any other comparable area in the world. Many buildings and other structures have been strengthened or purpose-built to make them earthquake-resistant, and the Loma Prieta was their first real test. The US geological Survey Report stated: '*Although the majority of facilities performed well, many failed the test.*' Strong-motion instruments were emplaced in many structures throughout the San Francisco Bay region and important lessons will have been learnt from their records. '*During the earthquake no engineering structure built on the basis of the latest codes collapsed*' (US Geological Survey Report). This sounds very positive, but it needs to be qualified. The report continues, '*Building codes aim to reduce, rather than to prevent, damage to structures during the most severe shaking likely to occur in the region.*' Thus, near the epicentre, homes built to code had serious failures, often resulting in the structure being sheared off its foundations. In downtown San Francisco, modern high-rise buildings up to 50 storeys escaped without structural damage (many of these were built on fill or bay mud but their foundations were securely fixed into layers at depths that have high-bearing strength). The particularly severe damage in the Marina district was partly caused by the liquefaction of the underlying silty sand, but also by inadequate building safeguards.

The collapse of parts of bridge structures in the San Francisco Bay region has received much attention. The failure of the Cypress Street viaduct in Oakland was responsible for 41 deaths out of a total of 62 in California. Basic design faults have been blamed for its collapse. Other viaducts within San Francisco of a similar design to the Cypress Street structure were also severely damaged.

FIGURE 3.22 Earthquake damage in the Marina district of San Francisco

FIGURE 3.23 Seismic zonation in San Francisco

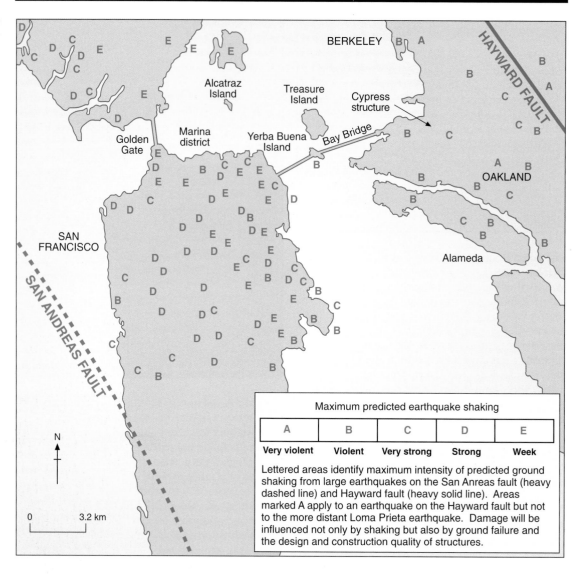

Maximum predicted earthquake shaking

A	B	C	D	E
Very violent	Violent	Very strong	Strong	Week

Lettered areas identify maximum intensity of predicted ground shaking from large earthquakes on the San Anreas fault (heavy dashed line) and Hayward fault (heavy solid line). Areas marked A apply to an earthquake on the Hayward fault but not to the more distant Loma Prieta earthquake. Damage will be influenced not only by shaking but also by ground failure and the design and construction quality of structures.

STUDENT ACTIVITY 3.9

Seismic zonation in San Francisco
In the San Francisco Bay area, the principle of **seismic zonation** has received considerable attention. This involves mapping the areas that are most vulnerable to seismic activity. The map in Figure 3.23 shows seismic zonation for the San Francisco Bay region.
1 Comment on the distribution of zones A and B which are prone to the most violent shaking.
2 How is the distribution of these zones related to the areas that were most severely damaged in the Loma Prieta earthquake?
3 What are the main uses of such a map to the San Francisco Bay region authorities?

The Kobe earthquake, 17 January 1995

The most devastating earthquake to strike Japan since the Tokyo earthquake of 1923 when 143 000 people were killed, occurred near the city of Kobe, on the Inland Sea, on 17 January 1995. The earthquake measured 7.2 on the Richter scale, and

its epicentre appears to have been located on a shallow fault zone some 200km from the main plate boundary between the Philippine and Eurasian Plates (see Figure 3.24). The **strike-slip** pattern of the earthquake is similar to the Loma Prieta event, with as much as 2m of surface slip on Awaji Island south-west of the epicentre.

Nearly 5000 people were killed in the earthquake, and 250 000 were rendered homeless. It occurred at 5.45 am local time, and clearly loss of life would have been much heavier if it had happened two or three hours later in the rush hour. With a high level of earthquake awareness in Japan, the structure of modern buildings is designed to withstand the strains imposed by seismic shocks. Thus, most of the buildings built to these stringent specifications seemed to have survived, but many older concrete buildings lacking this inbuilt protection collapsed. The worst devastation appears to have been in the traditional-style Japanese wooden houses, with whole floors collapsing into one another. Popular myth was that such buildings would survive in an earthquake, but experience in Kobe proved this to be untrue (Figure 3.25).

Considerable damage to the urban infrastructure inevitably occurred. The Hanshin Express Way collapsed in five places and the Bay Coast Highway failed over a section of reclaimed land. Lines for the high-speed 'bullet trains' collapsed at 36 places over a distance of 90km. Public utilities were damaged over a wide area, with water, electricity and gas supplies being disrupted. Supplies of gas to nearly 1 million households had to be discontinued because of the fire hazard.

'The Kobe disaster has been an important case study of how we cannot manage a crisis in Japan.' Professor Masashi Nishihara, of the National Defence Academy.

'The response to the earthquake of what many call the faceless and gigantic bureaucracy that controls Japan was dictated by territorialism, passivism and the inclination to follow precedent at times of emergency.' Mr Tatou Takayama, a commentator for the largest selling daily newspaper, the Yomiuri Shimbun.

Many comments similar to those above suggest that the response to the Kobe earthquake by the authorities left much to be desired. Even in one of the most technologically advanced countries in the world, flaws in its hazard management procedures were exposed:

■ the authorities waited five hours before calling in the Self-Defence Force;

■ government officials debated for days whether to designate the Kobe area 'a Particularly Terrible Disaster' – a legal requirement necessary to clear the way for special emergency relief;

■ offers from the United States military stationed in Japan were discussed for two days before being accepted;

■ there is a lack of a single powerful central authority to co-ordinate relief work. At the moment a weak ministry outside the cabinet, the National Land Agency, co-ordinates emergency responses, but is so weak that local government tends to bypass it and go straight to the services themselves;

■ bureaucratic delays in accepting foreign offers of help, e.g. discussion of whether Swiss sniffer dogs should undergo the statutory period of quarantine and the initial refusal to accept foreign medical teams because they were not qualified to work as doctors in Japan.

The Kobe earthquake also raises some important issues concerning seismological prediction research and the construction of earthquake-proof buildings. The Japanese Government has designated ten regions for the intensive monitoring of earthquakes, one of which covers the cities of Kobe, Kyoto, Osaka and Nagoya and the tip of Awaji Island. The most intensive observations, however, have been concentrated in the Kanto and Tokai regions around Tokyo, even to the extent that researchers claimed that they could predict the next earthquake in that region. Although small-scale foreshocks occurred at the Kobe epicentre, their significance was not correctly interpreted or understood. Harumo Aoki, head of the Co-ordination Committee for

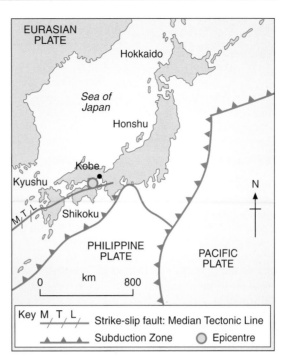

FIGURE 3.24 Seismic features of the Kobe earthquake

FIGURE 3.25 Buddhist monk prays at the devastated site where four people died in Kobe

Earthquake Prediction Research commented: 'We have repeatedly warned that the area around Kobe is riddled with active faults, but in practice only a few earthquakes have been felt, and the danger was not appreciated.'

Many experts now feel that the establishment of an effective and reliable earthquake prediction service is still a distant, if not impossible, goal. More research on a strong ground motion, which will provide data on the level of a disaster in different areas is required, since it will enable relief teams and other emergency procedures to be targeted effectively in the areas most requiring assistance. Data on strong ground motion is vital to future work on the design of earthquake-proof buildings.

The Armenia earthquake, 7 December 1988

This earthquake, which had a magnitude of Richter 7.0, devastated large sections of the three Armenian cities of Spitak, Leninakan and Kirovokan and appears to have resulted from a fault rupture on the southern side of the Caucasus mountains. Since all three cities were relatively close to the epicentre, serious damage was to be expected in an area not noted for its preparedness. Estimates of the death toll varied between 25 000 and 100 000. In Leninakan, 80 per cent of the structures collapsed or were seriously damaged; in Spitak all of the buildings were damaged; in Kirovakan damage was considerably less.

Loss of life and damage in Armenia would certainly appear to have been disproportionate. Soft sediments under Leninakan and Spitak were again a contributory factor, but certainly not the main one. Armenian and Russian engineers summarised the situation:

'The catastrophic earthquake that occurred on December 7, 1988 brought about heavy damage to most buildings and structures in many cities and villages. Initial results of our investigations revealed that in its manifestation most frame and nine-storey panel buildings were completely destroyed. Stone buildings with no anti-seismic measures of construction collapsed.'

A professor at a university in the USA has since written: *'Clearly, with regard to earthquake hazards, the system of prefabrication and site assembly of structural components in use in Armenia was deeply flawed.'*

The north-west Afghanistan Earthquake, 30 May 1998

North-west Afghanistan lies in a pronounced seismic zone running through Central Asia, where the Indo-Australian plate is in collision with the Eurasian plate. Earthquakes of magnitude 6.0 and above on the Richter scale are quite common in this belt. The epicentre of this particular earthquake appears to have been near the remote village of Shari Basurk, close to the border of Turkmenistan, and registered a magnitude of 6.9 (see Figure 3.26). It occurred barely four months after a similar event farther to the east near the small town of Rostaq, some 500km to the east. Both areas are hundreds of kms from Kabul, the capital of Afghanistan, and lie

FIGURE 3.26 The north-west Afghanistan earthquake, 30 May 1998

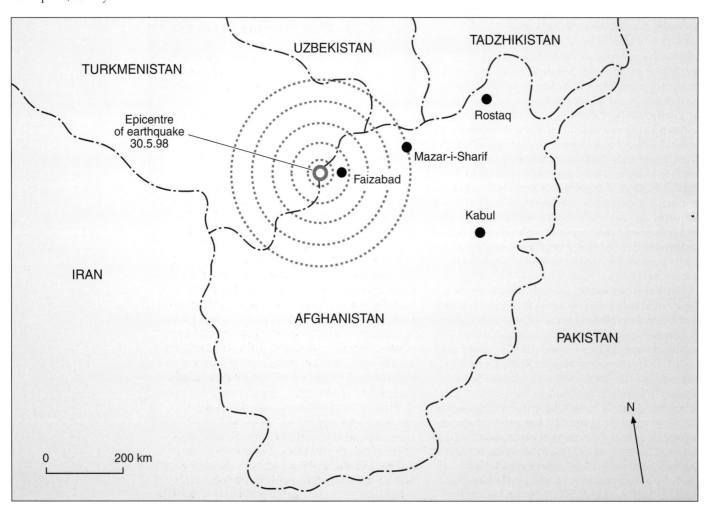

in mountainous terrain, which is penetrated by few roads and is served only by widely spaced airstrips, from which any rescue operations have to be organised.

Compared to the major urban areas affected by the earthquakes already described in this section, areas such as the inaccessible mountain areas of Afghanistan suffer from a whole range of additional problems in the immediate aftermath of an earthquake:

- many villages are built in very precarious physical locations, particularly susceptible to destruction in an earthquake;
- damage is often worsened by other physical events, such as landslides, triggered by the initial seismic activity;
- as a result of inaccessibility the scale of the damage to villages, and the number of casualties is not known for a considerable interval after the event;
- there is rarely, if ever, any contingency plan for dealing with the immediate physical effect of the earthquake;
- local medical and welfare facilities are rudimentary in the extreme, and are unable to respond to any emergency;
- the provision of water and sanitation is usually primitive, and the risk of post-event disease and infection is much greater;
- the majority of the dwellings in such areas are often constructed of adobe, which has a very poor earthquake survival rate, particularly if it has already been weakened by previous seismic activity;
- aid and supplies are often slow in reaching the stricken area because of its remoteness and poor communications with the rest of the country.

The earthquake struck during the afternoon of the 30 May 1998, and was followed by four aftershocks. The timing of the earthquake probably reduced the number of casualties since many people were not in their frail adobe houses at the time. Maps of the remote area were often inaccurate, and many of the stricken villages were not even recorded on the map sheets that the rescue organisations were using. As is often the case in such areas, where people live in very primitive conditions, up to 25 villages were completely destroyed, and it is unlikely that some of them will be rebuilt. Up to 100 villages were affected, an estimated 5000 people were killed and 95 000 rendered homeless in the aftermath of the earthquake.

Reports on the initial reaction and response of international organisations such as the United Nations and the International Red Cross were somewhat contradictory. In the period immediately following the earlier earthquake in February 1998, it took five days for emergency supplies to reach the afflicted areas. In the second earthquake aid was arriving within a matter of hours according to some reports; other accounts still complained of long delays in the arrival of help. Food and other supplies had been stockpiled after the previous

Rostaq earthquake, and the United Nations still had more than $1 million dollars in unused funds. Nevertheless, the severe physical conditions encountered in the area hampered relief activity. Landslides blocked most of the already poor access roads into the worst hit region of Bandakhshan, two days drive away from the relief centre of Faizabad under normal conditions. Poor visibility hampered helicopter operations over much of north-west Afghanistan, and the same adverse weather conditions were responsible for flooding in the areas affected by the earthquake, further delaying the relief operation.

Much of Afghanistan has suffered during the war against the U.S.S.R. in the 1980s and more so during the current ongoing internal conflict between the hardline Taliban militia, which controls much of the country and the Northern Alliance. Aid workers are naturally concerned about their own safety in a country so riven with conflict, and this, together with the damage done to the country's economy and infrastructure, further hampered the relief operations. Latif Shah, a farmer in remote Shari Basurk, perhaps summed up a stoic community's reaction: *'We must leave everything in Allah's hands, but sometimes I wonder why He is punishing the people of this country so much.'*

STUDENT ACTIVITY 3.11

Survival rates and relief priorities in remote earthquake locations

1 Summarise the reasons why survival rates in an earthquake in a remote area such as north-west Afghanistan are likely to be so much lower than in more developed areas?

2 What priorities would govern decisions that have been made by relief organisations operating in such remote areas?

The Colombian Earthquake, 25 January 1999

The location of this earthquake, in the Andean part of Colombia, lies in the seismic zone where the Nazca Plate is subducting beneath the South American Plate. The epicentre of the earthquake, which measured 6.0 on the Richter scale, was at Quindio, some 225km to the north-west of the capital, Bogota. The main city affected was Armenia, an important centre in the coffee-growing region of the country, although many of the other towns and villages in Quindio province suffered varying degrees of damage. Earthquakes are common in Colombia, with the most recent occurring in 1994, when 800 people were killed in the south of the country.

Much of Armenia was destroyed in the earthquake (see Figure 3.27), with most of its 200 000 population rendered homeless. Many of the residential districts were completely devastated, and in the centre few public buildings had been built to withstand earthquakes. The shanty towns on the edge of Armenia appeared to

FIGURE 3.27 Armenia City, Columbia

be some of the worst hit: in one, Brasilia, all 300 of the flimsy homes collapsed and 300 people died. Although international aid seemed to have reached Colombia fairly quickly, bureaucratic delays meant that relief was not reaching the areas affected quickly enough. Four days after the earthquake, inhabitants, despairing of receiving any kind of support from outside, began to take matters into their own hands. Looting of supermarkets was common, and security forces appeared to be able to do little to stop people who were desperate for food, and other essential items. At one stage matters deteriorated so much that international relief teams had to withdraw from the worst hit areas. Early reports suggested a death toll of approximately 1000, although as rescue work continued the final level was much higher.

STUDENT ACTIVITY 3.12

Earthquakes in Economically Less Developed Countries
1 Both Afghanistan and Colombia are economically less developed countries. Explain why the circumstances of the two earthquakes were different, and how this affected the response.
2 What lessons need to be learnt from the rioting and looting that occurred in Armenia, Colombia?

STUDENT ACTIVITY 3.13

Summary essay: earthquakes as hazards
Produce a detailed 250-word essay plan for one of the following two alternative essay titles.
1 More careful location of residential areas in earthquake-prone zones could reduce both property damage and loss of life. Discuss this statement with reference to a range of examples.
2 To what extent are poor building regulations responsible for high loss of life in earthquakes?

Volcanic hazards

Although many volcanic eruptions are spectacular (see Figure 3.13), and attract intense media attention, the volcanic hazard generally has far less impact than earthquakes. Like earthquakes the majority of volcanoes are found along plate margins, and many erupt in locations which carry little or no population. Indeed the most common eruptions are submarine ones along the mid-oceanic ridges which create new oceanic lithosphere. Many volcanic eruptions occur on islands either on the mid-oceanic ridges, e.g. Iceland, or an island arcs associated with subduction zones, e.g. the West Indies, the Indonesian archipelago, parts of the Mediterranean, or on the mid-plate volcanoes of the Pacific such as Hawaii. Where these islands are densely populated, as is often the case in the Caribbean and Hawaii, the volcanic hazard, although localised, has to be taken seriously. Volcanoes within the younger fold mountains are often in remote areas and thus present little threat to people, but where pockets of population occur near volcanic centres, as in parts of the Andes, the hazard is a very real one. The eruption of Nevado del Ruiz in 1985, in the Colombian Andes, although neither particularly large nor violent, was responsible for the largest loss of life in an eruption in the twentieth century since that of Mont Pelée in 1902.

Eruption styles

The nature of a volcano, and, to a certain extent, the severity of the associated hazard, depends on its style of eruption. This, in its turn, depends on the type of magma that is erupted. Generally lava of a basic composition (low silica content of 45–52 per cent), e.g. **basalt**, will result in quiescent eruptions, whilst more acid, viscous lava, produces more violent eruptions. A number of eruption styles are commonly recognised and distinguished by their increasingly explosive nature (Figure 3.28).

1 Icelandic style: eruption of predominantly mobile, basic basaltic lavas. It occurs in regions of crustal tension, e.g. mid-ocean ridges. Fissure eruptions lead to the accumulation of widespread sheets of basaltic lava.

2 Hawaiian style: although some mobile lava is erupted from fissures, most lava emissions occur from clusters of vents in central volcanoes.

3 Strombolian style: eruptions are slightly more explosive due to the existence of more viscous lava.

4 Vulcanian style: much more gas, ash and cinders are erupted in this type of eruption. Gases are trapped for longer time intervals, and thus when the pressure is suddenly released the eruptions are more violent.

5 Vesuvian style: long periods of quiescence mean that the viscous lava, usually andesitic, becomes highly charged with gases. Large, dark clouds are erupted high into the atmosphere.

6 Plinian style: this produces the most violent uprush of gas, charged with fine ash and pumice.

7 Pelean style: upward escape of explosive gases is prevented by solidified lava. Compressed material forces its way out in a huge lateral blast that destroys everything in its downward path.

Keith Smith, an environmental scientist, recognises seven main types of volcanic hazard resulting from the range of eruptions indicated above.

Primary volcanic hazards

Nués ardentes

Air fall **tephra**

Lava flows

Secondary volcanic hazards

Volcanic gases

Lahars

Landslides

Tsunamis

Nués ardentes (incandescent clouds) are huge

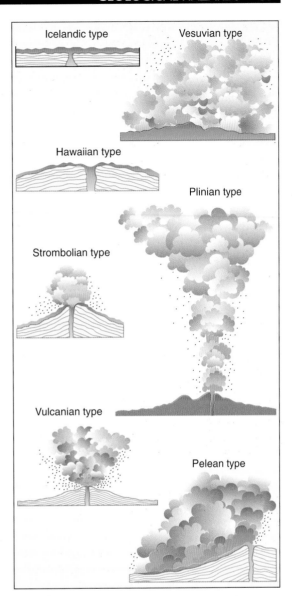

FIGURE 3.28 Styles of volcanic eruption

clouds of very hot gases (up to 1000°C) charged with all types of volcanic fragments, which rush downhill at speeds of 100km per hour. Little in their path survives.

Air fall tephra includes all solid material, of varying grain size, that is erupted and later falls to the ground. It includes material such as volcanic bombs and fine dust.

Lava flows vary in mobility according to their composition, but the most mobile basalts can travel at speeds of up to 50km per hour and can overwhelm people and buildings within a very short time.

Volcanic gases are released in eruptions, and encompass an astonishing variety of chemical composition. Only rarely, as in the case of Lake Nyos, are they the direct cause of volcanic disaster.

Lahars are volcanic mudflows. A mix of water, from heavy rain, melting ice and snow, or from draining crater lakes, and soft volcanic ash can have a devastating effect as it moves downhill, at speeds of up to 80km per hour.

Landslides occur when particularly viscous material is injected into the upper structure of a volcano. This sets up stresses that result in huge fractures in the volcano, and the structure can later collapse, as occurred in the case of Mount St Helens.

Tsunamis are more associated with earthquakes than with volcanic eruptions, although the tsunami resulting from the eruption of Krakatoa drowned some 30 000 people in 1883.

Case studies of volcanic hazards

Several volcanic eruptions and locations prone to volcanic hazards are examined in the following sections.

Mont Pelée, 8 May 1902

Mont Pelée lies on Martinique, one of the Lesser Antilles in the Caribbean, a volcanic island arc,

FIGURE 3.29 Lesser Antilles subduction zone and Mont Pelée

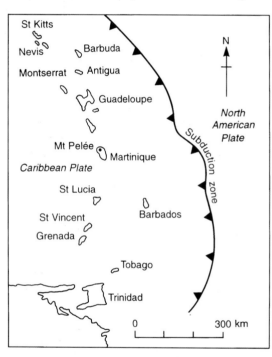

FIGURE 3.30 Mont Pelée with St Pierre, 1985

formed as the North American Plate subducts beneath the Caribbean Plate (see Figure 3.29). Mont Pelée lies in the north-west of Martinique (Figure 3.30), and developed from a submarine volcano, initially established some 500 000 years ago. Much of the present volcano has been built up in successive Plinian and Pelean eruptions. In the second half of the nineteenth century, there was little evidence to suggest that a major eruption would occur although minor eruptions occurred in 1792 and 1851.

Ominously, in February 1902, the nauseous smells associated with hydrogen sulphide were experienced in St Pierre, and in Le Precheur and other villages on the north coast. Ash erupted from the summit crater for the first time in late April. St Pierre, the 'pearl of the West Indies', an attractive town some 7km to the south of Mont Pelée, received its first coating of ash on 2 May. An eruption on 5 May sent a lahar down the Rivière Blanche, killing 23 workers in the factory at its mouth. Throughout the 6 May fine ash fell over St Pierre, and on 7 May the first nuées ardentes rippled down the upper slopes of Mont Pelée.

The Governor of Martinique had paid several visits to St Pierre to bolster morale during the previous week, and his latest arrival on 7 May was accompanied by increasing activity from Mont Pelée. The Governor and his party set off early in the morning by boat for the little fishing village of Le Precheur. They were never seen again. Shortly after 8am an initial blast ripped through the side of the volcano, followed by a powerful nuée ardente. The latter, at temperatures between 200°C and 450°C, swept down the Rivière Blanche valley and then turned swiftly southwards at speeds of up to 500km an hour and quickly devastated St Pierre. Its 28 000 inhabitants died within minutes, and few buildings were left standing, such was the force of the blast. Figure 3.31 shows the extent of the damage. Other nuées ardentes occurred later in May, and in June, July and August, when another 1000 people died in the town of Morne Rouge. Strange spines of hardened lava were forced up from the crater later in the year, and in 1903, but after 1905 the volcano fell quiescent and did not erupt again until 1929, and then continued to erupt until 1932.

STUDENT ACTIVITY 3.14

Mont Pelée
1 On 3 May 1902, the opposition candidate in the local elections called for St Pierre to be evacuated. Rehearse the arguments that could have been used for and against this plea.

Ruapehu, North Island, New Zealand: effective monitoring?

Ruapehu (2797 metres) is the highest of the three **stratovolcanoes** that dominate the Tongariro National Park in the centre of North Island, New Zealand (see Figure 3.32). They form part of the Taupo Volcanic Zone, which extends north-east-south-west for a distance of some 240km, and varies in width from 20 to 40km. This belt of volcanoes lies along the zone where the Pacific Plate is subducting steeply beneath the Fiji Plate. Eruptions along this line are usually violently explosive, with the production of large quantities of andesitic lava. Ruapehu itself has a long history of eruptive activity (see Figure 3.33), with the first eruptions beginning about 1 million years ago: in the last quarter of a million years there have been four main periods of cone building, with the volcano being particularly active between 10 000 and 14 000 years ago, although records only date from the eruption in 1861. A period of intense volcanic activity occurred on Ruapehu in 1945, which was responsible for dramatic changes in the crater lake beneath which the eruptions took place. Although the lake initially disappeared it began to fill again in 1946, and by 1953 the water had risen to a level 8m higher than before the eruption in 1945. In December 1953 water from the summit crater lake burst through the barrier of debris produced by the 1945 eruption, formed a lahar and poured into the Whangaehu valley. As this torrent of water swept down the Whangaehu valley it picked up great quantities of sand and boulders, and when it reached Tangiwai, 30km away it destroyed part of the bridge that carried the main railway from

FIGURE 3.31 Devastation in St Pierre after the 1902 eruption

Auckland to Wellington just before the Auckland express was due to cross it: 151 people were killed in the ensuing disaster. Further major eruptions occurred in 1969, 1975 and 1995, each involving the development of lahars, with consequent threat to the surrounding area. By virtue of its snowfields, Ruapehu has become a major skiing and tourist centre in North Island. The infrastructure that has been developed to service these recreational

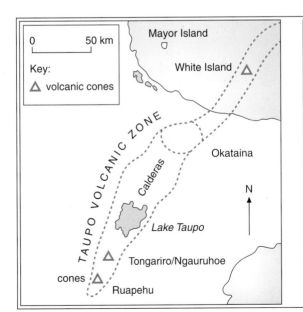

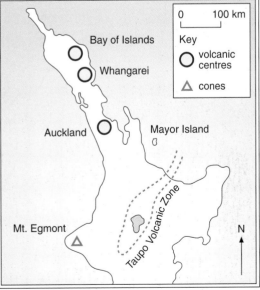

FIGURE 3.32 The Taupo volcanic zone

Source: *Tephra*, October 1995

FIGURE 3.33 Eruption
rates of Ruapehu over
the last 80 000 years

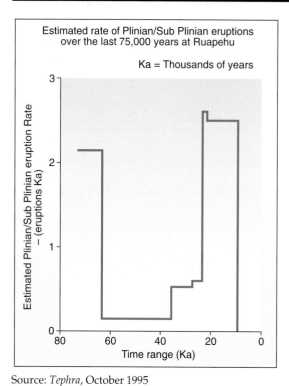

FIGURE 3.33 Eruption
rates of Ruapehu over
the last 80 000 years

Source: *Tephra*, October 1995

functions of the area is clearly under threat from these latter and future eruptions, and loss of life among tourists and skiers is a real possibility unless a thorough risk assessment and evaluation was undertaken.

Monitoring of physical and chemical changes in the volcanic environment in and around Ruapehu has been in place for some considerable time. Seismic activity in the Tongariro Volcanic Centre, of which Ruapehu is part, has been monitored since 1952, and regular surveys of the Ruapehu Crater Lake (including physical monitoring of the shape of the crater, and chemical surveys of the lake water), have been carried out since the 1953 disaster (see Figure 3.34). Monitoring of ground deformation on the surface of the volcano has been in operation since 1970. The Ruapehu Lahar Warning System has been in place since 1984. Later, in 1994, the Institute of Geological and Nuclear Sciences established a six-stage scientific alert programme for all of New Zealand's volcanoes (see Figure 3.35).

In October 1995, shortly after the eruptions of the previous month, the New Zealand Government

FIGURE 3.34 Monitoring
of Crater Lake, Ruapehu

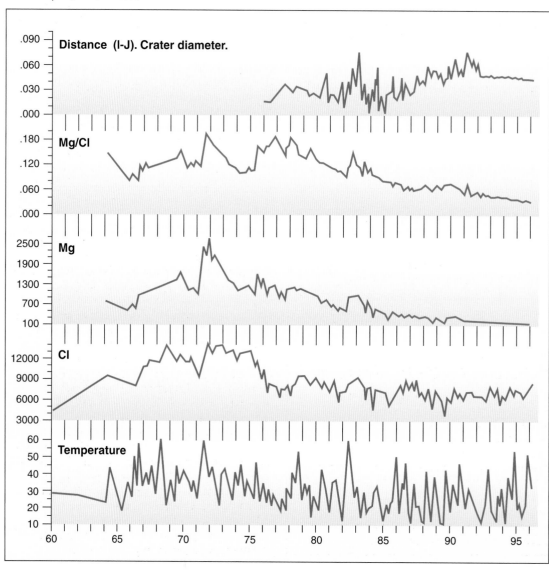

Scientific alert level	Phenomena observed	Scientific interpretation (volcano status)
0	Typical background surface activity: seismicity, deformation and heat flow at low levels.	Usual dormant, intra-eruption or quiescent state
1	Departure from typical background surface activity.	Minor phreatic activity.
	Apparent seismic, geodetic, thermal or other unrest indicators.	Signs of volcano unrest. No significant eruption threat.
2	Increase from low level of eruptive activity, accompanied by changes to monitored indicators.	Significant change in level or style of ongoing eruptive activity.
	Increase in seismicity, deformation, heat flow and/or other unrest indicators	Indications of intrusive proesses. Local eruption threat.
3	Increased vigour of ongoing activity and monitored indicators.	Significant local eruption in progress.
	Commencement of minor eruptions at reawakened vent(s). Relatively high and increasing trends shown by unrest indicators.	Increasing intrusive trends indicate real possibility of hazardous eruptions.
4	Significant change to ongoing activity and monitored indicators.	Hazardous local eruption in progress.
	Establishment of magmatic activity at reawakening vent(s), with acceleration of unrest indicators.	Large scale eruption now appears imminent.
5	Hazardous large volcanic eruption in progress.	Destruction within the Permanent Danger (red) Zone. Significant risk over wider areas.

FIGURE 3.35 New Zealand volcanoes – alert levels

Note: The frequently active cone volcanoes (White Island, Ngauruhoe, Ruapehu), require definitions different from all other volcano systems, hence the subdivisions of Stages 1, 2, 3 and 4. The yellow portion relates to the frequently active volcanoes, while the blue to the other systems (Auckland, Taranaki, Taupo, Okataina etc).

convened a series of meetings, where a formal risk assessment and evaluation was carried out. Officials consulted a wide range of expert and specialists, and their discussions revealed nine possible hazards relating to the main eruption event. At current levels of activity it is thought that risks to population are relatively small. However, should activity increase, public safety would be jeopardised in two ways: the magnitude of the various hazards would increase, and warning times would be reduced significantly. It has been concluded that monitoring of various physical and chemical parameters should be sufficient to detect upward trends. With current low levels of activity, this should give days', even weeks' warning of a major eruption, although if activity moves to alert level four, more intensive monitoring would be needed.

STUDENT ACTIVITY 3.15

Monitoring volcanic activity on Ruapehu
1   Why is Ruapehu regarded as a particularly dangerous volcano by the New Zealand authorities?
2   How useful do you think are the types of monitoring of Crater Lake as shown in Figure 3.34?
3   It has been concluded that, at the present, only basic levels of monitoring of Crater Lake are required. What other considerations might have influenced the choice of such a strategy?

Montserrat: disaster on a small island

Montserrat is a small island of approximately 102km square in the same volcanic arc as Martinique, where Mont Pelée erupted with such violence in 1902. The island is dominated by the volcanic peak of Soufrière Hills which rises to a height of 915m in the south of the island. Before the eruption of Soufrière Hills, most of the population was concentrated on the western coastal zone of the island, with the capital, Plymouth (see Figure 3.36), lying only four km west of the volcano (see Figure 3.37). The people of Montserrat are mostly subsistence farmers relying on the rich volcanic soil to grow a whole range of fruit and vegetables. More recently a modest tourist industry seemed to be developing, although the island is handicapped by having a small airport that cannot accept wide-bodied jets from Europe and North America. In common with Mont Pelée on Martinique, Soufriere Hills had lain dormant for some time – nearly four hundred years. Tourists were taken to see the **fumaroles** in the small subsidiary crater of Galway's Soufrière, but, for the most part, the potential volcanic threat of Soufrière Hills was ignored on the island. However, a volcanic hazard map for southern Montserrat did exist (Figure 3.37), which showed that the populations along the western coastal zone around Plymouth, and in the Paradise River valley to the north-east of Soufriere Hills were at risk from pyroclastic flows.

After its long period of dormancy, Soufrière Hills became active again in July 1995, when new

FIGURE 3.36 Plymouth, Montserrat

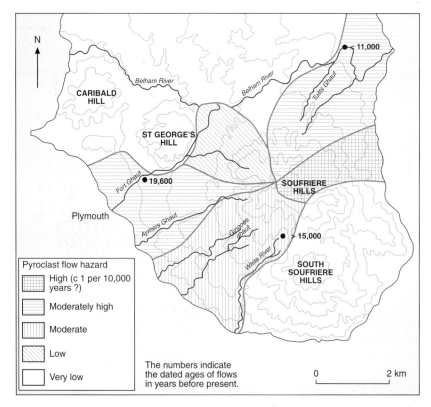

Pyroclast flow hazard

	High (c 1 per 10,000 years ?)
	Moderately high
	Moderate
	Low
	Very low

The numbers indicate the dated ages of flows in years before present.

0   2 km

FIGURE 3.37 Pyroclastic flow hazards – southern Montserrat

phreatic eruptions led to falls of tephra over much of the island. Activity continued though the next few weeks, with a further major eruption on August 21, resulting in large falls of tephra on Plymouth. Similar activity continued throughout 1995, with steam and tephra eruptions, and the development of new lava domes. Spines, similar to those that formed on Mont Pelée began to appear, and then subsequently collapsed. In December, Plymouth was evacuated as a precaution, although residents were allowed to return later, when activity subsided. Escalation of the eruptive activity occurred in April 1996, with pyroclastic surges threatening the slopes of the volcano, and in early 1997 a further renewal of activity saw more pyroclastic flows reaching the sea to the east and south of the volcano. By June 1997, the Montserrat Volcanic Observatory reported that the volcano was 'very dangerous', and on 25 June part of the dome of Soufrière Hills collapsed, sending a tephra plume 9000m high. Meanwhile a huge pyroclastic flow swept down the north-east flank of the volcano engulfing several villages, killing 19 people, and forcing the closure of Blackburne Airport.

In August 1997, pyroclastic flows poured down the western flank of Soufrière Hills into Plymouth itself, and within a matter of four days, 80 per cent of the buildings in the capital were destroyed, and ash deposits within the town had grown up to 1.2 metres thick (see Figure 3.38). The entire population of Plymouth had long since been evacuated, thus avoiding any further loss of life. Renewed activity later in August led the Governor to call for the evacuation of all the settlements in the middle belt of Montserrat, such as Flemmings, Hope, Olveston and Salem, which had previously been considered safe. Throughout the closing months of 1997 continuing activity manifested itself in further tephra plumes and pyroclastic flows. In early 1998, the volcano seemed to have entered a quiescent phase, and this appears to have continued for the remainder of the year. Further activity occurred in 1999 so the eruption phase is still continuing.

Throughout the period of the eruptive activity the Montserrat Volcanic Observatory, set up in 1995, was responsible for the day-to-day monitoring of activity on Soufrière Hills. Seismic measuring devices were in place at the base of Soufrière Hills to record earthquake swarms that would indicate levels of magma activity deep within the volcano. Daily helicopter flights were able to monitor ground deformation and dome growth on the volcano, and to plot the course of the pyroclastic flows. As a result of the work of geologists in the Observatory, the Government was able to define a number of hazard zones on the island (see Figure 3.39). Evacuation of the population from the most vulnerable zones was effectively based on the reports issued by the Observatory. In the first instance evacuation, from the southernmost two zones was advised, but at the height of the eruptive activity it was decided to evacuate the zone to the north as well, where a 'new' capital had been established at Salem. For those that were evacuated from the southern, most vulnerable part of the island, there were two options: they could move to the northern, relatively safe part of the island, where temporary shelter was available but overcrowded conditions were likely to create health and hygiene problems or they could leave the island altogether for one of the neighbouring islands, such as Antigua, or for the more distant Britain. 7000 of the island's population of 11 000 decided to leave, with 4000 remaining in the shrinking 'safe' zone in the north of the island, under deteriorating conditions.

Since Montserrat is still a dependent territory, the British Government has a direct responsibility to the island's population in providing relief and financial assistance. By June 1997, before the onset of the most violent phase of the eruptions, the British Government had pledged up to £41 million in relief for Montserrat. Air and sea links to the island were to be re-established, and new permanent housing was to be built to replace homes destroyed in the eruptions. In the first instance assistance packages were to be paid to encourage inhabitants to stay on the island, but these were later replaced by the offer of relocation packages of £2500 per adult. This sum was perceived as being inadequate by many of the islanders, and bitter arguments broke out between the island's representatives and the British Government over the level of assistance. The difficulties were compounded by the fact that two Government Departments were involved in offering assistance to the island, and unnecessary tensions existed between the two. Assurances were given by the Foreign Secretary, Robin Cook that there would be a change in the Government's strategy, with emphasis on assistance for those who wished to resettle in the United Kingdom, further infrastructure improvements for the north of the island, and additional help for Antigua where most of the Montserratians were likely to resettle.

In 1999 the arguments continued to rumble on. An inquest on the island found that the British Government was in part responsible for the deaths of nine people in the eruptions of 1997 because it had failed to buy farmland in the north of the island on which inhabitants in the vulnerable south of the island could be resettled. The response of the Government was to point out that those farmers who stayed to cultivate land in the south were well aware of the risks that they were taking, that Government-owned land in the north was unsuitable for farming, and that privately owned land there was not available for lease. In January 1999, 1000 islanders were still living in shared accommodation, and 400 were still living in shelters, and the island's coroner accused the British Government of a response that was 'unimaginative, grudging and tardy'. However, the Department for International Development pointed out that £59 million had been spent on Montserrat up to March 1998, and that a three-year development plan up to 2001 would receive an additional £75 million.

FIGURE 3.38 Plymouth under ash

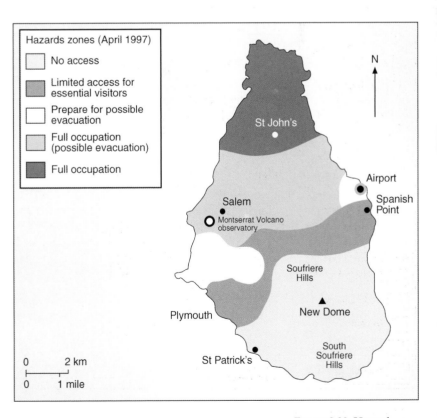

FIGURE 3.39 Hazard zones, Montserrat

Iceland: living with volcanic hazards

Unlike both New Zealand, and the Lesser Antilles in the West Indies, both located on subduction zones, Iceland lies astride the Mid-Atlantic Ridge, a constructive plate margin. On constructive margins volcanic activity is much less violent, and involves the eruption of mainly basaltic lavas. Although Iceland has an area of 103 000 square kilometres (slightly smaller than North Island, New Zealand), it only carries a relatively small population of approximately 250 000, and over two-fifths of these people are concentrated in Reykjavik the capital.

Figure 3.40 shows the main features of volcanic activity, and accompanying hazards, in Iceland. It will be noted that the main belt of volcanic activity extends from north-east to south-west across the island, and includes both fissure systems and central volcanoes. Figure 3.41 shows the distribution of population in Iceland, indicating that most of the population is concentrated around the coast of the island, although it is densest in the

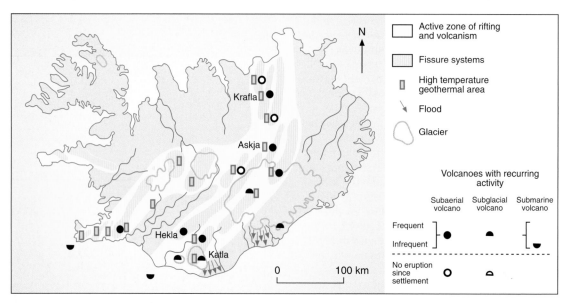

FIGURE 3.40 Volcanic hazards – Iceland

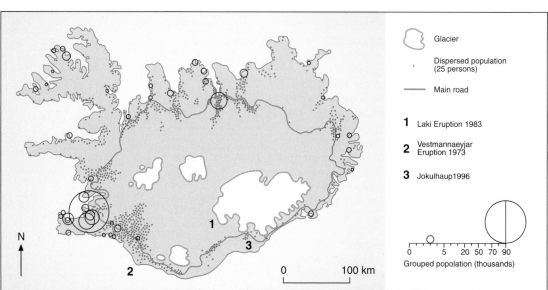

FIGURE 3.41 Population – Iceland

Frequency	Size	Details
(1) Decade	Less than 1km³	Small-volume eruptions of basalts from volcanoes such as Hekla and Katla. Products are both air falls and lava flows. Locally falls are dangerous to farmland and vegetation. Lava flows may cause semi-permanent sterilisation of land
	1–10km³	Large volume eruptions of basalts. Hazard is mostly from lava flows
Centuries	Less than 1km³	Moderately explosive eruptions from central volcanoes such as Hekla. Hazard mostly from fall deposits
(2)	10–20km³	Very large-volume fissure eruptions of basalts from eruption sites which are difficult to predict, e.g. Laki in 1783. Likely effects catastrophic
Millennia		Large-volume Plinian eruptions from central volcanoes

FIGURE 3.42 Volcanic hazards – Iceland

(1) Low-magnitude/high-frequency eruptions – also includes jokulhaups
(2) High-magnitude/low-frequency eruptions

south-west, in and around the capital Reykjavik. Although at first sight it might be thought that most of the population is not particularly threatened by volcanic hazards, much of the country's property, industry, infrastructure and power supplies lie in the volcanic zone. Iceland has derived considerable benefits from the availability of geothermal power in this zone, and now derives some 31 per cent of its power from this source. However, most of the power plants are located in the central volcanic zone, and would be very vulnerable in the event of an eruption. The Icelandic Government has inevitably been involved in research into the nature of volcanic activity on the island, in order to establish a prediction strategy for future events. Loss adjustments measures are also in place should any future activity prove to be particularly hazardous and result in damage to settlements and infrastructure. Iceland is only a small country, and its limited financial resources have placed some restrictions on the level of research that can be carried out, and on the implementation of a full programme of hazard prediction.

Iceland has only been permanently settled since the ninth century, and some 250 eruptions have been recorded during this period, with some particularly powerful events occurring in Vatnaoldur in 871, Eldgja in 934 and Hekla in 1104. Records of activity are somewhat sparse until the eighteenth and nineteenth centuries, when much more detail became available. The Laki eruption in 1783 has proved to be one of the most hazardous in Iceland's history, and, more recently, the Heimaey event attracted world-wide attention. Iceland also experiences **jokulhaups**, which are glacial outbursts caused by eruptions underneath the large ice caps that cover parts of the interior of the country. Although these usually occur in remote areas, the resulting floods can cause much damage to the tenuous infrastructure of Iceland's interior and coastal zones. Figure 3.42, above, indicates the range of volcanic hazards that are experienced in Iceland.

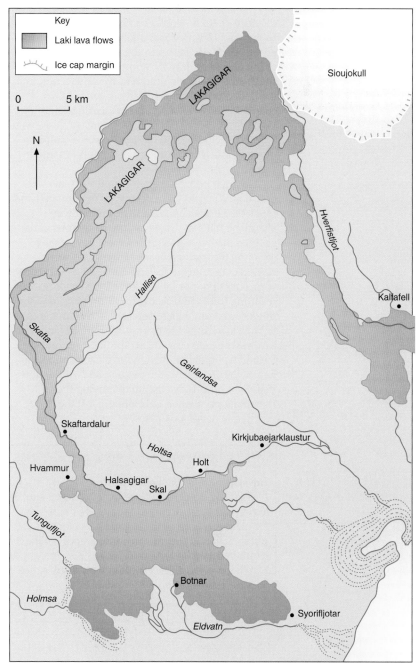

FIGURE 3.43 The Laki eruption

The Laki Eruption, June 1783 to July 1784

The Laki fissure is found in south-east Iceland, approximately 50km inland from the coast, and extends north-east-south-west for some 26km (see Figure 3.43). Rising from the feature are some 130 volcanic vents. In 1783 one of the most productive lava eruptions ever recorded occurred from this fissure, and is recorded in Icelandic literature as *Skaftaredlar* (Skafta Fires) and the ensuing catastrophe as *Moduhardindi* (the Haze Famine). In May and early June 1783 a number of earthquakes were felt in southern Iceland, and these were the precursors of the major crustal rifting that caused the Laki fissure to develop. The eruption of lava began on June 8, and was accompanied with the emission of ash, pumice and volcanic gases. By July 20 some farms were engulfed by lava and were abandoned: the lava front had moved a distance of 40km, finally coming to a halt a few km to the west of Kirkjubaerjatklaustur. Renewed eruptive activity began in the north-eastern section of the fissure on July 29, and the lava flowed south-east, destroying more farms. The eruption continued until February 1784: 15km^3 of lava erupted and covered an area of nearly 600km^2 (see Figure 3.43). Some 500 million tonnes of gases were erupted, including 140 million tonnes of sulphur dioxide. Much of the latter was converted into a sulphuric acid aerosol.

Although no lives were lost in the actual eruption, 20 farms were destroyed or damaged and much fertile farmland had to be temporarily abandoned. It was, however, the dangerous gases erupted that were to have the most devastating effects in the ensuing years. These gases were carried over much of Iceland, and as a result crops were either poor or failed altogether. The 'haze' resulting from the aerosol of acid droplets, and the fine-grained ash which persisted in the atmosphere led to a lowering of temperatures over Iceland, and to a lesser extent elsewhere. About 20 per cent of Iceland's population died in the Haze Famine and half of the domestic animals were lost. At the time there was serious discussion of moving the remaining population to Denmark, but the evacuation never took place.

STUDENT ACTIVITY 3.17

The aftermath of the Laki Eruption
1 The Laki event took place over 200 years ago. If a similar event occurred today, what would be the main reactions of the Iceland Government, and how would the human consequences of the eruption differ?
2 What aspects of the eruption would still cause possible problems today?

The Heimaey Eruption, 22 January 1973

The Vestmann Islands lie off the south-west coast of Iceland, and represent a seaward extension of the volcanic zone of Iceland as shown on the map, Figure 3.40. Apart from one small insignificant submarine eruption in 1896, no eruptive activity had been recorded in these islands since the settlement of Iceland in the ninth century. In the twentieth century attention was first drawn to the archipelago when the new island Surtsey was formed in a fresh series of eruptions between 1963 and 1967. Heimaey is the largest island in the group: its principal settlement, Vestmannaeyjar is its main fishing port and fish-processing centre, and it accounts for a fifth of Iceland's fish exports. The town is sheltered by a ridge to the north, whilst to the south-east there is a small cinder cone, Helgafell, that last erupted some 5000 years ago.

Earth tremors were first felt on Heimaey on 21 January, indicating that magmatic activity at depth would soon lead to eruptions at the surface. A 2km fissure trending from north-north-east to south-south-west opened up on the east of Heimaey on the 22 January, and was accompanied by a spectacular series of lava fire fountains. As these began to subside on 24 January, a Strombolian eruption commenced and a cinder cone, Eldfell, began to form at the northern end of the fissure, (see Figure 3.44) only 1km from the outskirts of Vestmannaeyjar (see Figure 3.45). Airborne ash set fire to some houses and others were crushed by the weight of the debris that fell on them. By the end of January alone, lava flows had added over a kilometre square of land to the eastern side of the island, and when, on February 19, the northern part of the crater wall of Eldfell collapsed, lava began to approach the eastern outskirts of Vestmannaeyjar, and threatened to fill the harbour. Submarine activity cut electrical power cables and the freshwater conduit from the mainland. From late February the eruption began to subside, although lava flows continued to threaten the town. By the end of April most eruptive activity had ceased.

Within a few hours of the eruption beginning, the whole of the population of Heimaey (5300 people) was evacuated to the mainland, using the vessels of the fishing fleet. Cattle and cars, deep-frozen fish stored near the harbour, money in the bank and municipal documents were transferred to Reykjavik. Firefighters from the town, Reykjavik and Keflavik fought to save as much of the town as possible. In early February it became apparent that measures would have to be taken to curb the flow of lava into the harbour. On 17 February a pipeline was completed, which enabled water to be sprayed on to the advancing front of the lava, thus cooling it and slowing its advance. This proved to be reasonably successful, but in late March lava began to flow into the town, and pumping equipment was brought in from the United States in order to stem this renewed threat, by spraying water on the advancing lava front.

An assessment of the success of the measures taken suggests that, given the circumstances, the authorities did all that they could. However, the response did depend on a plentiful supply of water being used against slow-moving lava on gentle slopes, at a time when the eruptive period was coming to an end, the lava flow was declining, and had completed most of its advance. In spite of all the efforts of the authorities, three of the five fish factories were destroyed, and 300 houses were lost in the eruption. In the aftermath of the eruption, US $36 million was made available for the necessary compensation, restoration and repair work and the cost of moving people back to Heimaey.

STUDENT ACTIVITY 3.18

Vestmannaeyjar: eruption, response and options
1 What were the particular circumstances that enabled the evacuation of Vestmannaeyjar to be carried out so successfully?
2 What lessons could be learnt from the progress of events on Heimaey between January and April 1973?
3 What arguments could be put forward for abandoning settlement on Heimaey altogether?

The Grimsvotn Jokulhaup (glacial burst) 5 November 1996

Vatnajokull is the largest ice cap in Iceland, covering some 21 497 square kilometres. Buried beneath Vatnajokull there are a number of volcanoes of which the most active is Grimsvotn, which appears to erupt quite frequently (about every 10–15 years). Grimsvotn is, in fact, a **caldera**, which contains a huge glacial lake, overlain by 200–250 metres of ice. The caldera is heated by a shallow underlying source of magma, and thus as ice flows into the caldera considerable quantities of it melt to form the water in the lake. The lake has an area of 8–10 square kilometres and its level rises slowly until it is emptied during successive glacial bursts. The rising level of the lake causes the icesheet above to lift, until the pressure at the lake bottom forces an exit at the glacier's bed (see Figure 3.46). The water then flows some 50km beneath Skeidararjokull until it reaches the Skeidara river, which drains across the Skeidararsandur outwash plains to the sea.

On 29 September 1996 an earthquake, registering 5.0 on the Richter scale was recorded near the caldera of Bardabunga, and subsequent tremors to the south suggested that magma was beginning to move towards the surface beneath that part of Vatnajokull. By October 1 two huge cauldrons or craters had appeared on the ice cap between Bardabunga and Grimsvotn (see Figure 3.47), indicating eruptive activity along a four km fissure. On the following day huge eruptions of steam and tephra were occurring from the cauldrons on the ice cap, and on subsequent days

FIGURE 3.44 Eldfell, Heimaey in eruption

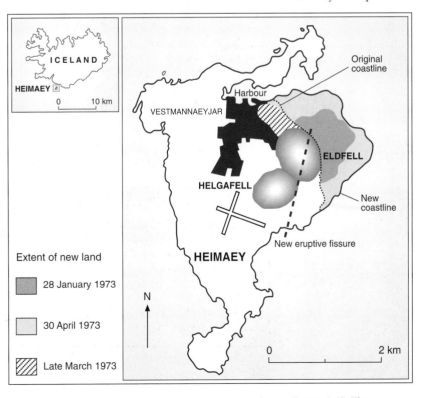

FIGURE 3.45 The Heimaey eruption

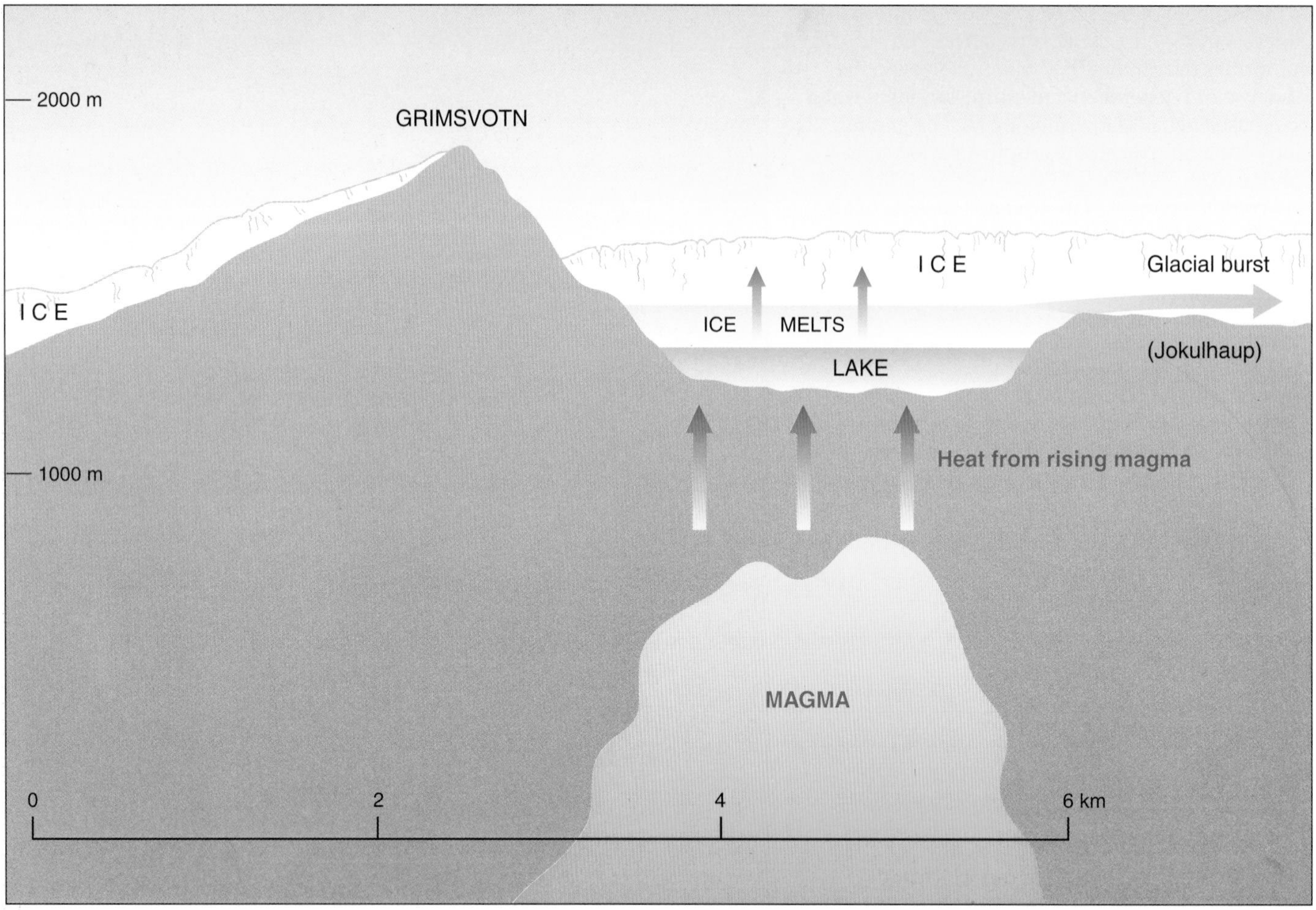

2000 m

GRIMSVOTN

I C E

ICE Glacial burst

I C E

ICE MELTS

(Jokulhaup)

LAKE

1000 m

Heat from rising magma

MAGMA

0   2   4   6 km

FIGURE 3.46 Jokulhaup
dynamics: Grimsvotn

FIGURE 3.47 Vatnajokull,
1996

the fissure grew to nine km in length. There was
concern that the caldera lake would fill rapidly,
leading to a jokulhaup within a matter of days. By
October 15, however, the eruption had ceased,
leaving an ice canyon 3.5km long on the surface of
Vatnajokull but no jokulhaup had yet appeared.
On November 4 seismographs indicated that the
ice dam had finally lifted and that the jokulhaup
was imminent, and on the following morning the
huge flood emerged from under Skeidararjokull.
The bridges carrying the Iceland Ring Road over
the Saeluhusavikl and the River Gigja were
destroyed very quickly and later sections of the
bridge over the Skeidara were carried away (see
Figure 3.48).

Because of the delay in the onset of the
jokulhaup, attempts were made to build dykes of
boulders to protect the bridges over the rivers
which cross the Skeidararsandur and also the
service centre of Skaftafell. In the event this
protective work was only effective at the bridge
over the Nuptsvotn and at Skaftafell itself. Intensive
repair works were begun immediately after the
jokulhaup had subsided, and the bridges and roads
that were swept away were rebuilt in the following
months.

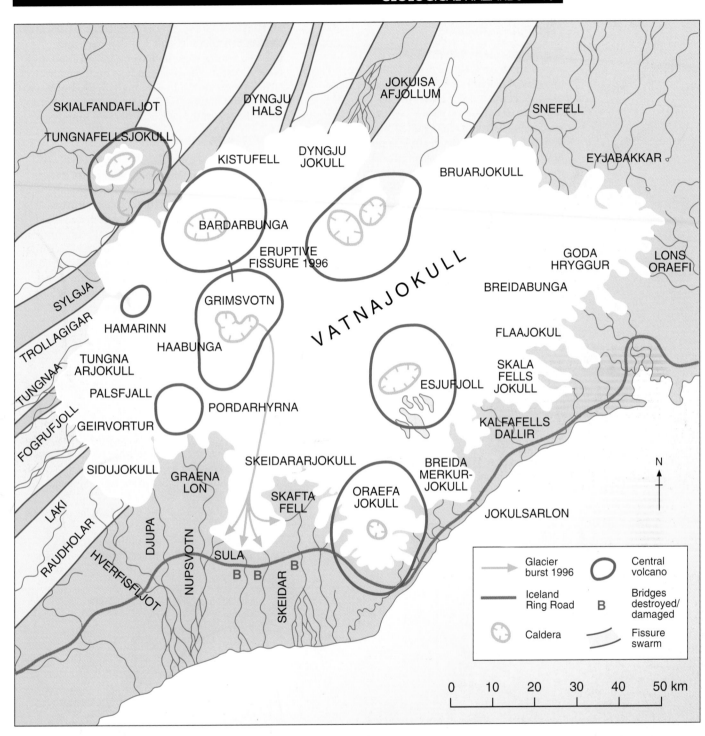

FIGURE 3.48 The Grimsvotn Jokulhaup, November 5 1996

STUDENT ACTIVITY 3.19

The Grimsvotn Jokulhaup
1 In the light of the information in the case study, do you consider jokulhaups to be a major volcanic hazard in Iceland? Give reasons for your answer.
2 Why is it difficult to take effective precautionary measures against the occurrence of jokulhaups?
3 What future response strategies might be adopted after the Grimsvotn jokulhaup of 1996?

STUDENT ACTIVITY 3.20

Summary essay: volcanic hazards
Produce a detailed 250-word essay plan or topic web for one of these two alternative titles:
1 Discuss the factors responsible for variations in the level of hazard around volcanoes.
2 'Volcanic hazards require intelligent, well-informed perception, and sharp, disciplined response.' Discuss.

Tsunamis as hazards

The word tsunami is derived from two Japanese words and means, literally, 'harbour waves'. The majority of tsunamis result from shallow focus earthquakes that occur under the sea floor, although some can be caused by particularly violent volcanic eruptions, e.g. those that resulted from the destruction of Krakatoa in 1883. Typically, tsunamis have particularly long **wavelengths**, sometimes up to 100km, but are also very low in **amplitude**, often only 0.5m. In deep water tsunamis travel at considerable speeds, up to 700km an hour: the tsunami generated by the 1960 earthquake in Chile took only 22 hours to travel across the Pacific to Japan, where it caused considerable damage and resulted in 100 deaths. The travel times for the tsunami resulting from the Good Friday earthquake in Alaska are shown in Figure 3.50.

When a tsunami enters shallow water it increases considerably in height. Its arrival is often heralded by draw-down of water from the shore, which rises up offshore to form the first of the waves. These waves can reach heights of up to 30m and are likely to cause great damage to buildings and infrastructure.

Between 80–90 per cent of all damaging tsunamis occur in the Pacific Ocean, and the majority of these result from earthquakes. Tsunamis can lift and carry away light structures, tear buildings apart, and wash away soil or loosely consolidated sediments.

The Krakatoa tsunami, 1883

The eruptions on the island of Krakatoa, which lies in the Sunda Straits between Sumatra and Java in Indonesia, caused one of the most devastating of all tsunamis. Waves were recorded as far away as the English Channel and San Francisco and induced waves were noticed on Lake Taupo in New Zealand. The coasts in Java and Sumatra were struck by waves up to 42m high. 5–600 boats were sunk in the Straits and 36 000 perished in towns and villages on the coasts of the two islands.

Crescent City, California, 1964

This Pacific coast town lies in the far north of California. The tsunami that hit Crescent City was generated by the earthquake in Prince William Sound in Alaska, and arrived on the coast of northern California 4.5 hours later. The waves that reached Crescent City were amplified by local configuration of the adjacent continental shelf. Sufficient warning had been given for evacuation of all low-lying areas. Several waves damaged the areas adjacent to the harbour: the third wave washed inland some 500m, flooded 30 city blocks and destroyed many one-storey buildings. After the tsunami, Crescent City was re-zoned and the waterfront was turned into a public park. All businesses in this area were relocated on higher ground.

The Papua New Guinea tsunami, 17 July 1998

'The ground was cracking before us. We saw the waves coming ... but there was nowhere to run. I tried but it caught me up, dumping me and my sister-in-law, Anna, who was holding her baby. It was like being in a huge washing machine. We were tumbled over and over, the wave was collecting coconut palms and houses and hundreds more people. We were dumped into the mangroves ... and Anna was clinging to the baby. They were both alive.'

Henry Harmutt, inhabitant of the village of Warapu, on the north coast of Papua New Guinea.

FIGURE 3.49 Tsunami!

FIGURE 3.50 Tsunami travel times

'I think they're saying tsunami – whatever that means'

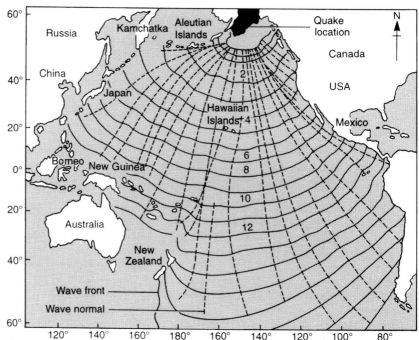

This eye-witness account of the tsunami that hit the north coast of Papua New Guinea at 6.30 pm on 17 July 1998 recalls the feelings of terror and helplessness experienced when a massive wave, some 7m high crashed on to this palm-fringed shoreline. Along this stretch of the coast a sand spit, some 70m wide, runs for just over three km from the village of Malo to Sissano in the west. Other small villages, such as Warapu and Arop are scattered along the spit, 'like jewels in a necklace'. They look out to the Bismarck Sea, rich in fish resources, whilst on the landward side of the spit is the shallow Sissano lagoon.

Records show that this coast has had a history of seismic activity, with the last major disturbance occurring in 1907, when local buckling of the crust led to the formation of the Sissano lagoon. All of the north coast of Papua New Guinea lies in an extremely unstable and complicated tectonic zone, where the Philippine plate appears to be subducting under the Indo-Australian plate. The tsunami appears to have been triggered by a major earthquake (7.0 on the Richter scale) on the subduction zone, at some depth beneath the Bismarck Sea to the north of the coast of Papua New Guinea (see Figure 3.51). Although there is a trans-Pacific tsunami early warning system based in Honolulu, no local warning system exists in Papua New Guinea: in any case the interval between the earthquake and the arrival of the tsunami may well have been too short for appropriate measures, such as evacuation of the coastal zone, to have been put into operation.

The initial wave was followed by two others, which struck the coast in the dark, making survival much more unlikely. The two villages of Arop and Warapu were completely destroyed, and most of Sissano and Malo were badly damaged (see Figure 3.52). The death toll in the villages was initially about 6000, although others will almost have certainly died from their injuries and subsequent infections and disease.

Response to the tsunami event appears to have been worryingly slow, for a variety of reasons:
■ roads, bridges and radio communication with the stricken area were knocked out;
■ the National Emergency Centre in the capital, Port Moresby, 900km away, received no information about the disaster until the following morning;
■ officials in the provincial capital, Vanimo (some 96 kilometres away) were not alerted for a similar period of time, although the shock waves from the earthquake were clearly felt there;
■ Australia was not asked for assistance until 24 hours had passed, and the first relief force did not arrive until two days after the event.

In the immediate aftermath of the tsunami, the rescue workers were faced with the inevitable problems of ensuring that survivors did not succumb to disease and infection. Very high humidity and temperatures carried enormous

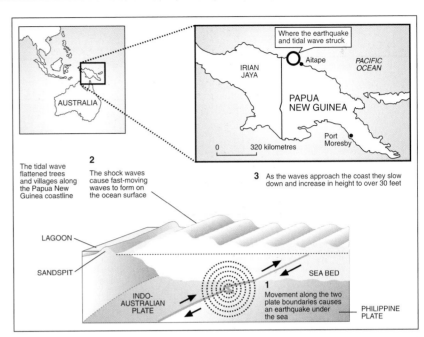

FIGURE 3.51 The Papua New Guinea tsunami

FIGURE 3.52 Devastation at Sissano

health risks, particularly with the large number of unburied dead both on the sand spit and in the lagoon. Many of the inhabitants fled into the rain forest behind the lagoon, and search and rescue operations were mounted to locate them, and bring them into temporary accommodation. Long-term rehabilitation of the community poses massive problems: it will not only involve rebuilding of the villages, but complete cleansing and sanitising of the polluted waters of the Sissano lagoon.

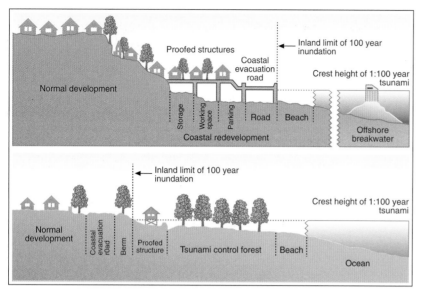

FIGURE 3.53 Designs for tsunami mitigation in vulnerable coastal areas

The management of geological hazards

Effective management of geological hazards is still an elusive objective for countries throughout the world. Experience has shown that, even in the most technologically developed countries, much remains to be achieved. Although considerable advances have been made in the field of geological hazard prediction, many geophysicists feel that accurate prediction of earthquakes may no longer be regarded as an achievable goal. Although the current view on prediction of volcanic eruptions is less pessimistic, few would claim that all of the many difficulties in accurate forecasting have been fully resolved. Increasingly scientists and hazard managers are turning their attention to improving and adapting buildings and infrastructures that will withstand earthquakes. Hazard mapping, and land-use zoning have important parts to play in the reduction of losses from both earthquakes and volcanic eruptions. The proper co-ordination of community awareness, evacuation procedures and effective response by public services is acquiring a much higher profile as a result of shortcomings revealed in recent events such as the Kobe and Armenian earthquakes. Administration of aid and relief programmes during the vital days after the occurrence of a disaster has often been criticised, particularly in the less economically developed countries (LEDCs), and much more competent use of resources is clearly required in many cases.

Prediction and forecast of geological hazards

Predictions of geological events are based largely on past patterns and generally tend to be imprecise. They are usually long-term, and as we have seen, in the case of earthquakes it is unlikely that the location and magnitude of an event can be predicted with any accuracy. Forecasts are based on the evolution of an event through a series of stages that are increasingly well understood. In contrast to predictions, forecasts are often short-term and thus offer little time for effective warning to be given. Again little progress has been possible with seismic hazard forecasting, although the future for some volcanic hazard forecasting is promising.

Earthquake prediction

There has been considerable investment into the scientific prediction of earthquakes in areas such as the Kanto and Tokai regions of Japan and in California. In such densely urbanised and technologically complex areas the search for accurate prediction methods clearly justifies research costs. Seismic variations in the San Andreas Fault are well known. The section around the town of Parkfield is currently the site of an ongoing seismic prediction experiment. It appears that slips occur along this section of the fault at fairly regular intervals, averaging out at 22 years. The window of occurrence for the latest slip and earthquake was between 1987 and 1993, but no major seismic event has yet occurred!

Tsunami forecast and warning

Compared to seismic events, tsunami forecast and warning systems are well established in the Pacific. A warning system was established in 1948. Seismograph stations around the Pacific relay data to

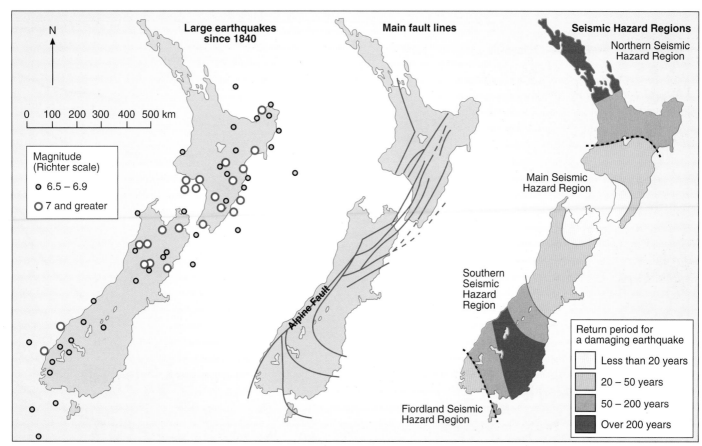

FIGURE 3.54 Seismic features of New Zealand

a central Warning Centre near Honolulu, on Hawaii. In the Pacific tsunami warnings operate at two levels. There is a Pacific-wide system where warnings are provided of large potentially damaging tsunamis to all countries bordering the Pacific. The second level is regional, where warnings are provided to areas that are particularly tsunami-prone. They aim to provide a warning within minutes for areas between 100 and 700km from source. These regional warnings appear to be very effective where they are in operation – the Japanese Meteorological Agency has operated a warning system since 1952. Before the introduction of this service, 6000 people were killed by 14 tsunamis. Since 1952 only 215 people have died in 20 local tsunamis.

Prediction of volcanic eruptions

Prediction and forecasting of volcanic eruptions have some obvious similarities with earthquake projections. Predictions of eruptions can be made by careful study of the past eruptive history of volcanoes, such as Etna, or groups of volcanoes, such as the Cascade group in the north-west of the USA. Forecasting of eruptions depends on the intensive monitoring of physical and chemical parameters in the immediate vicinity of the volcano, and this is clearly only possible for a very limited number of volcanoes – only about 12 around the world. With both prediction and forecasting a similar lack of precision to that discussed in the earthquake section is evident.

Differences exist when it comes to assessing the degree of danger involved. Volcanoes are less

---

STUDENT ACTIVITY 3.22

Earthquake prediction
Figure 3.54 shows various features associated with the seismicity of New Zealand.
1 Using Figure 3.54 and a good atlas, discuss the inter-related patterns shown by the three maps, and discuss the vulnerability of the major cities in New Zealand to a damaging earthquake in the first half of the twenty-first century.
2 Figure 3.55 displays the seismic pattern along the south coast of Alaska. Seismic gap theory suggests that where gaps in a seismic pattern occur, the risk of an earthquake is greatest. Locate the seismic gaps on the map and, with the help of a good atlas, discuss the vulnerability of Alaska's coastal population relative to these gaps. Why should such maps be treated with caution?
3 Recent research on earthquake prediction has focused on changes of physical parameters in crustal rocks in seismically active areas. Figure 3.56 indicates how these physical parameters change during the onset of an earthquake.
a) Comment on the changes in the physical parameters as shown in the diagram.
b) At this stage in seismic research, monitoring of these changes appears to have had little success in actually forecasting earthquakes. Suggest reasons why this might be so?
4 Given the long lead-times of earthquake prediction, suggest some of the social and economic problems that might result. You will find it helpful to use the structure of Figure 3.57. Complete an A4-sized version of this table.

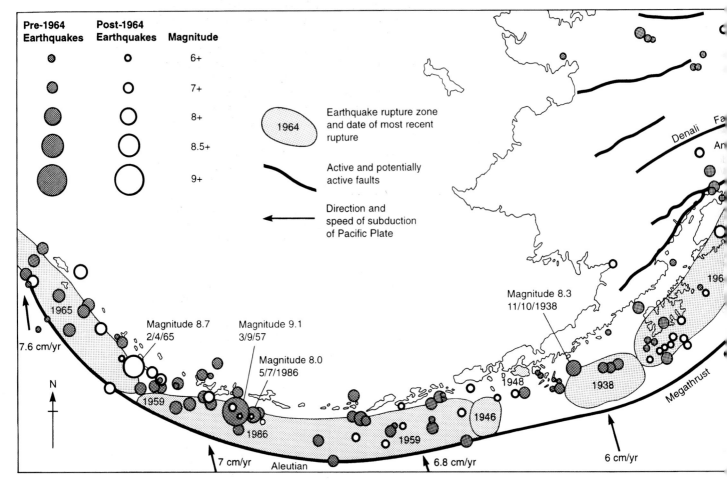

FIGURE 3.55 Seismicity – south coast of Alaska

threatening than earthquakes – only about 1 per cent of the volcanic eruptions in the last 100 years have caused fatalities. About 30–50 eruptions occur every year, and few last longer than six to ten weeks. Only about 70 000 deaths have occurred in the twentieth century from volcanic eruptions and more than half of those occurred in a few fatal minutes around Mont Pelée in 1902, and at Armero del Ruiz in Colombia in 1985. Many people live too close to volcanoes in Japan, and in Indonesia (see Figure 3.13) and these two countries account for two-thirds of the deaths caused by volcanoes since 1600. These inhabitants are, in fact, making their own predictions, based on their own imperfect knowledge of the eruptive history of the volcano.

Monitoring of volcanic activity

Surveillance of dangerous volcanoes involves sophisticated technology and skilled scientists and is therefore expensive. It is for these reasons that only the more economically developed countries (MEDCs) can afford such monitoring. Japan possesses seven volcanic observatories and 15 observation stations. Kilauea on Hawaii has been monitored for over 40 years, and the Mount St Helens eruption was probably the best documented.

FIGURE 3.56 Changes in physical parameters prior to an earthquake

Physical parameters	Precursor stages			Stage IV earthquake
	Stage I	Stage II	Stage III	Stage V
	Build up of elastic strain	Dilatancy and development of cracks	Influx of water and unstable deformation in fault zone	Sudden drop in stress followed by aftershocks
P-wave velocity				
Ground uplift and tilt				
Radon gas emission				
Electrical resistivity				
Number of local earthquakes				

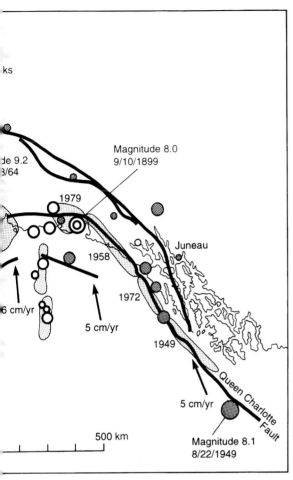

ks

Magnitude 8.0
9/10/1899

de 9.2
3/64

1979

Juneau

1958

1972

6 cm/yr

5 cm/yr

1949

5 cm/yr

Queen Charlotte Fault

500 km

Magnitude 8.1
8/22/1949

dominated by a single frequency. Such tremors were recorded at Mount St Helens, Mount Pinatubo and Nevado del Ruiz. However, problems exist with forecasting as the lead-time may vary considerably, from a few days to a year, and there is no certainty that an eruption may follow.

2   Tiltmeters and ground deformation

Rising magma will often result in ground deformation, often in the form of a bulge in the profile of the volcano. Tiltmeters can measure the amount of deformation very accurately – to 1mm in 1km. In Japan, Mount Unzen's summit bulged out by 50m before it erupted on 24 May 1991. The now almost notorious bulge on the slopes of Mount St Helens was a feature that could be seen with the naked eye, although when the eruption occurred the bulge itself was no longer increasing.

3   Gas and steam emission monitoring

Volcanic eruptions appear to be preceded by increased emissions of gas and steam from **fumaroles**, and **solfataras** on their flanks. Increases in a range of gases, such as hydrogen chloride, hydrogen fluoride and sulphur dioxide can be detected. Increased dissolution of acid volcanic gases will lead to increased pH values in crater lakes and other volcanic pools (the summit crater lake at Nevado del Ruiz virtually contained sulphuric acid before its eruption in 1985).

4   Other indicators

As the volcano is about to erupt, more heat is emitted. **Thermal anomalies** can be detected in the ground and in various water bodies associated with the volcano. Furthermore, heating will disturb other properties of volcanic rock, and thus magnetic, gravitational and electrical anomalies can be detected.

The Armero disaster: could it have been avoided?

Nevado del Ruiz is the most northerly active volcano of the Andes in South America. It has experienced major eruptions at least ten times in the last 10 000 years, with a recurrence interval in the range of 160–400 years. Serious eruptions occurred in 1595, 1845 (when 1000 people perished

Volcanoes in Kamchatka were carefully surveyed by the former Soviet Union for nearly half a century.

Figure 3.58 shows some of the parameters that can be monitored around volcanoes.

1   Seismographic monitoring

Magma rising within the earth's crust will set off a series of earth tremors. When the frequency and intensity of these seismic disturbances increases markedly, magma is approaching the surface. Sometimes **harmonic tremors** occur: these are a narrow band of nearly continuous vibrations

FIGURE 3.57 Impacts and adjustments to earthquake prediction

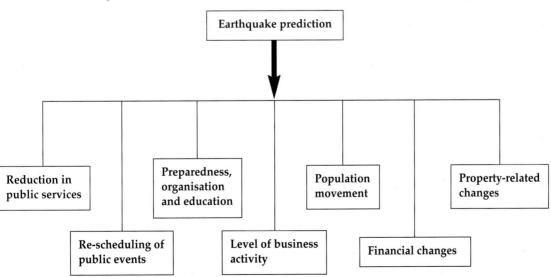

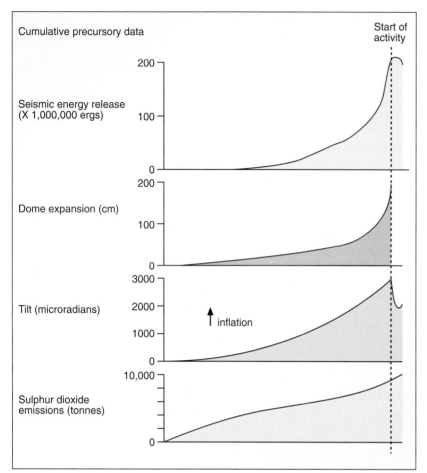

Cumulative precursory data

Start of activity

Seismic energy release (X 1,000,000 ergs)

Dome expansion (cm)

Tilt (microradians)

↑ inflation

Sulphur dioxide emissions (tonnes)

FIGURE 3.58 Physical parameters monitored around volcanoes

STUDENT ACTIVITY 3.23

Comparing Armero and Mount Pinatubo
Make a careful study of the table (Figure 3.60) which shows the chronology of events leading up to the Armero disaster, and the volcanic hazard map in Figure 3.59.
1 Using both of these resources, discuss the shortcomings of official reaction to the eruption potential of Nevado del Ruiz.
2 Make a series of realistic recommendations for the future monitoring of the volcano.
3 Monitoring of the Mount Pinatubo eruption in the Philippines in June 1991 appears to have been much better managed. Figure 3.61 records the volcanic and seismic events and reaction to them in the days leading up to 14 June 1991.
a) What crucial decisions were taken by the authorities?
b) Write a short summary of the way in which monitoring and forecasting differed from the eruption of Nevado del Ruiz.

as a lahar swept down the Lagunillas Valley), and in 1916. The eruption of 13 November 1985 was not particularly large, or violent, compared to Mount St Helens, but it caused damage of some US $1000 million, and lahars in the Lagunillas Valley caused the deaths of some 23 000 people in the town of Armero. This was the second worst volcanic disaster of the twentieth century after Mont Pelée.

Geological hazard mapping

Reference has been made in several case studies to the use and value of hazard mapping (Loma Prieta earthquake and Nevado del Ruiz eruption). In many areas prone to geological hazards the production of a hazard zonation map is seen as a key integral part of hazard management policy. The technique of hazard mapping may be divided into three approaches:
1 Single hazard-single-purpose mapping, e.g. lahar hazard mapping of risk to communities around Nevado del Ruiz.
2 Single hazard-multi-purpose mapping, e.g. seismic risks to housing, manufacturing industries and transportation in urban areas in Los Angeles.
3 Multiple hazard-multi-purpose mapping, e.g. landslide, seismic and flooding risks in an urban area.

Once hazard-prone areas have been identified it is possible to begin to move towards a planned system of land-use zoning. In this way, vulnerable areas can be zoned for uses where damage to property and loss of life can be minimised.

Geological hazard mapping on Hawaii

The island of Hawaii is affected by all three geological hazards considered in this section – volcanoes, earthquakes and tsunamis. Hawaii is located over a **hot spot** or **plume** where volcanicity occurs in a mid-plate location. The whole chain of islands, of which Hawaii is the most south-easterly, has been formed as the plate moves north-westwards over the hot spot. Intermittent activity over the last 70 million years has produced the volcanic chain.

FIGURE 3.59 Volcanic hazards: Nevado del Ruiz, Columbia

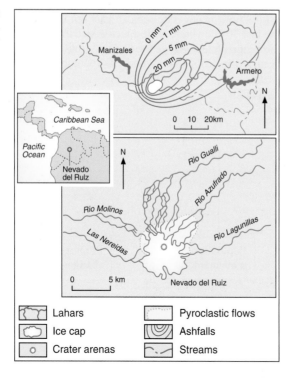

Manizales
0 mm
1 mm
5 mm
20 mm
Armero
N
0   10   20km

Caribbean Sea
Pacific Ocean
Nevado del Rulz

N
Rio Gualli
Rio Azufrado
Rio Molinos
Rio Lagunillas
Las Nereidas
0   5 km
Nevado del Ruiz

	Lahars		Pyroclastic flows
	Ice cap		Ashfalls
	Crater arenas		Streams

Year	Event	Scientific research	Government action	Monitoring
1595 1845 1916 1935 1950	Eruption Eruption Eruption Mudflows in Armero Mudflows in Armero			
1980 1982 1983 1984–5	 Increased fumarole activity	PhD Jaramillo PhD Herd Geothermal report: Italian scientists Studies by University of Grenoble. INGEOMINAS		No study forecast future volcanic activity: thus no monitoring
1985 January			Local business people and local government officials meet to discuss crisis	
February		Local scientists, alarmed by events, recommend early monitoring	Caldas civil defence informs civil defence chief in Bogota	INGEOMINAS visits volcano – assesses that anomalous activity does not warrant monitoring
March		UNDRO scientist visits – concludes Ruiz potentially dangerous	Civic committee recommends surveillance. Seminar recommends monitoring	INGEOMINAS advised by UNDRO to begin monitoring and hazard evaluation
April				
May		UNDRO scientist visits: concludes Ruiz in abnormal state		No INGEOMINAS studies commenced
June			Colombian Ambassador to UNESCO writes to Colombia Foreign Minister stating that UNESCO ready to offer help – letter is lost	
July			Civic committee presents report – local government contributes $2500	INGEOMINAS installs four seismographs
August				INGEOMINAS prepared report for UNESCO – but not sent. Swiss install three seismographs
September	Unusual seismic activity Eruption on 11 Sept Lahar in Azofredo valley		National government holds first meeting on crisis – order hazards map	No experienced seismologist present: thus warning signs not interpreted. New Zealand geochemist arrives but samples have to go to New Zealand for checking
October			Hazards map presented by Minister but withdrawn in order to be checked	Tiltmeters installed but only temporarily
November 13	Eruption 15.06 Eruption 21.08 Eruption 21.30 Lahar engulfs Chinchina 22.40 Lahar engulfs Armero 23.35	Scientists record but unable to send warning from volcano	Red Cross order evacuation of Armero but uncertain if order was ever sent	INGEOMINAS publishes report connecting harmonic tremors and eruptions but no action taken. Seismic and deformation monitoring ceases before eruption

INGEOMINAS: Instituto Nacional de Investigationes Geologico et Mineras – the Colombian Geological Survey
UNDRO: United States Disaster Relief Office

FIGURE 3.60 Chronology of the Nevado del Ruiz eruption and Amero disaster

Hawaii is made up of five volcanoes (see Figure 3.62) of which two, Kilauea and Mauna Loa are expected to erupt frequently in the foreseeable future. The main volcanic hazards are from lava flows, erupted either from the summits or from the flanks of the volcanoes. Ground cracking is a less serious volcanic hazard, only affecting areas near an active or recently active vent. Other volcanic hazards are gases, tephra, and the occasional **pyroclastic surge** from the infrequent explosive eruptions (see Figure 3.62a).

Most of the earthquakes on Hawaii are associated with volcanic activity, being largely related to movements of magma within the upper parts of the earth's crust. Figure 3.62b shows the location of damaging earthquakes of magnitude 6 or more. Only the earthquake located beneath Honomu appears to be unrelated to volcanic

---

STUDENT ACTIVITY 3.24

Multiple-hazard risk map for Hawaii
Given the difficulties of producing a seismic hazards map, attempt a multiple-hazard risk map for Hawaii suitable for use by the state government when making decisions about land-use zoning.

---

activity. Most of the island's earthquakes are concentrated between Kilauea and Mauna Loa. No seismic hazard map exists of Hawaii as yet, mainly because the hazards are highly localised, and it is difficult to define broad zones.

In the mid-Pacific, Hawaii is particularly prone to risk from tsunamis. Figure 3.63 shows the tsunami hazard risk for locations around the coast.

FIGURE 3.61 Chronology of the Mt Pinatubo eruption

Year	Event	Monitoring and surveys	Government action
4410–5100 BP	Eruption		
2500–3000 BP	Eruption		
400–600 BP	Eruption		
2 April 1991	Small eruption of steam ash coats villages 10km away	Seismographs installed on mountain, linked to Clark Air Force Base (US). Volcanic Observatory set up at Clark	
23 May 1991		Volcanic hazard map results from surveys. Throughout May seismographs record 1800 small earthquakes 2–6km deep, 5km north-west of summit.	Philippine Institute of Volcanology (PHILVOCS) publishes hazard map distributed by Government
13–28 May		SO$_2$ concentrations increase ×10	5 levels of alert published 1 = low level unrest 5 = eruption underway
1 June	Eruptions change to new focus – less than 5km deep		
3 June	Small explosion and then ash eruptions, harmonic tremors suggest magma ascent		
5 June			Alert level 3 – eruption within a fortnight. Areas threatened by nuées ardentes evacuated
6 June		Tiltmeter near summits indicates bulge in volcano	
7 June	Column of ash and steam up to 8km in height		Alert level 4 (explosive eruption in 24 hours)
8 June	Magma reaches surface		
9 June			Alert level 5 – evacuation of all inhabitants within 20km of summit
10 June			Clark Air Force base evacuated (1500 maintenance, security remain)
12 June	Two major eruptions. 08.51 major Plinian eruption sends column of gas, ash up to 19km in height		Evacuation zone extended to 30 km from summit. Manila Airport closed. More personnel leave Clark
14 June	Plinian eruptions up to 40km in height	Observations now difficult because of ash clouds	Remainder at Clark evacuated
15 June	Eruptions of increasing intensity. Nuées ardentes frequent. Ash widely deposited – made heavy by rain from Typhoon Yunga	Seismographs destroyed	

BP: Before present

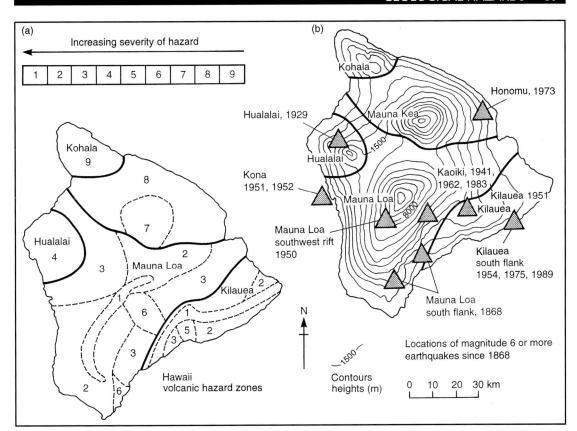

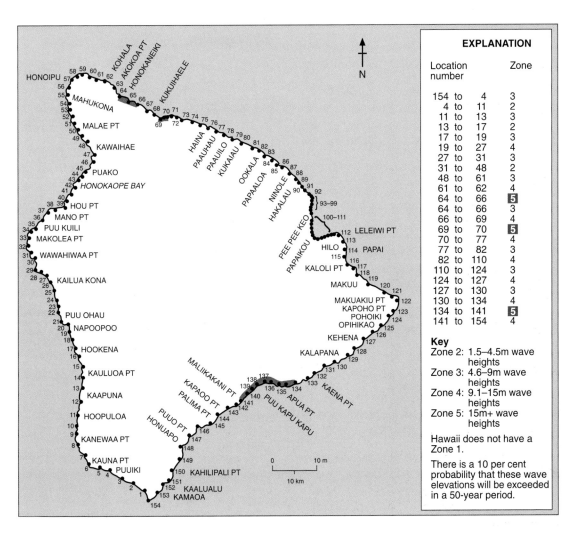

FIGURE 3.63 Tsunami hazards – Hawaii

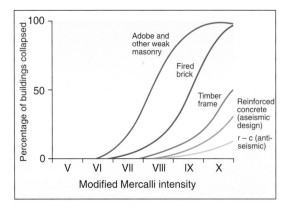

FIGURE 3.64 Impact of shallow focus near-field earthquakes on different building types

FIGURE 3.65 Problems and solutions to building in earthquake-prone areas

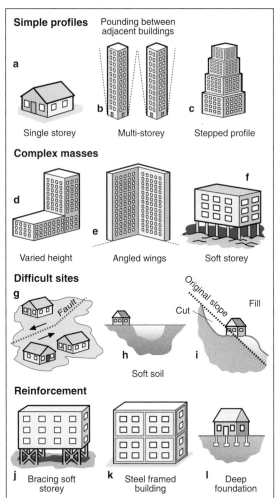

Hazard-resistant design of buildings and infrastructure

It is a truism that it is buildings that kill people, not earthquakes. The vast majority of deaths in earthquakes are caused by collapse of buildings and other infrastructure features such as bridges and freeways.

Future building codes will necessarily have to incorporate more stringent and expensive measures to ensure that structures have a reasonable chance of survival in an earthquake. The Loma Prieta experience has shown the importance of building structures to high standards of strain resistance. The Armenian experience reinforced the need for high building standards, but, sadly, from a different point of view. In areas where the volcanic hazard is the principal risk, heavy ashfalls from eruptions can cause collapse, particularly if buildings have flat roofs. New designs should incorporate steeply pitching roofs.

Environmental control of geological hazards

It would appear that little can be done to suppress earthquakes, or to stop a volcanic eruption once it has started. Research has shown that there may be a case for the adjustment of surface water in reservoirs in hazardous zones. The extra load of water in newly created reservoirs has, in some cases, triggered off small shallow earthquakes in sensitive seismic areas. Lowering reservoir levels could lessen this risk and would reduce dam failure and downstream flooding.

Frictional resistance in a fault zone may be reduced by the injection of water into these features. This could control the build up of strain, but it is a technique which has yet to be fully tested in the field.

Only one aspect of the volcanic hazard appears to be controllable. The control of lava flows was mentioned in the account of the recent eruptions of Mount Etna in 1983. There appear to be three main methods available:
1 Bombing of lava flows, or even of the summit cone so that lava spills occur more widely.
2 Artificial barriers can be constructed to protect towns or factories at risk. This has been proposed

for the town of Hilo in Hawaii, and barriers have been built to protect areas from the eruption of Krafla in northern Iceland.
3 The spraying of water on lava flows appeared to be effective in reducing their advance on the town of Vestmannaeyjar on Heimaey island off southern Iceland in 1973.

Review of key ideas

■ The earth's surface is made up of a series of plates, around the margins of which occur most of the world's earthquakes and volcanic eruptions.

■ Earthquakes, volcanoes and tsunamis are responsible for a number of geological hazards.

■ The severity of a geological hazard will depend on a range of physical factors responsible for its occurrence.

■ Loss of life and damage to property resulting from a geological hazard will depend not only on the severity of the hazard but also on human conditions in the area it affects.

■ Successful management of geological hazards can do much to lessen their impacts, but, as yet, cannot control the events responsible.

Glossary

Adobe – buildings consisting of mudbrick or rammed earth.

Amplitude (of a wave) – vertical distance measured from trough to crest of wave.

Andesite – lava type containing 52–66 per cent silica, referred to as an intermediate composition lava.

Aseismic – having no seismic activity.

Asthenosphere – plastic, partially molten layer of the atmosphere, underlying the lithosphere.

Basalt – lava type containing 45–52 per cent silica, referred to as a basic composition lava.

Benioff zone – steeply dipping zone of earthquakes associated with a subducting plate.

Earthquake intensity – measures the degree of shaking caused by earthquake waves, measured on the Mercalli scale.

Earthquake magnitude – measures the degree of energy released in an earthquake, measured on the Richter scale.

Elastic rebound – theory of cause of earthquake which envisages rocks on either side of fault returning to original positions after rupture.

Epicentre – point on the earth's surface, vertically above the focus of the earthquake.

Fault plane – plane of break between two sets of adjacent rocks.

Focus – location of rupture that causes earthquake.

Fumarole – a small vent in a volcanic area from which steam and other gases are emitted.

Harmonic tremor – series of small seismic disturbances that appear to be associated with rising magma close to the earth's surface.

Hot spot – point on the earth's surface located above a plume, a strong flow of heat from the earth's interior.

Island arc – chain of islands formed by volcanic activity at a subduction zone.

Isoseismal lines – lines of equal earthquake intensity around the epicentre of an earthquake.

Lahar – a mudflow of volcanic ash, lubricated by water, often from a crater lake, snowmelt, or heavy rain.

Lead-time – the time interval between prediction or forecast, and the actual event.

Lithosphere – the rigid outermost layer of the earth.

Locked section – section of fault along which there has been no significant seismic activity for some time.

Magma – rock material that is in a molten state.

Magnetic field (earth's) – magnetic field that exists around the earth resulting from the earth's magnetic properties.

Nuée ardente – incandescent cloud of gases, volcanic dust and super-heated steam ejected violently in a lateral direction from the flank of a volcano.

Ocean trench – deep elongated depression found on the oceanic flank of a subduction zone.

Parasitic cone – volcanic vents that develop on the flanks of volcanoes.

Plate – rigid section of the earth's lithosphere.

Plate boundary – the edge of plates that make up the lithosphere.

Plume – molten material that rises from the earth's mantle, causing a hot spot to develop in the crust.

Pyroclastic surge – similar to a nuée ardente, probably formed as a result of the interaction of magma and groundwater.

Sea-floor spreading – the process whereby oceanic crust spreads outwards from its source-region at the mid-oceanic ridge.

Seismicity – a measure of the extent to which an area or zone is prone to earthquake activity.

Seismic zonation – area zoning based on susceptibility to earthquake activity.

Seismogram – trace of earthquake waves on recording equipment.

Seismograph – equipment used to monitor seismic activity.

Solfatara – late stage of volcanic activity in which sulphurous gases and steam are emitted from vents.

Stratovolcano – volcano built of layers of lava and pyroclastic material.

Strike-slip – term applied to faults whose trend is transverse to the strike of the rocks and where relative movement is horizontal rather than vertical.

Subduction – process whereby oceanic crust returns to the mantle at a destructive plate margin.

Tephra – fragmented volcanic material ejected in an eruption.

Thermal anomaly – unexpected variations in the heat pattern of rocks.

Transform, fault – fault breaking the continuity of mid-oceanic ridge, thus causing it to be offset.

Tsunami – large ocean waves produced by earthquakes or volcanic eruptions.

Wavelength – horizontal distance from one wave crest to another.

References

Earthquakes, B A Bolt, revised 1993, Freeman

Environmental Hazards, K Smith, 1992, Routledge

Geohazards, Natural and Human, N K Coch, 1995, Prentice Hall

Geohazards, Natural and Man-made, G J H McCall, D J C Laming and S C Scott, 1992, Chapman and Hall

Institute of Geological Sciences: Volcanoes, 1974, HMSO

Institute of Geological Sciences: Earthquakes, 1983, HMSO

Natural Disasters, D Alexander, 1993, UCL Press

Natural Hazards, E A Bryant, 1991, Cambridge

Volcanoes, R Decker and B Decker, 1994, Freeman

Volcanoes, A Scarth, 1994, UCL Press

Volcanoes and Society, D Chester, 1993, Edward Arnold

4
GEOMORPHIC HAZARDS

In this chapter the focus is on some of the hazards associated with people living and working on slopes that are too steep. Case studies from events in Hong Kong, South Downs, Sarno and recent avalanches in Western Europe will illustrate the interactions between people and natural processes. A sound understanding of the processes of **mass movement** and **soil erosion** is essential and will be covered first.

Mass movement hazards

The rapid downslope movement of surface materials under gravitational influences represents an important group of environmental hazards, especially in mountainous terrain. Mass movement hazards are caused by large volumes of rock mixed with earth, water, snow or ice that can move at high velocity under the impetus of gravity and water. They can be classified depending on the dominant material. The main types are **rockfalls**, **landslides** (rock and soil), and **avalanches** (ice and snow). These hazards are currently increasing world-wide as land pressure forces new developments on to unstable slopes. Mass movements can be triggered by either seismic activity or atmospheric events including torrential rainfall. Some of the largest recorded events have been earthquake-induced.

During the 1970s an average of nearly 600 people per year were killed by slope failures world-wide, with some 90 per cent of these deaths occurring in the region around the Pacific Basin. This zone is particularly susceptible to mass movements because of combinations of rock type, steep terrain, heavy **typhoon** rainfall, rapid land-use change and high population density. Economic losses due to landslides have been estimated at more than $1 billion per year in several countries.

Landslides are complex and varied phenomena. They differ according to:
- the degree of sliding, flowing, creeping, falling or toppling involved;
- the wetness or dryness;
- their speed of movement.

Many landslides often show complex and interactive combinations of these phenomena, and it is difficult to incorporate all of these descriptions into a standard classification. The scheme proposed by Varnes (1978) has gained widest acceptance. Landslides can be classified both by speed (Figure 4.2) and type of movement/material (Figure 4.3).

Various engineering measures can be utilised to prevent landslides (Figure 4.4). Slope drainage is one of the most significant methods to prevent or control slope failure. Sound knowledge of the landslide hazard may allow evacuation, but vigilance, forecasting and monitoring are all necessary preliminaries. It may be possible to

FIGURE 4.1 Newspaper headlines featuring geomorphic hazards

500 Missing After Earthquake Triggers Mountain Landslides

A mountain village in south-western Colombia was yesterday reported to have been swept away in a landslide of rocks, ice and mud after a powerful earthquake.

"The avalanche from the river swept away the road," the reporter said. "The river is coming down with torrential force … houses and crops are totally destroyed. There is nothing there. The mud and the river have taken everything."

At least 64 people died in Toez alone, said national police General Jose Serrano. Another 36 people died in other villages along the path of the avalanche.

The US Geological Survey's earthquake centre in Colorado said the quake was the largest in Colombia since one measuring 6.8 on May 24, 1957.

The Guardian, 8 June 1994

One Killed When Trains Collide After Landslip

One person was killed and 31 others injured when two passenger trains collided after a landslip caused by heavy rain in the Lake District.

The accident involved the 4.26 pm Carlisle to Leeds service and the landslip happened at 7 pm at Aisgill, causing derailment of the train.

A spokesperson for the Fire Service said, "It was pitch black, raining very heavily and the ground was flooded on the fell side of the track." Mountain rescue teams brought the injured out to be taken to hospital on a special train.

November 1994

associate the duration and intensity of storms with critical slope conditions such as soil saturation and thus give time for action. Landslide hazards can be mapped and evidence of past instability is often the best guide to future landslipping. Not only can actual and potential mass movements be mapped, but so can vulnerable rock formations, soils and slope angles. It is possible to produce a map of slope stability categories, consisting of 'security zones' such as nil, low, moderate and high. A landslide probability classification is given in Figure 4.5.

Once landslide areas and unstable slopes have been identified in an area, and stability ratings assigned for planning purposes, the **geotechnical** and geomorphological information can be integrated with planning decisions in order to choose which zones to develop, and in which zones to prohibit development or to concentrate on slope stabilisation work. The bottoms and mouths of steep ravines and the bases of steep slopes should not be developed. It has been estimated that landslide costs could be reduced by 95–99 per cent if extensive site investigation work was carried out. In San Mateo County, California, landslide zoning regulations were adopted in 1975 on the basis of a hazard map developed by the US Geological Survey. 1055 properties developed in the subsequent ten years (375 on hillsides) have suffered no landslide damage.

World-wide, the average death toll in landslides may be about 600 per year. In Japan landslides are primarily related to annual snowmelt and the occurrence of typhoons, but earthquakes, volcanic eruptions and tsunamis also play a part in causing slope instability. Landslides in the Commonwealth of Independent States (CIS) predominate in upland areas where there is active mountain building. Snowmelt, heavy rainfall and earthquakes are all important causes of mudflows in the Caucasus and in Soviet Central Asia. In the Mediterranean basin, landsliding has been intensified by deforestation and poor environmental management. In tropical areas of the less economically developed countries (LEDCs) overgrazing and population pressure on land are the main causes of landslides. The next section explores these issues in relation to detailed case studies. Population pressure in Hong Kong occurs on steep, unstable slopes in deeply weathered granite and creates problems in this highly urbanised environment. This can be contrasted with the processes that are active on the South Downs, mudslides in Italy and recent avalanches in Western Europe.

STUDENT ACTIVITY 4.1

Research skills and essay planning
Attempt a detailed essay plan for the following title.

'Examine the causes and effects of land instability using a variety of named examples.'

Useful starting points for research are the Geographical Magazine and Geography Review, as well as recent newspapers. Try to find examples of hazard types from a variety of MEDCs and LEDCs.

3.0 m per second	Extremely rapid
0.3 m per minute	Very rapid
1.5 m per day	Rapid
1.5 m per month	Moderate
1.5 m per year	Slow
0.06 m per year	Very slow

FIGURE 4.2 Rate of movement scale for landslides (Varnes 1978)

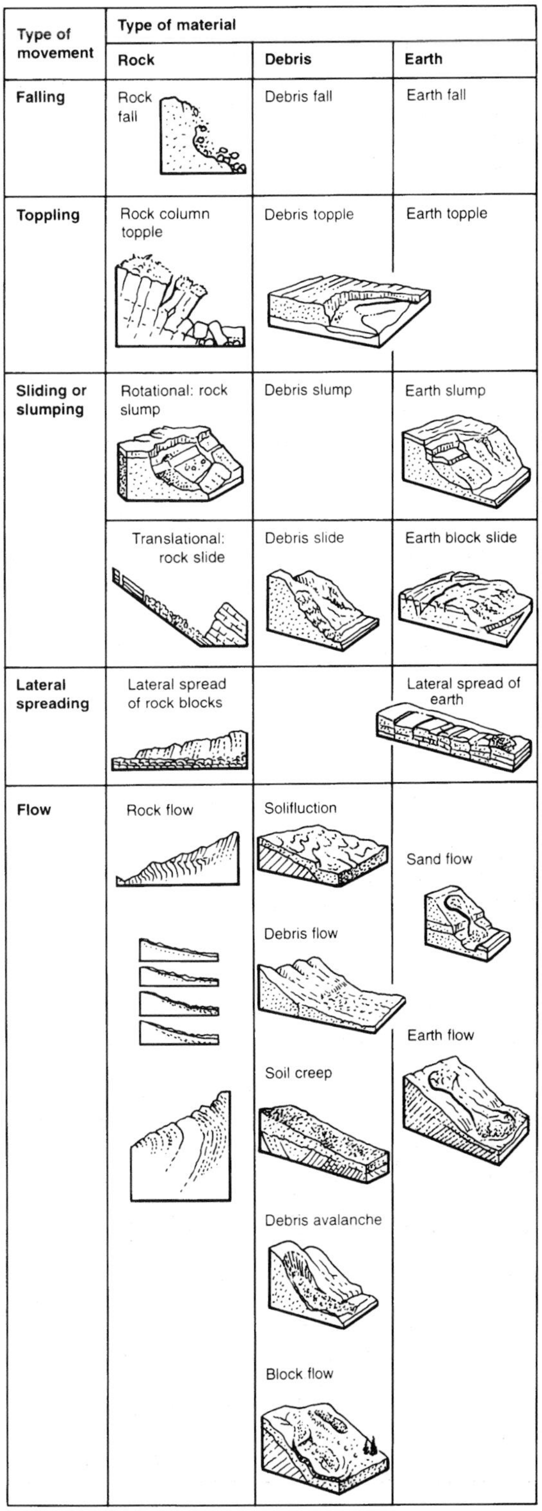

Type of movement	Type of material: Rock	Debris	Earth
Falling	Rock fall	Debris fall	Earth fall
Toppling	Rock column topple	Debris topple	Earth topple
Sliding or slumping	Rotational: rock slump	Debris slump	Earth slump
	Translational: rock slide	Debris slide	Earth block slide
Lateral spreading	Lateral spread of rock blocks		Lateral spread of earth
Flow	Rock flow	Solifluction Debris flow Soil creep Debris avalanche Block flow	Sand flow Earth flow

FIGURE 4.3 Varne's landslide classification

FIGURE 4.4 Methods of preventing and controlling slope failure

Major solution	Specific methods	Major solution	Specific methods
1 Avoidance *Control of location, timing and nature of development*	■ Remove, bridge or bypass unstable land ■ Land-use restrictions and controls ■ Hazard mapping and land-use zoning ■ Engineering geology or soil surveys before, during and after development ■ Redevelopment or moratoria on unsafe land uses ■ Use of sanitary codes to restrict development ■ Seasonal limitations to slope development ■ Grading and hillside development regulations ■ Acquisition, restructuring or removal of property ■ Warning and public education measures ■ Disclosure of hazard to property buyers ■ Establishing legal liabilities of property owners ■ Insurance against hazard ■ Financial assistance to promote hazard reduction	**2** Slope angle reduction *Control of cut and fill* **3** Infrastructural improvements *Improved drainage* *Retaining structures* **4** Surface protection *Protect surface* *Compaction*	■ Limit or reduce slope angles ■ Limit or reduce slope unit lengths ■ Remove unstable material ■ Surface drainage ■ Subsurface ■ Control irrigation ■ Buttress or counterweight at slope foot ■ Retaining walls ■ Foundation engineering ■ Control vegetation cover ■ Harden surface (e.g. concrete cover) ■ Chemical treatment ■ Control fill compaction

FIGURE 4.5 Landslide probability classification

Class	Description
I	Slopes which show no evidence of previous landslide activity and which are considered highly unlikely to develop landslides in the foreseeable future.
II	Slopes which show no evidence of previous landslide activity but which are considered likely to develop landslides in the future.
III	Slopes with evidence of previous landslide activity but which have not undergone movement in the previous 100 years.
IV	Slopes infrequently subject to new or renewed landslide activity. Triggering of landslides results from events with recurrence intervals greater than five years.
V	Slopes frequently subject to new or renewed landslide activity. Triggering of landslides results from events with recurrence intervals of up to five years.
VI	Slopes with active landslides. Material is continually moving, and landslide forms are fresh and well defined. Movement may be continuous or seasonal.

FIGURE 4.6 Major failure of a soil/rock cut slope (about 200–250m cubed) leading to the evacuation of 15 flats

Landslip disasters in Hong Kong

Hong Kong has a long history of slope failure, which has often directly affected the population. Experience has shown that these failures occur on a regular basis, are related to heavy rainfall, and range in size and character from minor earth or boulder falls to major landslides.

The territory of Hong Kong lies at the mouth of the Pearl River on the coast of southern China and comprises a mountainous piece of Chinese mainland and a number of hilly islands in the South China Sea. A building boom accompanied the influx of immigrants from the North of China after the 1939–45 war and industry and commerce flourished. Population pressure built up and the Government had to begin to build new towns. The population has risen from 3.6 million in 1963 to about 6 million in 1995. Urban development in the hilly terrain of Hong Kong has involved extensive earth **cutting and filling** in order to produce level platforms (terraces) on which to build roads and buildings. A significant hazard exists in the intensively developed middle and lower slopes of the mountains where large quantities of weathered rock are easily moved during intense rainstorms.

Intense rainstorms, which give rise to many landslides, are most likely to occur in summer, either when stationary troughs of low pressure settle near the South China coast, or during the close passage of tropical cyclones. Cyclones occur most frequently between July and September.

The hillside streams draining small steep catchments, quickly became swollen with storm water and have a potentially destructive power as roads and paved surfaces act as conduits for flood water. Unless well protected these steep slopes are easily eroded. The greatest hazard is posed by collapses of earthworks or natural landslips which can develop into large mobile flows capable of demolishing multi-storey buildings (Figure 4.6).

Although total elimination of landslip risk in Hong Kong is nearly impossible, much can be done to reduce the risk.

Landslip events in Hong Kong

In the last 30 years there have been over 2000 landslips causing over 200 deaths. Figure 4.7 provides some detailed statistics.

Development of slope safety systems

The landslip disaster prevention system that Hong Kong has developed over the last 30 years comprises of six main elements:
1 Squatter protection;
2 Geotechnical emergency services;
3 Geotechnical input to development control (planning);
4 Upgrading of substandard old slopes;

Date	Number of landslips	How many killed
June 1966	500	64
June 1972	2	138
August 1976	4	18
May 1982	689	27
May 1989	340	2
May 1992	350	3
June 1993	108	1
July 1994	*1	5

* Final figures not yet available

FIGURE 4.7 Landslip statistics

5 Routine slope maintenance;
6 Geotechnical input into land-use planning.
The illegal settlement (squatting) of people from China and other Asian countries has had a major impact on landslip disaster potential, since most of the squatters live in ramshackle huts on steep slopes.

Following the 1966 landslides, a landslip warning system for squatters was set up. Since 1982 some 65 000 squatters have been cleared from steep hillsides and rehoused. After the 1972 disasters a professional geotechnical advisory service was established to check landslip sites and evaluate plans for private building developments. A systematic study to locate and reinforce potentially dangerous slopes was a direct response to the 1976 disaster. The long-term programme to upgrade substandard slopes continues and about 25 engineers are directly employed and over HK $1 billion has been spent on the programme since 1976. Work on this programme will not be completed for another 15 years and the work load for newly recognised slope hazards has yet to be assessed.

The landslip disaster prevention system in Hong Kong is a product of past disasters. Even slopes that are designed and constructed to high safety standards are liable to become dangerous through deterioration if not properly maintained. The introduction of a slope certification system, under which owners of all registered slopes would be required by law to obtain an engineer's safety certificate, could be the next step in landslip risk mitigation.

Rainstorms and landslips in the 1990s: a proven link

1992: a very severe rainstorm occurred on 8 May 1992 bringing 350mm of rain in a 9-hour deluge to the western coast of Hong Kong Island. A total of 350 landslips were reported, two of which killed three people. An old masonry wall collapsed above the Baguio Villas estate releasing 2000m of soil into a drainage gulley which then struck the back of a block of flats displacing foundations and killing two people in the process. Over 1500 residents had to be evacuated. The event showed that many slopes were uncatalogued as serious hazards and that many private owners were unaware of their obligations to inspect and maintain slopes within their property. A public education campaign aimed at private owners began in September 1992 as a result of this incident.

1993: a severe rainstorm occurred on 16 June 1993 and 108 landslips were reported. One collapse in an old cutting resulted in the death of a pedestrian at a bus stop which attracted considerable media attention.

1994: July 1994 was unusually wet in Hong Kong. On 23 July an old retaining wall collapsed in the Western District killing five people. Rescue efforts continued for several days and more than 2500 residents were temporarily evacuated from their homes. The event was widely publicised and became a political issue in the District Board elections.

FIGURE 4.8 Landslide disaster

STUDENT ACTIVITY 4.2

Landslip disasters in Hong Kong

1 Below are nine statements which describe the sequence of events in a landslip. They have been deliberately mixed up.

a) Arrange the statements into a possible chronological order.

b) Draw a frame around each statement, link them with arrows and produce a flow diagram.

> Lubrication of surfaces;
> long, dry spell;
> slope failure;
> slip, slide, slump;
> water soaks into soil;
> dry open soil;
> saturation of the soil;
> sustained heavy rain;
> weakening of the structure

2 Study Figure 4.8. What issues does it raise and what nature of problems face the Hong Kong authorities?

3 Answer the following questions in the form of summary notes with annotated diagrams where appropriate.

a) What are landslips?

b) What causes landslips in Hong Kong?

c) How do landslips affect people in Hong Kong?

d) How do people increase the likelihood of landslips?

e) What can be done to decrease landslip hazards in Hong Kong?

'12 Estates at Risk' from Landslides

An estimated 20,000 slopes in Hong Kong are dangerous, many of them have not been examined, and another landslip disaster could strike any day, a government surveyor warned last night.

Wong Wai-hung, the chairman of the Association of Government Land and Engineering Surveying Officers, said up to 12 housing estates were at risk from dangerous and unexamined slopes.

He said sites at the Hing Wah estate in Chai Wan and the Shun Lee estate near Sau Mau Ping were particularly dangerous.

Wong said slopes on the two estates had never been surveyed – an allegation denied by the Secretary for Works, James Blake.

Wong said that it was only a matter of time before the Kwun Lung Lau estate tragedy, caused by the collapse of a retaining wall, was repeated.

The death toll rose to six last night when another body was pulled from the rubble.

Wong said the Government's geotechnical division had only 15 surveying officers with the necessary experience to inspect the territory's dangerous slopes.

If the number was increased to 25 it would take two years to inspect all the dangerous slopes, he said.

Blake confirmed there were up to 20,000 slopes which would have to be examined.

"The estimated number of slopes [to be examined] varies, but a number in excess of 20,000 has been spoken about," Blake said.

"In an original survey 10 years ago the figure was less, but a consultancy awarded in July will establish the number."

When asked if Hong Kong's dangerous slopes remained unsurveyed, Blake said: "Not necessarily."

When asked if he feared another tragedy he said "I'd be surprised if there were any new significant problems or features."

Blake dismissed Wong's claims about a severe shortage of survey officers.

"That's not ... an accurate reflection of the resources available to carry out geotechnical surveys," he said.

"Survey officers are not the sole source of expertise to survey slopes. Within the engineering profession in Hong Kong, the geotechnical field is well covered."

A government spokesman said the 15 survey officers were supplemented by 151 geotechnical engineers.

Wong blamed Saturday's Kwun Lung Lau tragedy on the Government's inability to monitor Hong Kong slopes and a shift of responsibility to private organisations that often cannot afford proper geotechnical advice.

"There is not sufficient [government] staff to monitor slope movements, which means we can't supply adequate information to the engineers who are actually involved in remedial slope work," Wong said.

He said the Government was "stupid" for suggesting that private organisations embody geotechnical engineers.

"Not all these firms have advanced, precision monitoring equipment, and they can't cope with so many requests."

Wong said at least 5,000 of the 20,000 slopes in the territory required constant checking.

July 1994

Soil erosion

The hazard of soil erosion is strongly linked to that of landsliding. Soil erosion is a natural process affecting all soil-covered surfaces, and only becomes a problem when the rate of erosion exceeds the rate of new soil formation. Seven main methods of erosion may occur as shown in Figure 4.9.

Many factors interact to influence the rate of soil erosion. Morgan (1979) has developed a model of soil erosion in which three groups and factors are recognised, and these are shown in Figure 4.10 along with an indication of the way they influence the risk of erosion.

Erosion can be severe on a hillside construction site where excavations may significantly alter surface slopes, making a steeper slope more prone to erosion and gulleying and landslide potential (Figure 4.11). Proper drainage and erosion control practices are shown in Figure 4.12.

Soil erosion risks have increased from 9300 to 24 000 million tonnes per year. The vast majority (96 per cent) of soil erosion is caused by rivers and 2 per cent by wind sources. Rates of surface lowering prior to human influences were 2–3cm/1000 years and have now doubled. In highly localised instances the rate has increased by many orders of magnitude. Soil erosion has been identified in virtually every country of the world, but it tends to concentrate in some of the poorest, such as El Salvador, where 77 per cent of land area is seriously eroded. Erosion rates reach a maximum in fragile environments which are seasonally arid or semi-arid. With annual precipitation totals of 250–300mm, rainfall is insufficient to maintain continuous vegetation cover, but in wet periods sudden torrential rain storms can cause serious erosion.

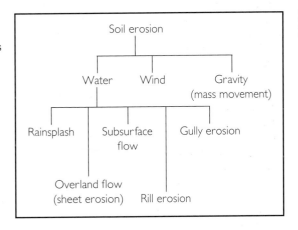

FIGURE 4.9 The main processes of soil erosion

Property damage on the South Downs

Causes and chronology

In the last 15 years there has been an increase in the incidence of property damage due to runoff from agricultural land in England. The prime cause of this has been a shift from spring-sown to autumn-sown or winter cereals as the dominant crop in the arable landscape. In non-agricultural circles this change has gone largely unnoticed, but for some rural and urban fringe communities the consequences have been considerable.

The widespread adoption of autumn-sown wheat and barley has meant that there are large areas of bare or relatively bare surfaces between October and December, generally the wettest months of the year in southern England.

Other factors which contribute to increased flooding include the following:
■ expansion of arable farming onto steep and vulnerable slopes beginning during the 1939–45 war and continuing in some areas until the early 1980s;
■ use of heavier and more powerful agricultural machinery with increased risk of soil compaction;
■ removal of field boundaries (hedges, banks, ditches) to form larger fields;
■ expansion of urban areas onto sites at risk of flooding.

Fields that are sown or prepared for sowing are generally smooth and sometimes rolled flat, and

---

STUDENT ACTIVITY 4.3

Soil erosion processes
1 Describe the major processes associated with soil erosion.
2 Examine the changes that may occur when agricultural activities modify slope processes.

FIGURE 4.10 The main factors influencing soil erosion rates

Energy factors	Protection factors	Resistance factors
Rainfall erosivity (+)	Population density (+)	Soil erodibility (+)
Runoff volume (+)	Plant cover (−)	Infiltration capacity (−)
Wind strength (+)	Amenity value (+)	Soil management (−)
Relief (+)	Land management (−)	
Slope angle (+)		
Slope length (+)		
Wind **fetch** (+)		
Slope shortening (e.g. terracing) (−)		
Fetch shortening (e.g. shelter belts) (−)		

Key
+ = increasing value therefore more erosion
− = decreasing value therefore more erosion

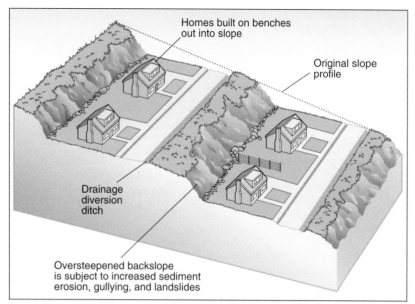

FIGURE 4.11 Slope and potential landslide problems in upland building sites

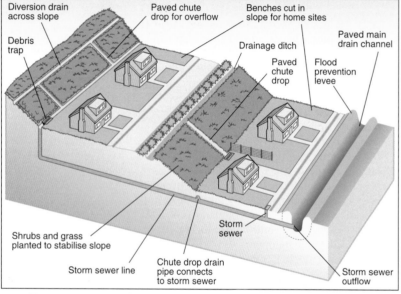

FIGURE 4.12 Proper drainage and erosion control practices in development of sediment pollution and flooding

until there is sufficient crop cover to inhibit flow, which may be two or three months later, there is a risk of runoff and erosion. Given optimal field surface conditions, unexceptional amounts of rainfall may result in runoff and erosion. On the South Downs, for example, rainfall of about 30mm over two days may cause erosion. Between 1 September and 30 November in each year from 1982 to 1991 this threshold was exceeded 22 times.

In areas with large expanses of winter cereals, farmed in an environmentally insensitive manner, there is a strong correlation between wet autumns, erosion and property damage. Flooding of houses in Sompting, West Sussex, occurred in 1980, 1987 and 1990. By 1990, 60 per cent of the normally dry chalk catchment above the houses was under winter cereals, an unusually high figure, constituting a severe risk of runoff in the autumn months.

On the South Downs damage has occurred

during ten of the 18 years from 1976 to 1994, most notably in the autumn and winter of 1982–3 and 1987–8. Of 39 dated incidents, 23 occurred in the month of October. Almost all damage was a result of runoff from winter cereal fields.

Costs: who pays?

In the first case of its kind at Highdown in Lewes during 1982, researchers Stammers and Boardman pointed out that costs of emergency and remedial action fell on the local district council because flooded householders were unable to cope and the farmer refused to accept any responsibility. In this instance damage to houses was slight, but in more recent events householder costs have been high.

In 1987, the Brighton area suffered from flooding at Mile Oak and Hangleton which led to expenditures of more than £106 000 by householders and £153 000 by the local authority; at Rottingdean the figures were about £300 000 and £120 000 and these excluded the fire and police service costs. Of the costs to individual householders, £112 500 of uninsured losses had to be borne directly by the householders. Repeated flooding of four houses at Sompting has so far cost Adur District Council in excess of £400 000 and costs in excess of £80 000 were claimed at Breaky Bottom vineyard. In all of these cases there were two common factors:

■ farming practices, including decisions regarding land use, were such as to cause or exacerbate the flooding;
■ no measures were taken to protect the neighbour.

The Breaky Bottom vineyard and farmhouse near Rodmell, East Sussex, were flooded in October 1987 by muddy water on about ten occasions. An estimated 635 tonnes of soil was dumped on the property and the farmhouse, built in 1827, had been previously flooded in 1976 and 1982 as a result of similar events. In 1987 the source of water and soil was not in dispute: field surveys and an air photograph showed it to be from recently sown winter cereal and ploughed fields of a particular farmer. There was also little doubt that the risk of erosion and runoff on steeply sloping cereal fields was known, with the farmer having chaired an NFU meeting on the subject and been interviewed by both TV and the press. The Agricultural Developments Advisory Service (ADAS), of the Ministry of Agriculture, Fisheries and Food (MAFF), had circulated a pamphlet on the problem of erosion to farmers on the South Downs and in a 1983 publication they had pointed to the dangers of cultivation of steep downland slopes.

After five years of preparation, the Breaky Bottom case was settled out of court a week before trial in January 1993, with the plaintiff recovering damages of an undisclosed amount. Thus no legal precedent was established. As is standard practice in such settlements, the defendants made no admission of liability. A judicial ruling on the issue of liability for runoff is therefore still awaited.

The future

European Union efforts to reduce expenditure on agriculture, to discourage overproduction of commodities including cereals, and to encourage environmentally sensitive farming practices should help to control the incidence of property damage by runoff. Set-aside regulations have the potential to take out of cultivation erosion-prone land, preferably permanently. At Steepdown in Sompting, the non-cultivation of steep slopes for the last two years under set-aside has significantly reduced, although not eliminated, the amount of runoff, and therefore the risk of flooding.

In the longer term, the issue of climate change and the introduction of new crops to Britain will have to be confronted. The emphasis may shift from runoff during winter due to cereals, to the effect of summer thunderstorms on maize, sugar beet and sunflowers, as altitudinal limits of crop growth rise and farmers are tempted to convert grassland to arable.

In a recent article in the Town and Country Planning Journal, J Boardman suggests, 'Imaginative development of set-aside regulations would seem to be the best hope for control of the problem.'

Figure 4.13 shows the problem of soil erosion in the eastern area of the South Downs. The extent of the problems can be seen in Figure 4.15. Figure 4.14 shows the time of year of the greatest risk of soil erosion. Agricultural activities, weather and soil erosion difficulties are also shown in Figures 4.16,

4.17 and 4.20, all of which show areas having suffered from soil erosion on the South Downs.

Albourne: a detailed case study of soil erosion and farm management

Research into the character of soil erosion in one field at Albourne Farm, 10km north-west of Brighton, showed that it was primarily the result of farm management methods rather than purely physical factors. The field in question is on Grade 2 farmland with fine loamy soil of typical brown earth character known as the Dundale Series, formed on the Lower Greensand sands. The slope of

FIGURE 4.15 Soil erosion on the South Downs, at Kingston nr. Lewes

FIGURE 4.13 Soil erosion on the eastern South Downs

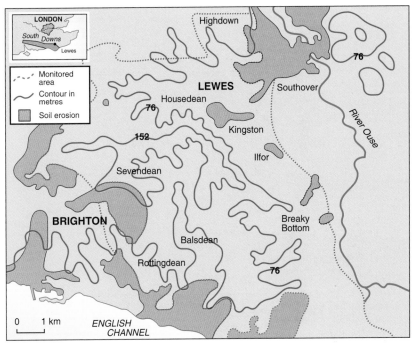

FIGURE 4.14 Periods of risk in relation to crop cover – winter cereals on the South Downs

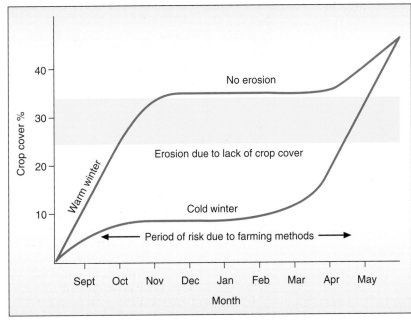

FIGURE 4.16 Rainfall (Southover) farming operations and erosion during Sept–Dec 1987

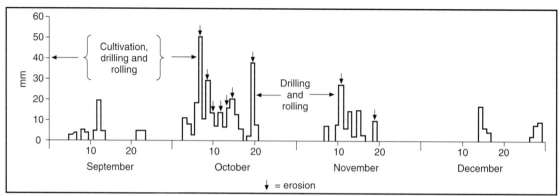

FIGURE 4.17 Sediment movement pattern in Breaky Bottom Valley

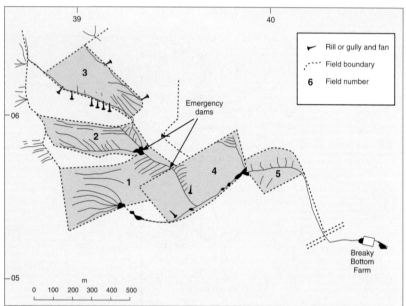

FIGURE 4.18 Soil erosion at Albourne, West Sussex

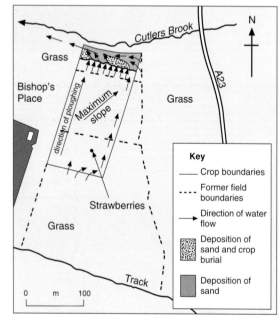

the field runs 335m down to a small stream, declining in altitude by about 16m. Figure 4.18 shows some of the characteristics of the field.

In June 1979 the field was planted to strawberries and by April 1980 extensive erosion had been noted. Loss of soil was apparent over the whole field and the furrows between ridges of strawberries had been filled in. Channels had developed at the head of the field, and at the bottom of the field the crop had been buried by deposits up to 10cm deep.

Research by J Boardman (1983) suggested the following factors as important in the occurrence of erosion in this field:

1 Field size. Prior to 1962 this area had consisted of five fields but by 1978 it was only one. The length of unbroken slope increased, therefore, from 90m to 335m;

2 The nature of the crop meant that large areas and channels of soil were left exposed throughout the winter;

3 The land was worked downslope rather than around the contours;

4 The soils are highly susceptible to erosion, consisting of low clay slit content (2–3 per cent) and with a tendency to form a crust or cap;

5 The farm manager suggested that a prime cause was the large number of autumn storms in 1979. However, although August and December were particularly wet, the frequency of intense rainfall events (days with more than 7.7mm) was below average.

The rates of erosion recorded at Albourne Farm were among the highest recorded in the UK with 200m³ of soil removed from 1.66ha in the period from July 1979 to March 1980. The surface lowering was about 12mm with an annual removal rate of 241 tonnes/ha.

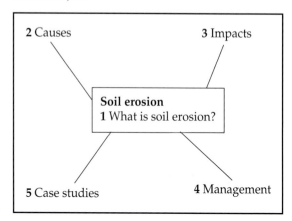

FIGURE 4.19 Topic web

STUDENT ACTIVITY 4.4

Soil erosion on the South Downs

1 Prepare an article for a newspaper detailing the impact of soil erosion on people's lives. Give your article an appropriate heading and use diagrams to illustrate the places, processes and mitigation of soil erosion hazards.

2 Study Figure 4.20 and carry out a hypothesis testing exercise, using Spearman's Rank correlation coefficient, to find out if there is an association between:

a) soil loss and slope length;

b) soil loss and slope angle.

3 Topic summary webs are useful in reinforcing the main ideas in this section. Prepare such a web using Figure 4.19 as a guide.

a) What is soil erosion?

b) What causes soil erosion?

c) How does soil erosion affect people?

d) How can people increase or decrease the likelihood or effects of soil erosion?

STUDENT ACTIVITY 4.5

Summary essay on soil erosion and landslides

To what extent do people's perceptions of landslides and soil erosion influence their responses to these events?

You may like to use the following basic plan as a study guide:

Introduction: proper definitions of hazard perception and responses. Definitions of land instability, landslides and soil erosions. Factors on which they depend (population, warning, speed of event, relief operations, hazard management and mitigation, economic development, etc).

Main part: selected case studies to show a range of perceptions and responses, i.e. different social and economic backgrounds, groups and organisations, national and international authorities. Use diagrams and maps to locate case studies and explain the processes.

Conclusion: summary of the main points. Significance of these to any response to reduce human suffering from erosion. Contrast responses of MEDCs and LEDCs.

Evaluate your work using this mark scheme:

a) Defining and describing the question, problem or issue.   5 marks

b Using and selecting appropriate reference material and extracting data.   5 marks

c Applying the results of research to the set question.   7 marks

d Evaluating and summarising conclusions.   5 marks

e Presenting the conclusions in a clear, logical order.   3 marks

Total 25 marks

FIGURE 4.20 Soil erosion

Field	Area (ha)	Slope length (m)	Maximum angle (°)	Relief (m)	Soil loss (m³)	Erosion rate (m³ ha²¹)	Lane use
1	12.4	550	15	70	979	79	ds/wc
2	8.4	540	15	70	527	63	ds/wc
3	9.7	500	13	60	371	38	ds/wc
4	15.0	230	20	42	461	31	ds/plo
5	5.6	150	12	20	181	32	ds/plo
6	14.0	830	13	70	200	14	ds/wc
7	22.8	1 250	15	125	1 605	70	ds/plo and wc
8	18.4	840	12	85	494	27	ds/har
9	12.6	410	12	65	2 543	202	ds/wc
10	14.9	490	15	50	950	64	ds/wc
11	20.0	300	15	54	1 606	80	ds/wc
12	10.8	300	12	38	408	38	ds/wc
13	22.9	640	16	50	500	22	ds/har
14	6.4	170	10	26	294	46	ds/wc
15	6.6	190	12	28	391	59	ds/har
16	9.5	600	15	50	131	14	ds/wc
17	7.6	450	18	85	100	13	ds/plo
18	19.4	700	9	70	388	20	ds/plo

ds = downslope, w/c = winter cereal, plo = ploughed, har = harrowed, relief = difference in height between highest and lowest point in the field

Mudslides in Sarno, Italy

Havoc wrought on Sarno in Southern Italy

The mudslides struck late on Tuesday and followed several days of torrential rain.

In the centre of town there is a square with a monument and a big house with turquoise shutters. Above it, half-ruined fortifications climb a slope dotted with olive groves.

But it looked anything but picturesque yesterday as earth movers and trucks moved to and fro slowly draining a swamp of sludge the colour of bitter chocolate. The mud had reached halfway up the door of the house with the shutters.

Alessandro Belmonte was among those surveying the devastation. He described how the sludge had swept past his house 150 metres away: "*It made the sound of an earthquake. But unlike an earthquake it passed on and then could be heard again at a distance.*"

Carlo Crescenzo had just returned from the US to Sarno after 35 years. He had dumped his things at his home in the hills and gone down to the town for dinner: "*When I tried to go back everybody was coming in the opposite direction. I tried to get to my house, but there was a wall of mud seven or eight feet high. I've got all of my luggage and all of my documents in the house. It's too much,*" he said, shaking his head and looking across the square. "*Whichever way you tried to get up the hills, sooner or later you ran into a barrier of mud. It got rapidly deeper until it slapped in the wheel arches and threatened to pour in through the radiator grill. It swamped vineyards, brought down houses, carried away vehicles – and ended lives.*"

In the nearby village of Bracigliano, witnesses described seeing a 34-year-old woman and her three sons aged seven, nine and thirteen being swept away. In the town of Quindici, a mudslide killed the former mayor, Olga Santaniello, who became a local hero in the 1980s by campaigning against the Camorra, a powerful organised power syndicate.

Piles of mud and boulders covered railway tracks and roads, bringing circulation to a standstill. Power and telephone lines were down in much of the area. The cause of so much death and damage lay in the recent forest fires that stripped hills of vegetation that held the earth, and the refusal of residents to leave their homes, officials said.

The chief of the civil protection agency, Andrea Todisco, said many homes had been built too close to rivers or in areas prone to landslides. Construction without permits runs rampant in Southern Italy.

Along the roads that criss-cross the valley floor, all that remained of the mud last night was a thick layer of powdery earth. The army lorries and police cars, ambulances and trucks laden with sludge threw up great clouds of dust as the light faded. It was a scene from a third-world refugee crisis. Overhead helicopters chattered back and forth carrying rescue teams still searching for the missing.

7 May 1998

FIGURE 4.21 Havoc wrought on Sarno in Southern Italy

FIGURE 4.22 Death roll climbs

Death toll climbs

The death toll from Southern Italy's disastrous mudslides rose to 54 yesterday as rescue workers continued to search for 98 people still missing since Tuesday, Philip Willan in Rome writes.

"As the hours pass the hope of finding people alive gets even fainter," said Andrea Todisco the head of the Civil Protection Department in Rome.

Rescue workers assisted by dogs were digging in the deep mud that swept down Mount Saro and rolled into the centre of Sarno town. As they worked, new landslides continued to rumble down the rain-sodden mountain.

In the neighbouring town of Quindici, rescuers found the body of a woman aged 35, clinging to the roof of her submerged house. In the ruins of the parish church, a head appeared from the bulldozed mud, but turned out to be part of a statue of the Madonna.

Italian newspapers were filled with criticism of national and local authorities.

In parliament Franco Barberi, under-secretary with responsibility for civil protection, said local administrators had allowed houses to be built without taking account of the geological risk factors, while the neglect of forests and the failure to ensure an adequate drainage network had done the rest.

8 May 1998

FIGURE 4.23 Unnatural disaster

Unnatural Disaster

The mud swamping Sarno and nearby towns began to stink yesterday. It holds vegetation torn from the surrounding hills when the earth collapsed under torrential rain on Tuesday night and the leaves, branches, grass and branches trapped in the sludge started to rot. But there was another rotten smell coming off the sludge: the all too human stench of self-ishness, corruption and negligence. The tragedy that befell the Sarno valley was only to a limited extent a natural disaster. True, the rain was exceptional. Officials said as much rain had fallen in the area this week as would normally fall in a year. True, the geology of Campania, the region surrounding Naples, is inherently perilous. Its volcanic soils are in a pre-carious alliance with its limestone rock, always threatening to slither off under extreme weather.

But the other reason why so many land-slides take place in Campania, and Italy, has nothing to do with rain or soil, but with a failure to obey or enforce the law. It has to do with a culture which puts a greater emphasis on forgiveness than on punishment. It even has to do with or-ganised crime.

Except perhaps for the involvement of or-ganised criminals, Italy is not unique in this respect. The process that brought death and destruction to the Sarno valley is the one that has increasingly visited lethal flash floods on eastern Spain and will soon bring death and destruction to areas of Portugal, Greece and Turkey, as they too become richer and more developed.

Across Southern Europe vested interests have combined to invent a system that eliminates the natural methods by which excess rainfall can be absorbed harm-lessly. The first step involves clearing for development land the authorities have designated as "green belt". The easiest way is a forest fire.

The growing incidence of such fires around the Mediterranean is not coinci-dental. Large numbers are started delib-erately by developers to ensure that the areas they have targeted lost their natural beauty. One of the side-effects is to loosen the underlying soil. Then comes the development itself. Throughout sun-belt Europe, the easiest way for an indi-vidual to add on an extension or for a builder to put up a house, is not to submit plans for approval but just to go ahead – often in August when most officialdom is on holiday. There is almost no risk that the new structure will be demolished.

Local councils depend heavily on con-struction licence fees. Even if they cannot be persuaded, or bribed, to accept a fait ac-compli, there is rarely long to wait before the next central or regional government amnesty. Then illicit construction can be legalised overnight with the payment of a fine – an infinitely simpler procedure than obtaining planning permission.

Right now the autonomous government of Sicily is using its extensive powers to legitimise 20 000 holiday homes built on beaches, cliffs and wetlands in defiance of planning regulations.

In the past 5 years, according to the environmental group Legambiente, 207 000 houses have been built without permission in Italy. Together they would cover an area more than 10 times that of the City of London. Like hundreds and thousands of other houses thrown up since Italy's "economic miracle", many are without proper drainage or foun-dations. Or else they stand by riverbeds that seem empty, and remain empty until the next once-in-a-century storm.

The Naples area is where the process reaches its delirious apogee, exacerbated by the intimidatory power of the local mafia, the Camorra. Probably the most as-tonishing single example of rogue devel-opment in Europe is a Campanian town of 15 000 inhabitants called Villaggio Coppola di Castelvolturno, which was created entirely without authorisation.

The rising frequency of what Italians call "hydro-geological" disasters in the area underlines the human cost of such un-planned development. Landslides caused multiple deaths in Campania in 1973, 1978, 1986 and 1997. But last year there were no fewer than three.

It is just possible that the tide could now turn. The horrific choking deaths of those who died in the mud that swept into Sarno have given a chilling resonance to the warnings of environmentalists. Something considered a hobby horse of the greens has suddenly become the common wisdom of opinion makers.

The centre-right Il Messagero newspaper spoke yesterday of "collective suicide"; the centre-left La Repubblica of "en-vironmental pillage". By far the most un-compromisingly damming words came – encouragingly – from a politician. As he flew over the devastated valley in a heli-copter the interior minister, Girogo Napolitano said: "I am witnessing scenes unworthy of a civilised country".

8 May 1998

STUDENT ACTIVITY 4.6

Mudslides in Sarno, Italy
1   Describe the impacts of the mud slides in Sarno on the people and property. Locate the area on a sketch map.
2   To what extent can the event be described as an unnatural disaster?
3   Write a brief report on the lessons to be learnt following the disaster.

STUDENT ACTIVITY 4.7

The Chamonix Avalanche
1   Draw an annotated diagram to show the events leading up to the avalanches in the Chamonix valley at Montroc and Le Tour.
2   Describe the processes involved in an 'aerosol' avalanche.
3   What impacts on people and property have the avalanches had in
    (i) The Chamonix Valley
    (ii) Ski resorts in Europe
4   Produce a map and report using the modified Swiss Avalanche Zoning System, and methods of modifying and prevention of avalanches for the Chamonix Valley. You should consider protecting settlements, cost-benefit analysis and evaluate and justify your final decisions.

90 mph wall of snow hits Chamonix

As police, firemen and scores of volunteers searched Le Tour near the fashionable resort of Chamonix under the first blue sky for days, the scale of the tragedy became clear. Captain Jean-Claude Gin of the mountain police said:
"Avalanches are very quick and very strong. It hit like an explosion. The rescuers found people as they were when the avalanche hit, sitting sleeping or eating. It looked like an earthquake had hit the area. Everything was destroyed and covered with 10 to 15 metres of powder snow." Another rescuer, John Cristou, said: *"There is debris everywhere. It looks as though a bomb has gone off. Cars are mangled, chalets have disappeared."*

Details slowly emerged throughout the day of the dead and injured. Claude Marin, a spokesman for the mairie said the 12 people killed were French, including four locals. Four of the victims were children. He said 18 people had been rescued. Six people were still in hospital last night including the 12-year-old boy who was rescued early yesterday. Doctors said he was recovering after suffering from severe exposure. The remainder were slightly injured and suffering from shock. The tragedy had a shattering impact on holidaymakers and locals, with people openly crying in the town of Argentiere, the closest to the scene of the avalanche.

As the snow had been heavy since Sunday, ski-lifts in most of Chamonix had been closed. Many of the people killed or injured had been sheltering from the weather inside their chalets.

The weather improved greatly yesterday (10th), and the rescuers, the fireman and the gendarmes worked under sunny skies. Despite the tragedy many skiers headed for Les Houches, the only area where skiing was possible. However, roads to Argentiere from Chamonix were closed off by police with only residents and journalists being allowed through. Hundreds of people in neighbouring hamlets have been moved to hotels in the centre of Chamonix for safety. The snow covered everything in sight, with cars completely enveloped except for the tips of their windscreen wipers, which had been raised. An army helicopter was being used for the first time yesterday afternoon after fears that it would set off further avalanches. Mountain rescue experts were also carrying out controlled explosions to create avalanches in safe places. Captain Blaise Agresti of the mountain police said: *"It is a very bad condition of snow. We have this maybe once a century."*

Mr Marin and the rescuers were having a particularly difficult job as the snow had become "like concrete". It was very unlikely that the two people who were still missing would be found alive. "The avalanche was powder snow," he said. "But when it came down on the chalets it was like concrete. For the rescuers it is a mixture of concrete, wood, beds and all that you would find in a chalet."

Chamonix, which nestles in the shadow of Mont Blanc, is generally regarded as the skiing capital of Europe. The resort is popular among families with young children. It has a reputation for offering excellent skiing at a reasonable price. Accommodation ranges from dormitory-size youth hostels to four-star hotels. Although predominantly known as a skiing resort, Chamonix is also a popular destination for climbers in the summer.

11 February 1999

Blizzards strand thousands of holidaymakers

Army helicopters were drafted in by the Austrian authorities yesterday to lift essential supplies to some 25 000 holidaymakers now trapped in the country's resorts by some of the heaviest snow in decades. The popular Austrian resorts of St Anton, Lech, Zuers, Stuben and Ischgl are among those sealed off by snow since Saturday. Many of the resorts are short of basic supplies such as eggs and milk and the army is expected to airlift supplies of these to the villages.

The Lötschbergbahn rail line through the Alps remained closed because of avalanche threats. As the severe weather moved south, it dumped large quantities of snow on the Austrian province of Carinthia and neighbouring Slovenia, forcing the closure of Ljubljana airport. The Simplon Express train between Venice and Paris was derailed by snow on the track in the French town of Frasne.

In Italy, wind, rain and snow caused severe traffic problems and sparkled a landslide alert in Umbria where more than 100 people died under tons of mud last year. Temperatures fell to 12°F (minus 11°C) in some areas of north-east Italy.

Snow grounded flights in Budapest yesterday, preventing Janos Martonyi, the Hungarian foreign minister from flying to Strasbourg. He was due to attend meetings of the European Parliament and of the Council of Europe, which he currently heads.

Flights were also grounded in most of central Europe. Further afield ice and snow caused traffic disruption in the Netherlands, with some 373 miles of tailbacks reported during the morning rush-hour, officials said.

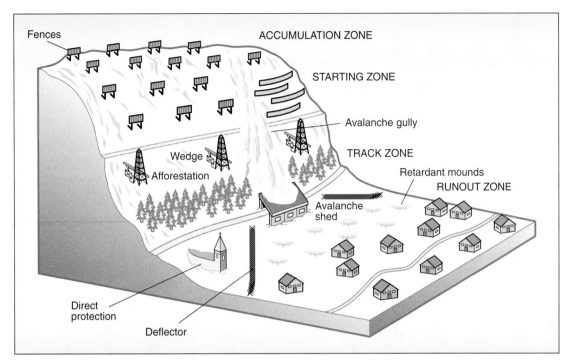

FIGURE 4.26 Methods of controlling avalanches

High-hazard (red) zone
- Any avalanche with a return interval of less than 30 years.
- No buildings or winter parking lots allowed – special bunkers needed for equipment.

Potential-hazard (blue) zone
- Avalanches with return intervals of 30–300 years.
- Public buildings that encourage gatherings of people should not be erected. Private houses may be erected if they are strengthened to withstand impact forces. The area may be closed during periods of hazard.

No-hazard (white) zone
- Very rarely affected by avalanches. Return interval greater than 300 years.
- No building restrictions.

FIGURE 4.27 A modified version of the Swiss Avalanche Zoning system

---

Size	Potential effects	Order of magnitude estimates		
		Vertical descent	**Volume (m³)**	**Frequency of occurrence**
Sluffs	Harmless	Less than 10m	1–10	10^4 per year
Small	Could bury, injure or kill a person	10–100m	$10–10^2$	10^3 per year
Medium	Could destroy a timber-frame house or car (localised damage)	100–500m	$10^3–10^4$	10^2 per year
Large	Could destroy a village or forest (general damage)	500m–1km	$10^5–10^6$	One per decade
Extreme	Could gouge the landscape (widespread damage)	1–5km	$10^6–10^9$	Two per century

FIGURE 4.28 The potential effects of avalanches

FIGURE 4.29 Avalanche and snow-related incidents in Europe, spring 1999

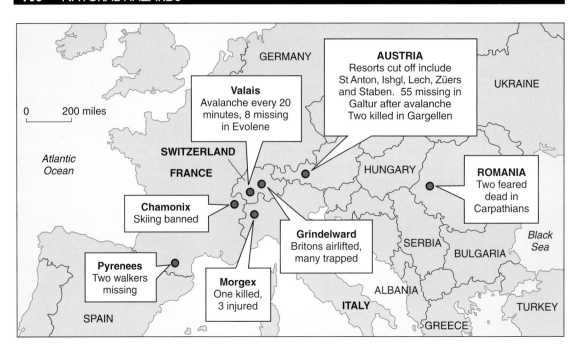

FIGURE 4.30 The Chamonix avalanche

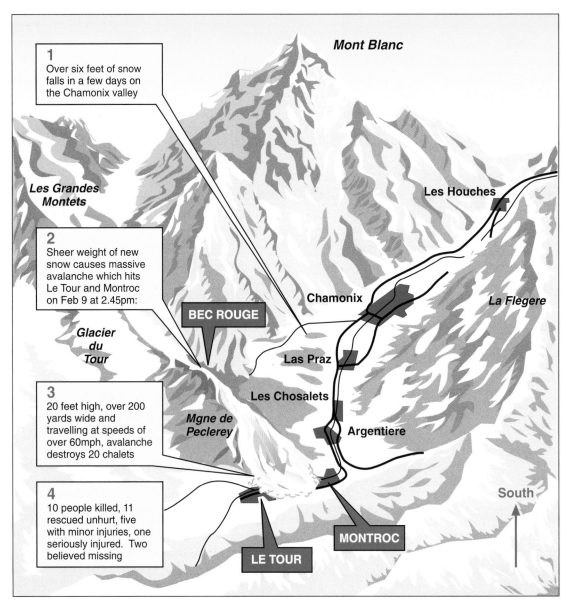

Review of key ideas

■ Mass movement hazards can be classified and perceived in a variety of ways.

■ Landslides are becoming more common as land pressure forces people to use unstable slopes.

■ Landslides can be classified by both speed and type of movement.

■ Landslide hazard mapping can be used in landslide probability classification and hazard mitigation.

■ Successful management of mass movement hazards can do much to lessen their impact but as yet, cannot control events responsible.

■ Soil erosion is only a problem when soil removal exceeds soil formation.

■ Loss of life and damage to property depend not only on physical factors but also on human activities in the area affected.

■ Soil erosion risks are increasing globally, but particularly in fragile environments with seriously arid or semi-arid climates.

■ Human activities and government policies often make the impacts and costs of soil erosion significantly greater.

■ Mass movement hazards have social and psychological effects as well as physical and economic effects.

Glossary

Avalanche – The rapid descent of a large mass of rock, ice and snow (sometimes all three) down a steep mountain slope.

Cut and fill – An engineering term referring to the practice of digging out material to form a terrace upon which constructions can take place on a slope.

Fetch – The distance of open land (or sea) over which winds (or waves) have travelled before striking a barrier (or the coast).

Geotechnical – Application of science and engineering techniques to the management of the surface of the earth, particularly slopes, rivers and coasts.

Landslides – A type of mass movement in which material is displaced along a clearly defined plane of sliding. Landslides often result from large accumulations of soil water, rainfall, springs or melting snow.

Mass movement – An inclusive term covering general types of processes responsible for the transport of weathered materials on slopes, without the action of running water. Mass movement occurs when the gravitational force acting on particles on the slope exceeds the resistance of the particles to displacement.

Rock fall – The free fall of masses of rock, detached by weakening or rock failure, to the base of a cliff or steep slope.

Set-aside – Arable land taken out of cereal production under the Common Agricultural Policy of the European Commission.

Soil erosion – The removal of soil by processes such as gulleying, rain wash and wind more rapidly than by natural processes.

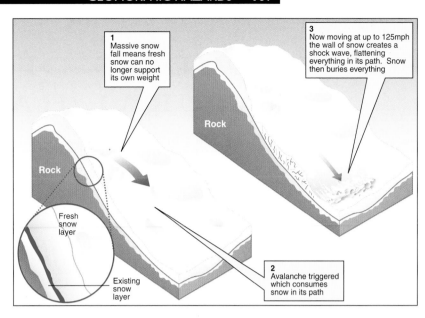

1 Massive snow fall means fresh snow can no longer support its own weight

3 Now moving at up to 125mph the wall of snow creates a shock wave, flattening everything in its path. Snow then buries everything

Rock

Rock

Fresh snow layer

Existing snow layer

2 Avalanche triggered which consumes snow in its path

Typhoon – A tropical revolving storm characterised by winds of very high velocity and torrential rainfall, occurring in the China Seas and along the western margins of the Pacific Ocean. Typhoons are a local type of tropical cyclone.

FIGURE 4.31 How an aerosol avalanche happens

References

National Disasters, D Alexander, 1993, UCL Press

Natural Hazards, E A Bryant, 1991, Cambridge University Press

Geohazard, Natural and Human, N R Coch, 1995, Prentice Hall

The Physical Geography of Landscape, R Collard, 1988, Unwin Hyman

Environmental Hazards, C C Park, 1991, Nelson

Environmental Hazards, K Smith, 1992, Routledge

Disasters, J Whittow, 1980, Pelican (out of print)

Hong Kong landslides

Hong Kong Rainfall and Landslides in 1992, Geotechnical Engineering Office, Hong Kong

Hong Kong Rainfall and Landslides in 1993, Engineering Department, Hong Kong

Learning from Landslip Disasters in Hong Kong, A Malone and K Ho

Soil erosion on the South Downs

Property damage by runoff from agricultural land, J Boardman, 1994, Town and Erosion Planning, 63. 9, 249–51

The Sensitivity of Downland Arable Land to Erosion by Water in Landscape Sensitivity, J Boardman, 1993, ed D S G Thomas and R J Allison (1973), John Wiley & Sons

Severe Erosion in Agricultural Land in East Sussex, UK October 1987, J Boardman, 1988, Soil Technology Vol 1, pp 33–348, Cantena Verley

5

CASE STUDIES OF MANAGING NATURAL HAZARDS

Managing coastal flooding: Chesil Sea Defence Scheme

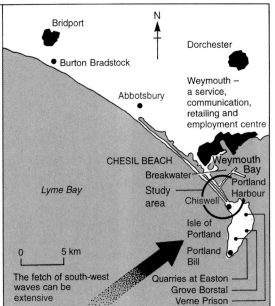

Chesil Beach Special Site of Scientific Interest (SSSI)
This is a natural barrier 27km long and 200m wide. It is a coastal feature of international significance, being one of three major shingle beaches in Britain, and its only simple storm beach. It is composed mainly of chert and flint, with grain size increasing from west to east, with the cobbles at Chiswell averaging 75mm diameter. It has been argued by Lewis that Chesil Beach is slowly shrinking as no new shingle is being added by lateral shingle drift or offshore replenishment, and that abrasion and attrition is continually reducing the size of the shingle components. Yet until 1972 beach material was extracted for commercial purposes. He also argues controversially that the beach has moved landward due to progressive overwash.

FIGURE 5.1 Chiswell and Chesil Beach location map

What is the nature of the hazard?

The Chiswell settlement has been flooded many times. The first major report of note occurred in November 1824 when, as a result of a catastrophic storm, 26 people were drowned and about 80 houses destroyed or damaged. Since that time, 22 events that have endangered lives and properties have been worthy of record, the most celebrated of which occurred in November 1936, when King Edward VIII had the misfortune of being on board a train which was stranded by flood water at Chiswell. The most recent severe floods were in December 1978 and February 1979.

The flood hazard did little to dissuade people from living in the area, or the authorities from systematically reclaiming the low-lying marsh land of the mere at the northern end of the settlement from 1865 and 1977 (see Figures 5.1, 5.2 and 5.3).

FIGURE 5.2 The vulnerable Chiswell area in Portland

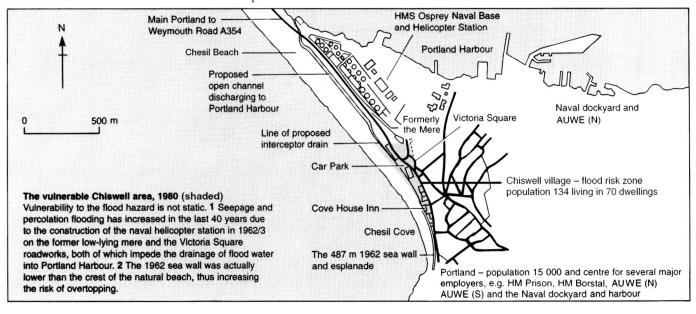

The vulnerable Chiswell area, 1980 (shaded)
Vulnerability to the flood hazard is not static. **1** Seepage and percolation flooding has increased in the last 40 years due to the construction of the naval helicopter station in 1962/3 on the former low-lying mere and the Victoria Square roadworks, both of which impede the drainage of flood water into Portland Harbour. **2** The 1962 sea wall was actually lower than the crest of the natural beach, thus increasing the risk of overtopping.

What are the physical and human causes of the hazard?

A case study of the events of 1978 and 1979

The hazard problem at Chiswell is almost unique in the UK and is a function of the interaction of human land use and extreme natural events.

There are two types of marine flooding at Chiswell:

FIGURE 5.3 (a) A field sketch of the Chiswell area, 1978
(b) The Chiswell area in the late 70s

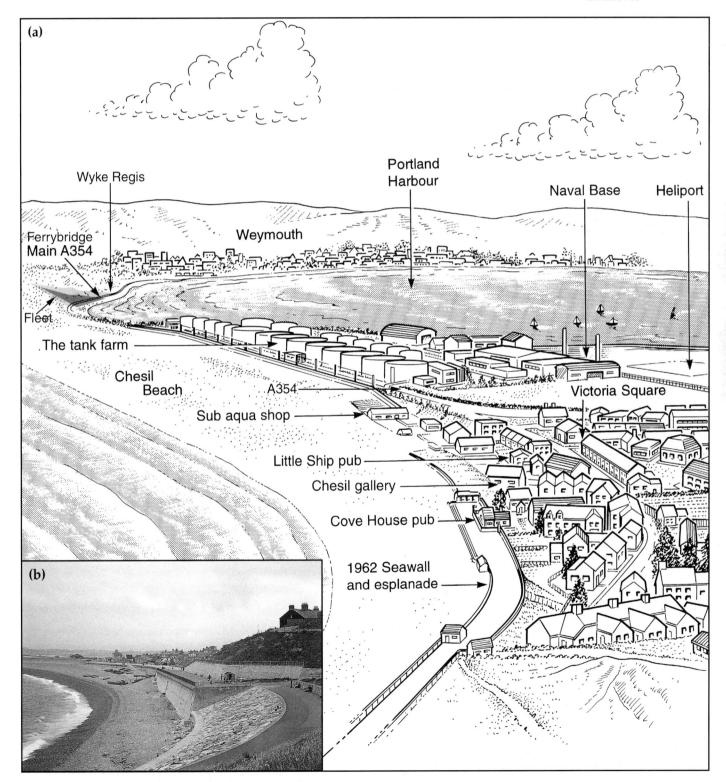

(a)
Wyke Regis
Portland Harbour
Naval Base
Heliport
Ferrybridge Main A354
Weymouth
Fleet
The tank farm
Chesil Beach
A354
Victoria Square
Sub aqua shop
Little Ship pub
Chesil gallery
Cove House pub
1962 Seawall and esplanade

(b)

FIGURE 5.4 A general model for the physical processes producing flooding at Chiswell

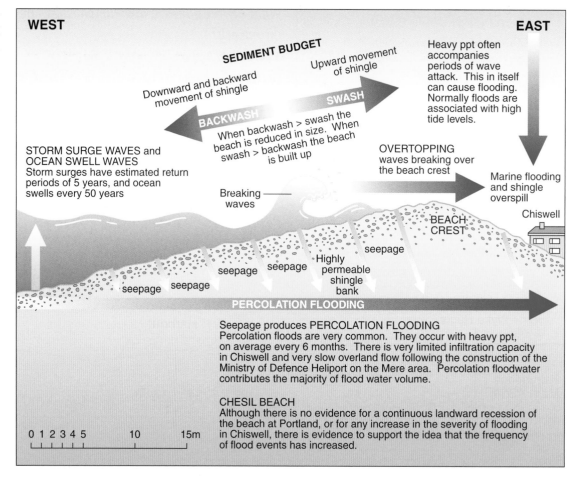

1   seepage or **percolating flooding**;
2   **overtopping** or overwash flooding with associated shingle **overspill**. In addition the situation can be compounded by heavy rainfall (see Figure 5.4).

On 13 December 1978 and again on 13 February 1979, Chiswell was flooded, but the physical causal processes were significantly different in each case.

Description of hazard events

Coastal flooding 13 December 1978: Chiswell

Storm surge flooding with percolation flooding

An Atlantic depression with associated local high onshore winds, caused surge conditions, with the predicted tide level exceeding 0.5m.

Wave height was estimated at 4.5m, and these steep waves occurred every 12 seconds. They were destructive plunging breakers with very strong backwash and weak swash. Consequently the storm beach was removed, and the main Chesil Bank was severely denuded, steepened and became highly unstable. A huge volume of beach shingle was moved offshore. The beach crest was lowered opposite the car park for 40m, and the leeward side of Chesil Beach was seriously eroded by seepage flooding and overtopping.

At the junction of the sea wall and Chesil Beach

there was extreme overtopping and shingle overspill. The beach itself was not breached, but was in serious danger of so doing. Chiswell was flooded to a depth of 1.2m; over 30 commercial and residential properties near Victoria Square were flooded; and families were evacuated to emergency rest centres. All public utilities were cut for 24 hours. Emergency services were required for 5 days.

Fortunately, within a week, constructive waves built up the beach material and the stepped beach profile reappeared. The flooding had been predicted and was associated with local storm conditions, with strong onshore winds. These storm conditions were estimated to occur at 5 to 10 yearly intervals. (See Figure 5.6).

Coastal flooding 13 February 1979: Chiswell

Ocean flooding

Without warning on the morning of 13 February 1979 Chesil Beach was overwhelmed by long constructive swell waves every 18 seconds. They were travelling on exactly the same course and at the same speed as a depression travelling up the English Channel. The beach was flattened under such wave action and there was very severe overtopping and massive shingle overspill. Tonnes of shingle were carried over the beach crest. Although Portland was temporarily isolated from the mainland, there had been no breaching or lowering of the beach crest. When the seas subsided the beach was left in a stable condition although traces of the stepped beach profile had been removed. Locally there were no winds.

Thirty Chiswell properties were flooded, the same families were evacuated again, and public utilities were cut for 24 hours. Portland was cut off from the mainland. Emergency services were committed for 10 days. There was massive trauma and stress for both the residents and emergency workers alike.

STUDENT ACTIVITY 5.2

Construction of hazard profiles
Make two A4 copies of the beach profile using Figure 5.4. Annotate these to explain the physical causes of the floods of 13 December 1978 and 13 February 1979. In addition begin to construct a hazard profile table for each event. (See Figure 1.8). Contrast:
a) wave height and type (destructive or constructive);
b) swash/backwash ratios;
c) net sediment movements;
d) effect on entire beach profile;
e) magnitude and frequency of this event;
f) seriousness/severity (breaching, extensiveness of the flooding and damage to property);
g) advance warning/predictability;
h) local weather situation;
i) tide situation if known;
j) type of flooding (percolation or overtopping).

STUDENT ACTIVITY 5.3

Human land use at Chiswell
1 Use Figures 5.1, 5.2, 5.3, 5.5, 5.6, 5.7, and 5.13 to explain how human land use in the Chiswell area has created the real problem.
2 How could the closure of the A354 affect the population of the whole Weymouth and Portland area?

What were the consequences of the 1978 and 1979 floods?

STUDENT ACTIVITY 5.4

Hazard impact analysis
Study Figure 5.5 and the newspaper articles in Figures 5.6 and 5.7. Produce two tables to summarise the socio-economic impact of the floods on:
a) local residents;
b) the broader community of Weymouth and Portland, who travel to or from the Island for work, post-16 education, healthcare etc.
Use the following headings for each table.
1 Short-term impact: a) social problems; b) economic problems.
2 Long-term impact: a) social problems; b) economic problems.

What options were available to alleviate the consequences of flooding?

On 14 February 1979 the two legally responsible authorities, Wessex Water Authority and Weymouth and Portland Borough Council, instructed a firm of consultant engineers to identify options to alleviate the flood hazard. In addition a **Cost-Benefit Assessment** (CBA) was carried out for a Chiswell Flood Scheme, which would protect and keep open the critical A354 Weymouth Road.

Under the Land Drainage Act of 1976 the authorities could apply for 65 per cent grant aid, if approved by MAFF. The rest of the money would come from: the County Council (8 per cent); Wessex Water Authority (13.5 per cent); and the local borough council (13.5 per cent). The cost to the rate payers would be 1p in the pound for 10 years.

FIGURE 5.5 The scale of the problem (a) Chiswell and the A354 to Weymouth (b) Victoria Square, Chiswell

The anguish of Portland

THE angry sea surges against the grey rocks of Portland 200 ft below Underhill School matched in its anger by that of the flood hit Chiswell residents staying there.

Bearded Roger Fells lounges in an armchair: "I've decided to make this my home. I'm not going back. If necessary I'm going to be here at Christmas."

I later saw why. His home at 10 Westbay Terrace – the worst hit part of a badly battered Chiswell – smells like an estuary.

The flood water that surged through has left a slime over the floors at best. An inch of mud carpets the bathroom, where the bath has obviously filled and emptied dirty water several times.

In the side alley crystal clear water was running out of a small drain and into the street, which was yesterday still covered with sand and shingle.

Mr Fells added: "I want the council to purchase our houses – not only mine, but all West Bay Terrace.

"They're not safe to live in with the constant threat – well, certainly – of flooding."

His neighbour, Mrs Sylvia Reed, added: "It'll need more than welfare people to clean my floor."

They had three floodings before they were evacuated. Her husband Ken found water coming over his wellington boots before he got to the bottom of the stairs.

And with the house under four feet of water, they had a fire.

Mr Reed heard gurgling in the flood water and thought it was the wind blowing down the chimney – until smoke billowed out from under the stairs.

Like many of their neighbours, he found the mains cable into the house was smouldering. The fire brigade had to have the electricity to Chiswell cut off.

The Reeds, too, are planning to stay at the Underhill rest centre in protest.

"We've all had offers of homes from friends and neighbours, but think by staying here and sticking together the council will have to do something," Mrs Reed said.

Meanwhile her son Steve mourns the death of his £30 worth of tropical fish.

In Victoria Square council workmen shovelled sludge and gravel. Earlier one of them had told a television cameraman to "pick up a shovel instead of taking bloody pictures" because he had been asked to turn towards the camera.

But it was from the beach that the power of the sea could be seen. Several places along the top of the beach were bare of pebbles and gullies had been cut on the landward side.

The public toilets near the Little Ship Inn were filled with a couple of feet of sand and pebbles.

At the Cove Inn workmen were reinforcing the corner of the sea wall while the sea dragged at pebbles with a noise like the Navy's Hunter jets make when they fly over the area.

Beyond the inn is a scene of devastation. Six fishermen's huts once stood there, now there are two – and one of those is shored up to stop it toppling over.

The whole area is littered with smashed wood, some of it just recognisable as former boats. The scene is not surprising when Mrs Eddie Mumford recalls what happened at the Cove Inn early on Wednesday.

She and her husband Jim were woken by coastguards knocking at the door at 5 am. "I looked out and all I saw was the sea," she said. "A huge wave was going up past the bedroom windows and over the house."

Outside the sea had smashed everything in sight.

A solid stone porch over the cellar door was torn away and the door hurled to the back of the large cellar – yet it was unmarked.

A six foot high wall of foot-thick stone blocks between the inn and its skittle alley was completely demolished – better than any Irish demolition expert could manage.

The Mumfords found stone blocks from the wall laying 15 ft from their original site. Their car, parked under the wall had been moved about 12 ft from it with £500 worth of damage to it.

The family turned to go down to Chiswell, but the water there was too deep and they were told to go past the fishermen's huts.

Up the terrace Mr Charles Yeoman had the water get into his home for the first time in the 28 years he has lived there.

Normally a few sandbags at the door stop it, but this time the water level was so high it came through the floorboards.

"It was the worst I've ever seen, and I've lived here near on 50 year," he said.

Dorset Evening Echo, 15 December 1978

FIGURE 5.6 The anguish of Portland

A perceived lack of consideration for local residents' opinions and of housing assistance, led to the formation of the Chesil Residents Action Group (CRAG), formed on 17 February 1979. Their prime aim was to lobby for: *'a scheme(s) that will end for all time the days of flooding at Chiswell and ensure that the environment of Chiswell reflects the expectations of the resident population.'*

They wanted hazard mitigation engineering schemes and a social policy to save and preserve their community.

CRAG were very successful. They co-ordinated local residents' opinions and actions; gained a 30 per cent rate reduction compensation; applied to the EEC Disaster Fund; established links with the consultant engineers and had their case publicised in regional and national media and in the House of Lords. They secured consultation with the Borough Council, got their scheme approved and Chiswell was granted General Improvement Area (GIA) status, encouraging the social redevelopment and enhancement of the community.

The Nature Conservancy Council (NCC) were also consulted in respect of the potential environmental impact of the scheme on the Chesil Beach SSSI. Although unenthusiastic about the project, they did acknowledge the need for a scheme to *'enable the very existence of Chesil Beach itself as both protective bastion and scientific entity'*.

The NCC raised two key issues.

1 That the landscape should retain the original pre-scheme appearance.

2 Natural local materials should be used.

The Terrifying Wave

WITHOUT wind or warning the sea has invaded Chiswell again – exactly two months after its last attack.

But yesterday, on February 13, it hit far harder than it did on December 13.

This time there was no warning. It took only half-an-hour for the Reed family to be flooded out of their home in West Bay Terrace.

It caught Chesil Beach Motors with cars still in their showroom.

It carried a police car off the sea wall, seconds after the driver leapt out.

And it finally knocked down the Little Ship pub's skittle alley – which used to have holes in the wall to let the water through.

Cars, boats and pebbles have been heaped up against the buildings on the seaward side of Chiswell, with many walls giving way under their weight.

Once more Mr Roland Smeeton, a Dorset County Council Social Services worker who fortunately lives on Portland, was running the rest centre at Underhill Junior School. He said some of the people who had been evacuated to the school had been very upset and shaken up.

It was hardly surprising that even these veterans of Chiswell's flooding should have been shaken up this time.

It had already started when Jennie and Alex Wellman, both aged 58, woke up at their home at 16 West Bay Terrace, opposite Chesil Beach.

Still a little shaken, Mrs Wellman said: "A wave came over the top of the beach, picked up our car from the car park opposite and smashed it down the road.

"It smashed in our bay window and our front door and the wave landed at the top of our stairs. I screamed out terrible."

The sea had hit their car with such force it had pushed it through the iron railings round the car park.

Mr Wellman said: "The flood this time was twice as bad as last time." But his wife said "it was ten times worse."

Even Mrs Wellman's attempt to lessen the flood damage by moving her dishes to a high shelf had not worked – the wave knocked them down.

Their neighbours from No 8, the Reed family, were expecting the insurance assessor to arrive at 3 pm yesterday to look at the damage caused in December.

Mr Ken Reed said: "You kid yourself it's

never going to happen again but..." His wife, Sylvia, said: "We just woke up to it this time, there was no warning at all."

She said Ken had left for work at 5.55 am and everything was "high and dry". But at 6.30 am she heard their Siamese cat wailing, so she went downstairs to find her home knee-deep in water.

She added: "We watched the waves smash the skittle alley of the Little Ship and smash up cars. We saw a freezer washed through the cafe window."

Mrs Reed added: "This time we've lost everything. Some of the things we were only just replacing after last time."

Outside their home lay a cement mixer which had been carried through the wreckage of the skittle alley by the waves.

Police said yesterday that everyone was accounted for.

Portland councillors have been visiting people in their homes and at the rest centre.

Mrs Helen Clissold even got the Navy to take her by boat to check everyone was all right in the flooded homes.

Mr Alan Martindale was worried that someone may have got washed off the beach. "There were people on the ridge when the wave hit," he said.

But most of all they were angry.

"The time is coming that we've got to

have some Junior Ministers come down," Mr Martindale said. "It is a disaster. We've got to have some financial help before someone is killed."

Mrs Clissold said: "The beach is on its way out. The sea is coming through and over. It's been happening gradually over the years, but they said it wouldn't happen. Those in authority always wait until two or three people are killed. They should have done something before."

Ken Reed added: "We're like rats in cages and they'll wait till we drown."

Mr Martindale suggested: "The only answer is to evacuate Chiswell and knock it down."

Several people at the rest centre called for a breakwater of some kind. Mr Wellman said: "It doesn't have to be above the water, just something to slow the seas down."

Tom Gibbs is a seaworn fisherman who has lived on Portland all his 78 years and has not seen Chiswell hit this badly.

"In '42 it was bad, but more sea's come in now than in '42," he said in his broad Dorset accent.

He felt the waves were the result of a ground swell from the storms in the Bay of Biscay. Out on the sea wall you could see the waves were not storm waves.

They rolled in about two hundred yards apart ... long, unbroken humps of water disappearing into the mist. On the sea wall Tom explained that in the past only three of the Navy's oil tanks had been visible from there.

"In the later part of last year I could see seven from here," he said. "I knew the beach had gone down and this was going to happen." Yesterday we counted 13 oil tanks showing above the beach.

Walking along the top of the beach, I could see the damage done. Walls were knocked down by water and debris. Cars were piled up where the water could move them no further.

Outside the clearing work went on. Sailors from HMS Osprey worked alongside council workmen and mechanical diggers. Lorries, including tippers from the quarries, carted off the rubble to tip it back on the beach.

As I "hitched a lift" back to the Royal Maritime Auxiliary Service tug Harlech, the predictions were for more flooding to come...

Dorset Evening Echo, 14 February 1979

FIGURE 5.7 The terrifying wave

FIGURE 5.8 Cost-benefit
analysis, April 1980

Cost-Benefit Analysis April 1980

Main areas to benefit

1 Chiswell – 110 houses
2 Users of the Weymouth to Portland A354

Types of benefit in summary

1 Tangible – direct
2 Tangible – indirect
3 Intangible

Types of benefit

1 Tangible direct benefits of the scheme, (i.e. measurable in financial terms)
Reduced property damage – houses, cars, public utilities, and the Royal Naval facilities at Portland.

2 Tangible indirect benefits
Reduced losses due to economic disruption to traffic flows, trade, loss of business profits and employment earnings, cost of emergency services.

3 Intangible benefits, (i.e. less easy to measure financially)
Preventing loss of life and injury, alleviating fear and anxiety and ill-health, preventing loss of community and quality of life.

Summary of probable financial damages

	PERCOLATION FLOOD	STORM SURGE FLOOD	OCEAN SWELL FLOOD
Direct damage	£6647	£263741	£263741
Indirect damage	£93591	£262173	£695305
Total cost damage	£100238	£525914	£923046
Return period estimate	0.5 years	5 years	50 years

Best estimate of the present value of total flood alleviation

Percolation flood – £1.83m
Storm surge flood – £12.12m
Ocean swell flood – £14.50m

i.e. the amount it is worth spending to prevent future flood damage.

Cost–Benefit Analysis

STUDENT ACTIVITY 5.5

The cost-benefit analysis
The engineering consultants advised that it was practicable to provide £5 million of protection against a storm with an estimated return period of five years, and to alleviate the consequences of more severe storms. Annual maintenance costs were estimated at £37 000 per year.

The Flood Hazard Research Centre of Middlesex Polytechnic presented a Cost-Benefit Analysis suggesting the project would be reasonably viable.

Using the CBA data sheet in Figure 5.8 explain why there was a positive benefit:cost ratio and justify the real benefits of the scheme.

The Chesil Sea Defence Scheme

STUDENT ACTIVITY 5.6

The Chesil Sea Defence Scheme: the preferred option
1 Why does the scheme only seek to alleviate the flood problem and not prevent flooding? Study Figures 5.4–5.13.
2 Identify the individual components that make up the integrated preferred scheme.
a) Produce a map to show the location of these measures.
b) The scheme was divided into four stages. Colour code your map to highlight these phases.

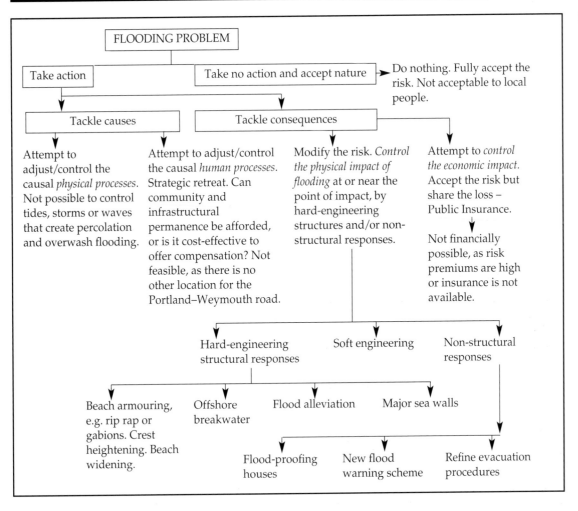

FIGURE 5.9 The options

FIGURE 5.10 Chesil Sea Defence preferred Scheme, Portland

1981 Experimental stage The construction of a trial length (150m) of gabion mattresses raised the beach crest level to 14.5m. The intention here is to raise and strengthen the crest of the beach in order to prevent breaching of prolonged short-period wave attack. The trial length is being regularly monitored and may form the prototype for strengthening a 1500m length of the crest as recommended by the consulting engineers. The cost was £150 000, and expected lifetime is 20 years with maintenance (see Figures 5.11 and 5.13a and b).

1983 Stage 1 This involved modifications to the 300m-long esplanade wall constructed some 30 years ago. A concrete stepped apron extending some 5m below the esplanade level with steel toe piles 5m long to prevent undermining of the wall was constructed. A new wave wall along the landward perimeter of the esplanade reduces the risk of water overtopping the structure during high wave conditions.

Provision has been made to maintain easy access to the esplanade for pedestrians and disabled persons by incorporating flood gates and ramps along the length of the new wave wall. Facilities have also been provided to enable the local fishers to readily remove their boats from the foreshore through gates in the wave wall. Cost of £350 000 (see Figure 5.13c and d).

1985/1986 Stage 2 This is the most expensive part of the work and provides for the interception of potential flood water percolating through the beach. A large culvert with openings in the seaward side and top allowing water to enter has been constructed along the landward side of the beach. Water is prevented from bypassing underneath the drain by long steel piles driven through the beach into the underlying Kimmeridge clay, which is approximately 17.5m below (see Figure 5.12).

The **culvert** discharges north of the Recreation Ground into an open channel excavated in beach material and this in turn outfalls into Portland Harbour via culverts under Weymouth Road at the north end of the tank farm of HMS Osprey Naval Base. Cost of £2.5 m. (see Figures 5.13e, f and g)

Stage 3 In June 1987 the A354 was raised over the length from the Recreation Ground to the north end of the tank farm. The design road level has been fixed to be above the flood level of the December 1978 flood. Cost of £600 000 (see Figure 5.13h).

Stage 4 1996–8 Further strengthening to the crest of Chesil Beach by an extension to the Steel Mattresses offered increased protection for both the A354 and local residential properties. In addition assistance of funding from the Portland Single Regeneration Budget Programme has enabled small-scale social housing redevelopment schemes to be implemented, resulting in visual improvement and an enhanced community confidence. The Environment Agency are however, becoming increasingly concerned about global warming and increased storminess, and have asked WPBC as the local planning authority to review its policy for social regeneration of the area as it increases the hazard risk.

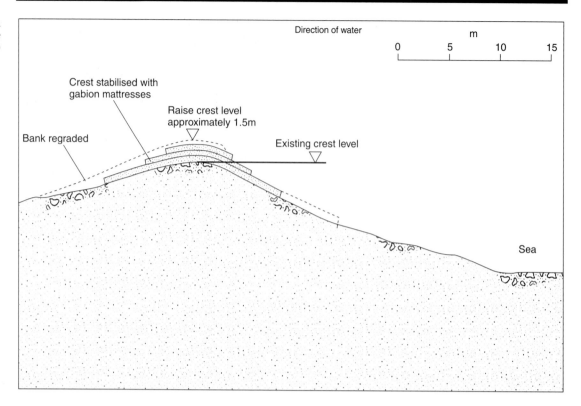

FIGURE 5.11 Gabion protection to crest (see also Figure 5.13a)

Direction of water

m

0   5   10   15

Crest stabilised with gabion mattresses

Raise crest level approximately 1.5m

Existing crest level

Bank regraded

Sea

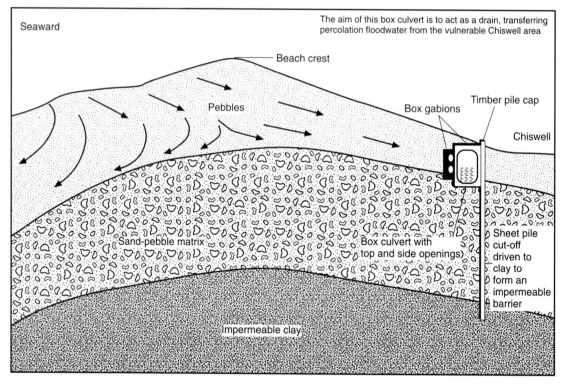

FIGURE 5.12 Percolation through beach into the box culvert (see also Figure 5.13e, f and g)

Seaward

The aim of this box culvert is to act as a drain, transferring percolation floodwater from the vulnerable Chiswell area

Beach crest

Pebbles

Box gabions

Timber pile cap

Chiswell

Sand-pebble matrix

Box culvert with top and side openings

Sheet pile cut-off driven to clay to form an impermeable barrier

Impermeable clay

Has the scheme worked?

An evaluation of the scheme: the present position in 2000

The construction of the scheme was completed in 1988 with the exception of the recommended 1500m length of **gabion** crest protection.

The severe storm on 16 December 1989 proved the effectiveness of the sea defence scheme in all its components: flooding was minimal and the interceptor drain flowed full.

The Council, maintaining its commitment to support the community of Chiswell, has actively pursued its GIA procedures, offering grants to encourage owners of properties in the area to carry out improvements. The Council itself has provided environmental improvement works, and has recently completed a small new house-build scheme

a) Gabion mattresses (experimental stage)

b) Gabion mattresses and esplanade seawall

c) Esplanade seawall (Stage 1)

d) Floodgate (Stage 1)

e) Installation of Stage 2 culvert

f) Open channel (Stage 2) Chiswell end

g) Open channel, Tank Farm end (Stage 2)

h) Stage 3, raised road

Figure 5.13 The Chesil Sea Defence Scheme, Portland

within the former flood-risk area, aimed at demonstrating to the community the Council's confidence in the region. Chiswell is beginning to demonstrate an air of well-being and optimism.

The sponsoring authorities have considered the completion of the scheme by implementing the remaining recommendation of the consulting engineers, namely the construction of the beach crest protection northwards from the end of the experimental length. This 400m extension was installed before the winter of 1998/9.

STUDENT ACTIVITY 5.7

An evaluation of the alleviation scheme
The following criteria can be used to evaluate the success of the preferred option.
1   COST
2   ENVIRONMENTAL IMPACT of the scheme
3   EFFECTIVENESS
4   DURABILITY.
Attempt your own evaluation after reading the text above and studying Figures 5.14 and 5.15.
In hindsight was this scheme the best option?

Review of key ideas

■ Chiswell suffered from frequent percolation flooding on a regular basis, additionally **storm surge** (December 1978) and **ocean swell** flooding (February 1979).
■ The hazard is the result of the human land use of a high-risk area of severe coastal flooding.
■ The **direct impacts** of flooding include damage to property, and public utilities. **Indirect impacts** involve the disruption to transport routes and cost of emergency services. Additionally there were **intangible impacts** including injury, anxiety, ill-health and the loss of the community spirit.
■ Five options can be recognised. Accept the risk; attempt to adjust nature; accept nature and **strategically retreat**; share the loss through a national public insurance scheme; or attempt to modify the vulnerability of the population using engineering solutions and non-structural responses.
■ The total financial benefits of the scheme were estimated at £1.83 million for a percolation flood protection, £12.12 million for **storm surge** flood protection and alleviation and £14.50 million for ocean-swell flood alleviation.

FIGURE 5.15 3 photos of winter storms, 1989

FIGURE 5.14 Battered – sea defences defended

BATTERED
Sea defences defended

PORTLAND'S £5million sea defence scheme has been defended by a top Borough councillor despite the island being cut off by one of the worst storms to batter the Dorset coast this century.

It left a trail of wreckage in its wake with sea walls breached, homes and businesses flooded, boats wrecked and roads under water.

Some people criticised the scheme for not withstanding the sea, but it was today backed by Borough Council leader David Hall who opened it in March 1987.

He said: "The scheme when designed was meant to cope with normal storm surges, but this was one of the worst storms this century.

"The London Meteorological Office told me it was worse than the 1987 hurricane, a once-in-50-years storm, and it was always known that the sea would come over the defences if this happened."

Dorset Evening Echo, 18 December 1989

■ The total capital costs of the scheme were £5 million and annual maintenance was estimated at £37 000 per year. Consequently the cost-benefit ratio was very favourable.

■ A four-stage scheme was implemented between 1981 and 1988.
a) Experimental phase 1981. Construction of 150m gabion trial.
b) 1983 Sea wall modifications.
c) 1985/6 Interception drainage scheme.
d) 1987/8 Road raising.

■ The scheme has had an environmental impact on the Chesil Beach SSSI and has not prevented flooding, but it has successfully alleviated some of the consequences of the flood hazard and reduced the risk for the local community of Chiswell and kept the Weymouth to Portland road open.

STUDENT ACTIVITY 5.8

Consolidation exercise
Either attempt one of the following essays or construct a topic web for this case study covering the following key points.
1 Location.
2 History of problem.
3 Human land use.
4 Physical processes.
5 Possible solutions.
6 Preferred option.
7 Costs and benefits.
8 Who was responsible.

Essay A
'Causal physical processes and natural systems must be fully understood in order to produce effective risk assessment and hazard management.' Discuss with reference to the **Chesil Sea Defence Scheme**.

Essay B
'Hazards can never be totally prevented, but their consequences and causes may be alleviated by hazard prevention methods, education and hazard management techniques.' Use the **Chesil Sea Defence Scheme** to assess how far you agree with this viewpoint.

Glossary

Cost Benefit Assessment (CBA) – ratio of financial benefits of a scheme in relation to capital and maintenance costs.

Culvert – a drain.

Direct impacts (CBA) – damage to property measurable in financial terms.

Gabion – a cage or mattress of boxed shingle.

Indirect impacts (CBA) – financial measurement of the economic disruption costs of a hazard to trade, communications and emergency services.

Intangible impacts (CBA) – effects not measurable in simple financial terms, e.g. stress.

Ocean swell waves – long constructive, often unpredictable waves, that originate in mid-ocean, in that they are not associated with local storm weather.

Overspill – movement of beach sediment over the beach crest.

Overtopping (overwash) – flooding due to waves washing over the top of the crest of a beach.

Percolation flooding – flooding due to water seepage through a beach.

Return period – estimated frequency of a hazard of a set magnitude.

Storm surge – severe localised event dominated by low pressure and high winds and short destructive waves.

Strategic retreat – compensated movement of communities from a high-risk hazard zone.

References

BJ Hook and JR Keeble, Proc Institution of Civil Engineers, Paper 9611, 1991, August 783–798
The Fleet and Chesil Beach, Fleet Study Group
Dorset Evening Echo, 15 December 1978, 18 December 1989, 14 February 1979, 13 February 1979
Middlesex Polytechnic Flood Management Research Centre, CBA at Chiswell 1980
Dorset County Magazine, Issue 78, pages 5–14

Further reading

East Anglia – Battling the Tide, Flood Defences in East Anglia, NRA Information Unit, Anglia Region, Peterborough – a contrasting UK study
Guyana, New Scientist, 31 March 1990 – a good LEDC contrasting case study

Multiple hazard management in the Los Angeles city region

Los Angeles has grown rapidly from its original site on the coastal lowland to infill the surrounding flat-floored basin of San Fernando, San Gabriel and San Bernadino. Rising abruptly from the low plains and valleys are the substantial San Gabriel and San Bernardino mountain ranges. These form a topographic and climatic barrier to the rest of California and Los Angeles is physically isolated in its basin. The region has a semi-desert climate of rainless summers and very mild winters. This

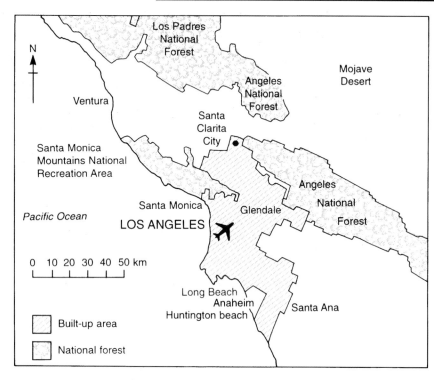

FIGURE 5.16 Los Angeles
city region

attractive climate, combined with sandy beaches, subtropical vegetation and backdrop of snow-capped peaks creates a striking environment, and yet it is one of the most hazardous places in the world. Los Angeles suffers periodically from earthquakes, tsunamis, sinking coastlines, landslides, high winds and brush fires, floods, drought and smog. Potentially it is one of the most hazardous areas in any MEDC, and requires effective integrated hazard management at local and regional scales.

Earthquakes

The most serious and devastating of the hazards in Los Angeles is the threat of seismic disturbance. The San Andreas Fault marks the boundary of the Pacific and North American Plate and is but one of a whole mosaic of faults underlying southern California and Los Angeles in particular (see Figure 5.17). In one historically recent seismic event, the 1971 San Fernando Valley earthquake damaged 1000 buildings, destroyed the freeway system, killed 65 people and damage costs came to $500 million. Computer predictions suggest that an event of similar intensity to that of the 1906 San Francisco earthquake would carve devastating rifts over 65km from the epicentre and that a major proportion of the city of Los Angeles would lie within this seismic

Scientists get a lesson on 'moderate' earthquakes

The Northridge earthquake woke Los Angeles up to the disturbing discovery that an otherwise moderate tremblor could shake a steel-framed building so badly that its joints crack.

"The strong ground motion is the real story," said Jim Mori, the seismologist who heads the US Geological Survey office in Pasadena.

"We really began to see for the first time how buildings, bridges, lifelines behave in an earthquake," Mori said. "There's a lot of ... evidence that the ground shakes harder than we might expect."

The quake that struck in the wee hours of 17 January 1994 is giving scientists a case study in urban Los Angeles tremblors, something seen only a few times in the last six decades.

By exploring links between geology and ground shaking, scientists hope to locate the areas most vulnerable to life and property losses.

They're still marveling at the surprisingly powerful motions from last year's quake, which at magnitude 6.7 is considered moderate by geological standards.

James F. Dolan, an earthquake geologist at the Southern California Earthquake Center in Los Angeles, said Northridge ground motions, some approaching twice the force of gravity, were "among the highest ever recorded and will probably have profound effects on future engineering philosophy and policy in metropolitan California."

"Northridge is a wakeup call," said John A. "Trailer" Martin, a structural engineer.

The failure of modern, steel-frame buildings leaves engineers "pretty high and dry," Martin said.

"As a profession, we've been put in a real tough spot where people think we have the answers and we really don't," he said.

Without a proven alternative design, it's hard to advise building owners, especially when the cost of replacing broken joints can run to a prohibitive $4 million or $5 million, he said.

It was Martin who recommended that the Olympic Center, a West Los Angeles commercial building, be vacated months after the quake because its joints were too compromised to withstand further shaking.

Repairs will make the building functional again, he said.

In the year since the earth slipped some 11

miles below the San Fernando Valley, seismologists have learned more about buried faults, or those that never come to the earth's surface.

They now warn that ruptures on such faults pose a potentially greater threat to Los Angeles than the feared "Big One" on the mighty San Andreas.

In a paper published in the 13 January issue of the journal Science, Dolan argues that Los Angeles is in store for additional Northridge-sized quakes, or even larger ones, to release unrelieved stress in the earth.

He found so much strain has built up that 17 Northridge-sized quakes should have occurred since 1800 – yet there have been only two.

Alternatively, the area's six major fault systems could generate one 7.2 to 7.6 magnitude quake every 140 years to release the same stress, but there hasn't been such a large occurrence in 210 years.

Thomas Anderson, a California structural engineer on a two-year fellowship at Rand Critical Technologies Institute in Washington, said the potential for multiple urban quakes must be anticipated with tougher construction codes and techniques for retrofitting existing buildings

FIGURE 5.17 Remembrance and recovery

hazard zone. Emergency planning has been made for the evacuation of high-rise buildings and hospitals, disconnection of nuclear power plants, halting of industries, shutting down of oil pipelines and lowering of water levels in dams. Most Angelenos are fatalistic – one entrepreneur considered erecting spectator stands to the north-east of the San Andreas Fault so that people could witness the great event if and when it happens! Figure 5.18 documents some worrying news.

Coastal hazards: tsunamis and flooding

Pacific Ocean coastlines are particularly prone to tsunamis generated by submarine earthquakes or volcanic eruptions. The coastal fringes of Malibu to Redondo Beach are under the greatest threat. A sizeable tsunami generated by the sudden release of locked undersea faults could strike Los Angeles beaches with virtually no warning. Considerable residential development and most transport infrastructure follows the cliff foot and would be damaged by such an event, especially in the region between Santa Monica and Malibu.

The Long Beach area of Los Angeles has become a flood hazard zone as a result of coastal subsidence due to oil extraction. At the Wilmington oil field behind Los Angeles the greatest subsidence is found with descents of as much as 9m during the space of 40 years. Major sea walls and injecting water have not totally removed the threat. Global warming and associated sea-level changes present a significant future threat.

Landslides, flooding and drought

Natural landslides occur within Los Angeles virtually every year, but are most prevalent in the long winter rains. Slumping and sliding of the hill slopes are largely the result of soft rocks such as unconsolidated gravel, sand and silt giving way, but also because of the steepness of coastal cliffs. The most dangerous zone is the area of 50m-high sea cliffs along the Santa Monica Bay which extends for some 10km. Numerous residential developments are found here because of the desirability of the sea view and cooling influences of ocean breezes. Figure 5.19 shows the effects of building on the hazardous quick clays. Figure 5.20 details the recent events of flooding in January 1995. Floods have damaged Los Angeles on many occasions. Major damage has occurred in 1914, 1934, 1938, 1969, 1978, 1980 and 1995. Flash flooding occurs when intense winter rainstorms wash out debris from the canyons above the city which sweep away everything in front of them including homes, factories and roads. Figures 5.21 and 5.22 highlight that the same story repeats itself nearly every year. The real problem is that an overwhelming flood may only occur six times a century and localised moderate flooding once a decade and so the risk is infrequent and lulls residents into a false sense of security. Most people soon erase the horrors of the flood and simply rebuild.

More big quakes forecasted for Los Angeles

Twelve months after an earthquake killed 60 people and damaged thousands of buildings, the residents of Los Angeles have been told to expect worse.

The area is long overdue for a series of large tremors or maybe the long-awaited "Big One". The epicentre of last year's quake was almost directly under the town of Northridge, northwest of central Los Angeles but most of the energy was released in the thinly populated Santa Susana Mountains, six miles further north. Seismologists consider it had enough energy to bring down modern steel-framed buildings.

Three articles in today's issue of *Science* show that Los Angeles has been enjoying an earthquake lull for 200 years and that building codes may not be tough enough.

In the past 195 years there have only been two earthquake events measuring 6.7 on the Richter Scale, when on average there should have been one every 11 years. This suggests that the period during which Los Angeles has become a major city has coincided with the quietest period of earthquake activity.

13 January 1995

FIGURE 5.18 Experts forecast more big quakes for Los Angeles

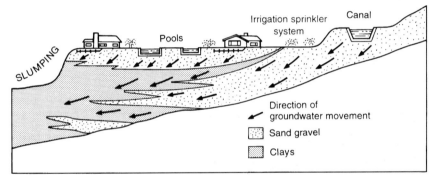

FIGURE 5.19 The hazardous effects of groundwater seepage on a typical Los Angeles housing development located on clays

Violent Storms Flood California

Eight people died when the main highway between Los Angeles and San Francisco was severed by floods and a collapsed bridge as violent storms hit California at the weekend.

Thirty-eight counties were declared emergency areas after being hit by the storms. Napa Valley vineyards and a 200-mile section of Interstate 5 highway were submerged.

Some 15 inches of rain fell on Saturday in the Central Californian area and winds gusted up to 130 mph.

Mud slides buried 12 house and damaged 70 in Malibu, the coastal retreat of film stars and surfers west of Los Angeles. Residents said that the mud slides were the worst since the 1950s.

The Golden State has had an unusually grey and sodden winter, with more storms forecast and new theories being offered to account for them. One idea is that global warming and its impact on the Pacific Ocean is to blame. The El Nino effect, a powerful moist wind, has been blamed by some scientists for the record snow falls in the Sierra Nevada.

Many mountainsides are saturated and unstable, bringing the risk of serious landslides. Nine homes were destroyed when a bluff above the village of La Conchita, north of Los Angeles, gave way last week.

Flammable sagebrush is expected to grow faster and in greater quantities than usual on the Southern Californian hills. This will replenish fuel supplies for the autumn bushfire season.

13 March 1995

FIGURE 5.20 Golden State declared federal disaster area

Golden State Declared Federal Disaster Area

Flooding and mud slides on an epic scale brought chaos to much of California yesterday. President Clinton declared 24 counties in the Golden State as Federal disaster areas after a day of five deaths, $41 million (£26 million) property damage and mass evacuations of flooded homes. He assured flood victims that the Federal Government would be "with you for the long haul". The President will visit California on Monday or Tuesday. The trip was originally planned to mark the anniversary of the Northridge earthquake last January.

In less than a day some parts of Southern California received their whole year's rainfall, turning dry valleys into rampaging rivers and cutting off the resort of Malibu.

As helicopters rescued stranded people, an evacuee from Santa Paula,

north of Los Angeles said "January has not been our month", she moved there after her San Fernando home was destroyed in the Northridge earthquake a year ago. On the Pacific highway, expensive sports cars drowned in mud.

Experts blamed the unprecedented rains on a so-called "storm door" forced open by 190 mph jet stream winds that have driven off the high-pressure system that normally sits off the Californian coast, bringing its famous hot and dry conditions.

The storms may be a symptom of the slight rise in the temperature of the Pacific Ocean. More rain is forecast in the devastated Russian River area, north of San Francisco. In Malibu, a resident said "Yes, its like this now; but next week we'll be back on the beach."

12 January 1995

FIGURE 5.21 Californian mudslide and flood crisis

FIGURE 5.22 Flood hazards in Los Angeles

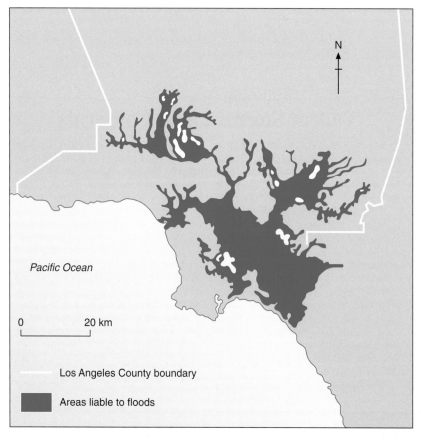

In addition, ironically water shortage is the rule rather than the exception, since rainfall and high evaporation combine to produce a runoff of less than 12.5cm per year. It is probable that few Angelenos think about water when millions of litres are used for drinking, bathing, car washing, irrigating and filling swimming pools. Most water comes from northern California including San Francisco, Owens Reservoir and the Colorado River. The last drought was 80 years ago but Los Angeles may face an increasing waterless future as nearly all of its water is utilised and very little reaches the ocean.

High winds and brush fires

During severe storms considerable damage is often caused in exposed areas such as the beach resort at Malibu. During the March 1978 storms many Hollywood stars such as Burgess Meredith, Rod Steiger and Merle Oberon lost their homes or suffered property damage (Figure 5.23).

The desiccating local wind known as the Santa Ana is often responsible for increasingly widespread brush fires. In 1970, 72 000ha of land was burnt, 295 houses destroyed and three people killed as fires ravaged hill top properties in the Santa Monica Mountains. The brush wood, known as chaparral, becomes highly flammable every autumn and the Santa Ana wind soon changes a small fire into a major conflagration. Householders often line hill crests and canyon floors with brush wood to reduce erosion and removal costs. This juxtaposition of brush and houses sets the scene for future disasters. Ten-metre brush clearance zones around all houses are now demanded by Californian law.

Smog

Air pollution is seen as the second most important environmental threat by most Angelenos. The city has a reputation for its smog and Figure 5.24 shows the process of inversion and smog formation. Ninety per cent of the smog is generated by vehicle exhausts and so it is a daytime phenomena. The Los Angeles Public Health Service monitors pollution levels and gives warnings when ozone levels are too high. Sea breezes tend to concentrate the smog around the central business district at midday and then it filters east in the afternoon.

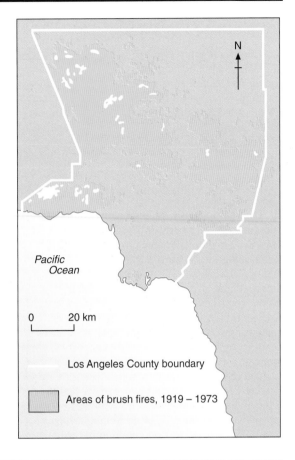

FIGURE 5.23 Areas of brush fires in Los Angeles County, 1919–73

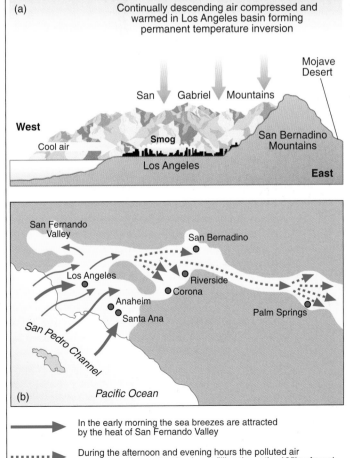

When the subsiding air mass compresses against the mountainous walls of the Los Angeles Basin, generating heat as the air molecules jam together to create an upper level of warm air, there is a so-called "Bowl" effect

The mass of air, warmed by the tightly jammed molecules creates an inversion layer over the Los Angeles Basin.

The subsidence above the basin is much heavier and massive during summer months, when the sun is in the northern hemisphere. The sun's proximity increreases the amount of subsidence and heating in the upper strata above the basin.

The inversion layer prevents dispersal of smog from industry and vehicles. A layer of warm air forms on sunny days above the basin. The cooler sea breeze from the ocean remains close to the surface, collecting ozone, and then moves eastward to inland cities and finally disperses in the desert air beyond San Gorgonio Pass.

It is an area of waste from 12 000 000 people living and working in a basin that has been unable to cleanse itself.

FIGURE 5.24 Smog and weather conditions in the Los Angeles basin

Los Angeles: hazard city

1 Make a tabulated summary of the hazards facing Los Angeles using the headings: Earthquakes; Coastal Hazards; Landslides, Floods and Drought; High Winds and Brush Fires; Smog.

Your table should include:

a) causes;

b) consequences;

c) spatial occurrence;

d) management.

2 The Los Angeles City Region environmental planning office recognises the need to effectively inform all key decision makers and local people about integrated hazard management at both the regional and local level. As part of the International Decade for Natural Disaster Reduction (IDNDR) they have been allocated a kick-start budget of £250 000 with the aim of increasing both public and specialist awareness leading directly to loss of life and property damage.

You have been given the role of project manager for this task, and have been asked to prepare the following.

a) An overall strategy to improve public hazard awareness leading to a reduction in hazard inputs.

b) A sustainable strategy to improve overall planning integration and improve awareness of key decision makers.

c) Sample design(s) to support your programme.

d) A budget bid for further funding of your project.

Emergency planning: Santa Clarita City, Los Angeles

Earthquakes are considered to be a major threat in the city of Santa Clarita due to the proximity of several fault zones. A major earthquake could cause many casualties, extensive property damage, fires, flooding and other hazards. The effects would be aggravated by aftershocks and the secondary effects of fire, landslides and dam failure. A catastrophic earthquake on the south-central San Andreas Fault of a magnitude of 8.3 has been predicted to occur before the end of the twentieth century. Property losses could reach $20 billion with 3000 fatalities (if at night) or 14 000 (if in the day), and a further 12 000–55 000 are expected to be hospitalised. Damage control and disaster relief support would be required from other local government and private organisations and from the state and federal governments for an extended period.

Some of the necessary aid would include the following:

- removing debris and clearing highways;
- demolishing unsafe structures;
- re-establishing private services/vehicles;
- providing search and rescue operations;
- providing medical care, food and temporary shelter;
- burial of the dead;
- mass evacuation of residents – particularly below dams;
- monitoring and managing other related effects such as landslides, dam failure, flood explosion, fire, chemical spills and pollution.

The city of Santa Clarita is located on tributaries of the Ventura River system. It could expect river overflows, dam/levée failure and soil erosion. Landslides are a major hazard of the rainy season. Wildland fires are a major threat during the Santa Ana wind season and particularly hazardous areas include: Los Padres National Forest; Angeles National Forest; San Gabriel Mountains; and the Santa Susana Mountains. Large destructive fires have burned through local mountains and areas near the city on a regular basis.

Integrated hazard management planning in Los Angeles County

Decision-making exercise

Study Figures 5.25–5.29.

1 Produce an annotated map to highlight the likely location and impacts of hazards occurring in the Los Angeles basin.

2 Use appropriate techniques (written and mapping) to decide on priorities for action in the event of a major earthquake disaster measuring 7.6 on the Richter Scale in the San Gabriel Mountains.

3 Identify criteria and justify recommendations for an integrated hazard management plan for the Los Angeles area. Try to use a weighted matrix (where criteria are given a score according to importance) in your answer.

Your answer to this exercise should take no longer than 3 hours and the word limit is 1500.

References

Disaster, John Whittow, 1980, Pelican (out of print)
Natural Disasters, D Alexander, 1993, UCL Press
City of Santa Clarita, 1990, Emergency plan

S Cochrane
27 Bushmills
CROYDON

D Mize
Emergency Planning Officer
Los Angeles County

Dear Stephen,

Thank you for your application for work experience with our office during your year out between school and university. I am now able to give you details of the report we should like you to write whilst you are with us. The report will be in three parts.

(1) A summary of the causes of hazards in the LA region and the likely location of their impacts. Overlay maps and annotated details would be very helpful here.

(2) Written and mapping techniques to decide priorities in the event of a major earthquake in the LA area. The survival guide by Pacific Bell may be of great use here.

(3) Identify criteria in the production of an integrated hazard management plan and make recommendations for an emergency document to cover the LA area. A weighted matrix such as a Leopold Matrix would be very useful here.

We hope you enjoy your stay with us and we look forward to reading your report on Integrated Hazard Management Planning in Los Angeles County.

D Mize,
LA Emergency Planning Officer.

FIGURE 5.25 Integrated hazard management planning in Los Angeles

FIGURE 5.26 Santa Clarita Earthquake Planning Services

First Aid and Survival Guide

Before the next earthquake

Be prepared. Take the time NOW to read the following checklists and take the necessary actions to minimise risks to yourself, your loved ones, your home and your office.

For more information on earthquake planning, check the following:

1 Yellow Pages, under "Earthquake Products and Services" (not available in all directories).

2 Local American Red Cross chapter.

3 Local Office of Emergency Services (see County Government listings in White Pages).

4 Governor's Office of Emergency Services Earthquake Program (510) 893-0818 or (818) 304-8383.

During an earthquake

1 If indoors, DUCK or drop down to the floor. Take COVER under a sturdy desk. HOLD on to it and be prepared to move with it. Don't rush outside. DO NOT try using the stairs.

2 If outside, get into the OPEN.

3 If you are driving – STOP if it is safe – but stay inside. DO NOT stop on or under a bridge, overpass or tunnel, under trees, light posts, electrical power lines or signs. Stay calm.

After the earthquake

1 Check for injuries.

2 **Safety check.** Check the following potential risks: fire; gas leaks; damaged electrical wiring; downed or damaged utility lines; downed or damaged chimneys; spilled medicines, drugs or other potentially harmful materials; fallen items in closets and cupboards. Check that each telephone is on its receiver. Wear sturdy shoes and gloves to avoid injury from broken glass.

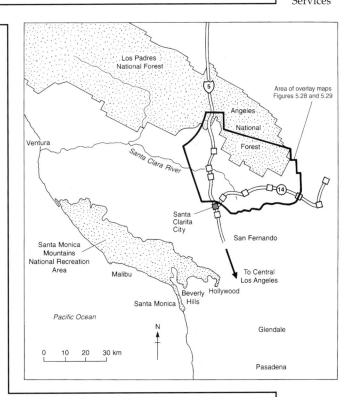

3 Check your food and water supplies.

DO NOT use lighters, candles, open-flame appliances or smoke until you are sure there are no gas leaks.

DO NOT operate electrical switches or appliances, including telephones, if you suspect a gas leak.

DO NOT use your telephone except for an emergency.

DO NOT go sightseeing afterwards, especially in beach and waterfront areas where seismic waves could strike.

FIGURE 5.27 Customer guide: First Aid and Survival Guide

FIGURE 5.28 City of Santa
Clarita Emergency Plan:
fire hazards

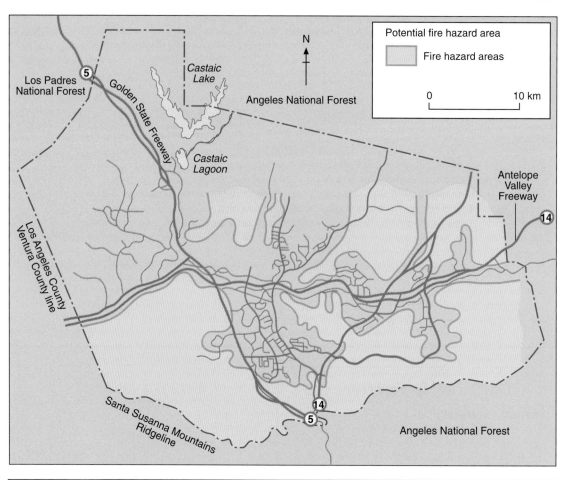

FIGURE 5.29 City of Santa
Clarita Emergency Plan:
flood hazards

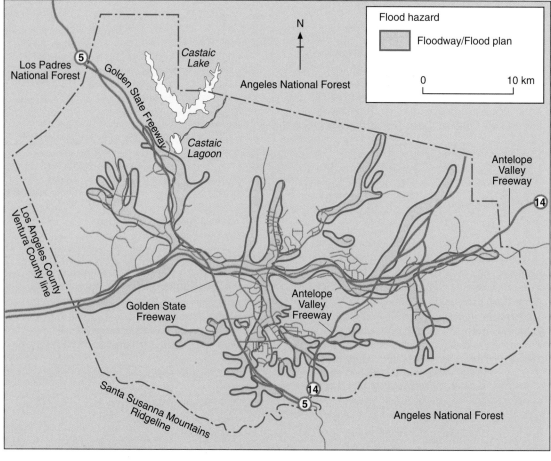

Managing floods in northern Italy

Possible causes of flooding in the Piedmont region

The flood event of 5–6 November 1994 in the Piedmont region of north-west Italy was the region's fifth in the past 13 months, part of the general increase in flooding events in Italy in recent years. Between 1950 and 1975, there were 60 recorded flood events in the country. Since then a further 66 have been documented, representing a 50 per cent increase in frequency.

Centred on the city of Torino, the Piedmont region is surrounded by mountainous terrain. The Swiss Alps are to the north, the French Alps to the west and the Alpi Maritime and Appenino Ligure border the Mediterranean on the south. The region is the principal catchment area for Italy's largest river, the Po, which flows eastward through Torino across northern Italy to join the Adriatic south of Venice.

A major southern tributary of the River Po in the region is the River Tanaro, but there are hundreds of other tributaries in Piedmont which combine to give a total watercourse length of around 5000km. The town's watercourses most affected by the 5–6 November 1994 flood are shown in Figure 5.30.

Following major floods in the past 50 years – notably in 1948, 1951 and 1968 – the River Po has been contained by flood defence works in its delta region and in areas adjacent to larger cities such as Torino. The defences are said to be typically designed for a 100-year flood, i.e. a flood which can be expected on average once in every 100 years.

However, the tributaries of the Po, especially those in Piedmont, have been left largely in their natural state, meandering across wide alluvial floodplains. This is primarily due to the prohibitive costs and difficulties of attempting to control what are fundamentally unstable river channels. In recent decades there has been substantial commercial and industrial development within Piedmont's undefended floodplains, significantly increasing the region's overall exposure to flood risk.

The catchment-wide rainfall which triggered the 5–6 November 1994 floods was unusually high. On 5 November 1994, 170mm of rainfall was recorded at Torino, representing the highest figure in a single day since 1951. In the upstream catchment areas, up to 212mm was recorded on 4 November with as much as 60mm falling in an hour.

The maximum flow from the Tanaro catchment was estimated at $0.43m^3$ per km^2, compared with $0.39m^3$ per km^2 in 1951. River levels exceeded the previous records of 1900 and 1951 but flow meters were largely destroyed by the flood. Flow in the River Po, upstream of the Tanaro, was measured at $10\,000m^3$/second – around 25 times the flow rate of the mean annual flood in the fluvial part of the River Severn in the UK.

The flood wave was estimated as moving at approximately 5km/hr (or 1.5m/second), which was fast enough to transport silt in suspension. As the water extended laterally from the main channel of the watercourse and into the floodplain, flows were reduced to 0.5m/second or less, precipitating silt out of suspension.

The silt and mud content of the flood waters was further increased by soil slips in the marly and sandy sub-strata of the steeply sloping upstream catchment areas.

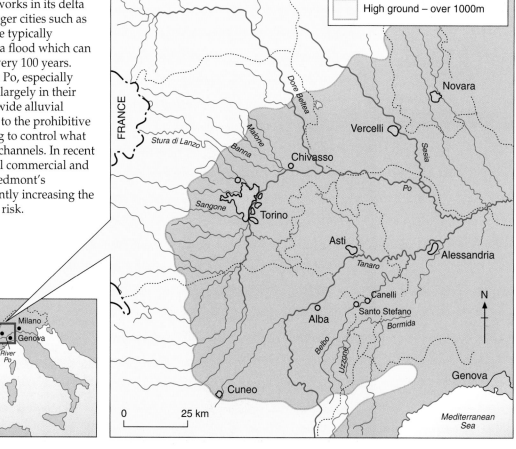

FIGURE 5.30 The Piedmont Region showing areas worst affected by the floods 5–6 November 1999 in N. Italy

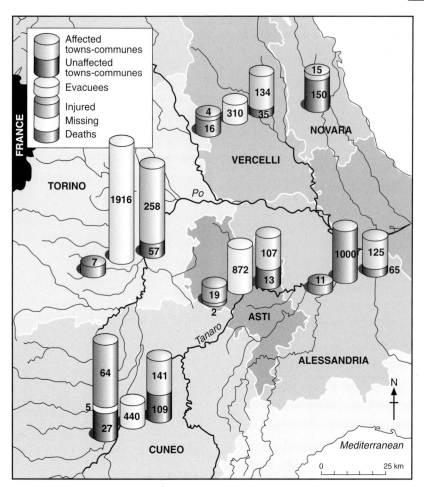

FIGURE 5.31 Personal injury, evacuation and community damage statistics for the six provinces in the Piedmont region

FIGURE 5.32 Flooded street with debris floating past hotel

STUDENT ACTIVITY 5.11

Causes of the Piedmont flood
1 What were the human and physical causes of flooding in the Piedmont region?
2 Draw a simplified annotated map based on Figure 5.30 to supplement your answer.

The consequences of the Piedmont floods

Provisional statistics from the Piedmont Department of Civil Protection in Torino for the 14 November 1994 showed 63 people dead, five missing, 87 injured, 4538 evacuated and 780 out of 1209 towns and communes affected. Provincial breakdown of this data is shown in Figure 5.31.

Global damage is provisionally estimated at 20 000 000 000 000 lire (approximately £8 billion). This is at least three times greater than the costs of the 1990 storms in southern England.

Insurance cover for household and small businesses appears to be the exception in Piedmont, and funds made available by the Ministry for the Interior are only likely to cover building fabric and structural damage. Damage to furnishings, contents, stock and cars will be mostly borne by the owners. National charitable appeals may help to cushion the loss.

Larger businesses had both the workforce and motivation to clean up and repair flood damage efficiently and quickly, whereas the rest of the community relied mainly on volunteer help. Clean-up operations within domestic and small business communities thus lagged behind the more organised industrial concerns.

Flood damage to property increases with depth, duration, velocity and sediment or effluent content of flood water. The velocity of flood water at Piedmont was generally low and durations short – typically less than 12 hours. Nevertheless, the depth (almost everywhere greater than 1m and not unusually greater than 3m) and high sediment load of the flood water caused significant damage to contents.

Furnishings and contents of households in flooded basements, cellars and ground floors were mostly destroyed with little or no residual values. Business premises were equally affected, though painstaking cleaning operations were undertaken in an attempt to salvage equipment where susceptibility to water and mud damage was low. However, items with electrical components had limited salvage value. Most communes were typified after the flood by mounds of muddy furniture and household goods waiting to be transported to municipal dumps for disposal. Vehicles caught in the wake of the flood were covered with thick mud and a large proportion of vehicles submerged by the flood water were written off.

Building construction is generally of masonry or reinforced concrete which mitigated against structural failures and damages. Fabric damage was typically confined to rendered brickwork, paintwork, carpentry, garage doors and windows, though in extreme cases, hydrostatic pressure ruptured floors and destroyed partition walls and some external masonry walls. One of the most severe failures was the collapse of an entire wing of a seven-storey riverside apartment block at Venaria just outside Torino. Pumping out cellars, basements and low-lying open areas was the most time-consuming aspect of the clean up.

Water marks (rack marks) on buildings, indicating the maximum level of flooding, were clearly visible on all buildings (Figure 5.32). These marks were horizontal, illustrating the steady vertical rise of flood waters rather than erratic lateral surges.

In the main towns of the Tanaro Valley, residential dwellings are largely five to eight-storey apartment buildings. Typically there is low economic use at ground level (open parking, garages, storage or workshops) and thus the potential for flood damage was limited.

Low-rise commercial buildings with large glass facades at ground floor suffered severe structural as well as contents damage. Single-storey businesses, such as garages and petrol stations, also suffered severe damage, mainly to equipment. Warehouses suffered high damages to inventory stock. Agricultural businesses also suffered significantly from loss of land use, crops and livestock.

Examples include the Ferrero Rocher chocolate factory in Alba, with a workforce of some 3800, where damages were estimated at over 100 billion lire. The Alba textile plant of the Mirglio group, Italy's third largest textiles and clothing manufacturer, suffered damage to plant and machinery and lost production worth around 30 billion lire.

Community damage should not be under-estimated. The widespread nature of flooding has affected the entire economic heart of those towns, e.g. the railway and bus stations, the central business districts, hospitals and communication networks, 3–4km from the main river channel of the Tanaro at Alba, Asti, and Alessandri.

The railway network in Piedmont was severely disrupted. Many routes between main towns, commonly only single track, were closed. In several places the ballast forming the base for rail tracks was washed out leading to severe buckling. At other places, the tracks remained water-logged or engulfed in mud.

The bus services also suffered. Some main bus terminals and dozens of buses, covered in mud, were out of action. Bridges across the rivers generally suffered low structural damage. However, the road bridge at Chivasso over the River Po, downstream of Torino, was totally destroyed.

Scour, erosion and failure of parapets, road surfaces and road embankments close to water channels forced the closure of several main roads in the area. This led to congested detours for through traffic. In addition, due to the torrential rains, there were thousands of minor landslips in the hills, many affecting roads. These landslips also disrupted gas and water and other underground distribution networks.

Hazard management pre-1994

It has been argued that poor hazard management was the real problem in Piedmont. Susceptibility to flooding was exacerbated by poor catchment and floodplain management (to mitigate against the effect of rapid runoff) and aggravated land slippage as a result of hills denuded of vegetation cover. Poor communication between provincial authorities during the flood emergency, and excessive development in the floodplains are further factors contributing to the severity of the November 1994 event.

On 4 November 1994 the Italian Government declared a state of emergency and vested responsibility for co-ordinating civil protection in a commission led by the Minister of the Interior in Rome with the President of the Piedmont Region as second in command.

However, though the disaster management plan was drawn up by the Piedmont Department of Civil Protection earlier in 1994, in accordance with a state law passed in 1992, no local preparatory plans were in force at the time of the flood. Local responsibility for civil protection was also unclear to the complicated government structure within each province.

As such, flood warnings were not passed from one province to another, which would have been particularly beneficial to the two downstream provinces of the River Tanaro. With a lead-time from Alba to Alessandria of up to 24 hours, a well-prepared and implemented emergency evacuation plan could have prevented death, injury and damage. The Department of Civil Protection is well aware of the problem and it is hoped that the 1994 disaster will provide the impetus for change.

Environmental management

Environmental groups in Italy are concerned that natural river beds, which attenuate flow and act as an effective sponge to flood water, are being replaced by narrower, concrete channels which act as effective hydraulic conveyors. In extreme flood the concentrated flow will reduce the time to peak flow and intensify residual flooding beyond the capacity of these channels. This may be true but on the River Tanaro, where some of the most catastrophic flooding has taken place, the river is rarely 'trained' but left to meander across its wide and natural floodplain.

Deforestation of the Piedmont and Alpine foothills has reduced the permeability of the land, and therefore retention of rainfall, and aggravates the erosion of the friable marls and sands. These factors combine during periods of torrential rainfall to exacerbate flooding in the river valleys and deposit tracts of displaced sediment in the wake of the flood.

In addition to managing forest clearance and land-use practice to stabilise the soil, the release of flood water should be contained naturally through buffer zones (wetland, alluvial forests and other valley ecosystems etc) at the edge of the floodplain.

Floodplain development

Environmental mismanagement will not in itself produce the high level of damage caused by flooding and heavy rainfall. These ultimately occur because property development has been allowed to encroach on the highly vulnerable land of the natural floodplains and the steep slopes of the valleys.

STUDENT ACTIVITY 5.13

Evaluation of management plans
1   Evaluate the regional and national hazard management plans drawn up by the Piedmont Regional Government and the Italian Government.
2   To what extent do you agree that poor hazard management planning was the real problem?

The aftermath of the 1994 floods: hazard management for the future

The November 1994 flood in Piedmont represents only one phase in a repetitive cycle of flooding. Climatic models have forecast an increased frequency in extreme atmospheric phenomena, consistent with the projections of the greenhouse effect.

It is important that victims of the recent flooding should be educated and made aware of the risks of living in areas subject to periodic flooding, and be party to the development of effective preparatory plans to mitigate the effects of future flooding.

River management can be seen as a blend of structural engineering and non-structural planning. The concept of floodplain zoning and 'guided growth' away from vulnerable areas can be used to discourage further floodplain development. Procedures for flood warning, complemented by effective dissemination and warning response measures, can significantly reduce the consequences of flooding, particularly damage to moveable property, death and injury. Maintenance of the floodplain and river channel in conjunction with the natural environment can no longer be ignored.

However, with regard to the Piedmont rivers, it is not easy to build flood defences. Concrete channelisation may be hydraulically efficient but it is an anathema to riverine ecology.

The very name Piedmont or 'foot of the mountains' implies that the river flow slackens as gradients level and efficiency of flow is maintained through meandering across wide alluvial floodplains. The rivers constantly change their course making the construction of embankments impractical. Embanking the very limits of the floodplain is not a cost-effect option. Dredging the channel to create a stable profile and to enhance carrying capacity can also be expensive and contrary to the environmental lobby's ideal of a natural river.

FIGURE 5.33 Flooded street showing high water mark

Nevertheless, strategic maintenance and a regionally co-ordinated philosophy are required to provide protection for areas adjacent to urban populations. Mitigation measures would include tree clearance, dredging in the direct flood way and the creation of buffer zones at the edges of the alluvial floodplain to retain water and attenuate flood flows.

The River Po basin authority has estimated a cost of 3 billion lire per km (£1.2 million) for a sensitive embankment and stabilisation programme and up to 300 million lire per km (£120 000) for tree clearance. However, the budget of the whole Piedmont region for the next three years is only around 60 billion lire. With the River Tanaro alone covering 150km, progress, when approved, will be slow.

Ironically, the authority in Parma established an urgent initiative for flood defence on the Po on 25 October 1994. The scale of the flood disaster that followed two weeks later may precipitate action for a concerted and integrated policy of structural and river maintenance works, in conjunction with the development of an effective flood preparatory plan for all stricken communities.

STUDENT ACTIVITY 5.14

Evaluation of recent hazard management plans for flooding in Piedmont. Identify and evaluate the measures since 1994 to reduce the impact of any future floods and modify their causal processes. It is important that you consider:
a) social;
b) technological;
c) ecological;
d) economic factors in your analysis.

A national case study of New Zealand

New Zealand is classified as a high-risk country in terms of natural hazards. It is slightly larger than the UK with an area of 270 000km^2 and a population of 3.5 million. The country stretches from 48° south to the fringes of the area affected by cyclonic storms at latitude 34° south. A broken snow-topped ridge of collision for two tectonic plates, New Zealand is subject to frequent earthquakes and occasional volcanic eruptions. Its eastern coasts look across 10 000km^2 of open ocean to Chile and Peru, from whose vicinity tectonic activity may at any time trigger fast-travelling tsunamis. Landslips are also common in the steep geologically youthful New Zealand landscape. Mount Cook, New Zealand's highest peak, lost 15m from its summit in the 1991 rock avalanche.

In this section you will be expected to explore the following three key topics as a route for enquiry.

1 Hazard risk assessment: meteorological and geological threats
New Zealanders are at risk from a number of natural processes as can be seen in Figures 5.34 and 5.35. Flooding is a risk to a maximum of 2.4 million people in most inhabited areas. Volcanoes expose over 2 million people to risks in Auckland and Central North Island. Earthquakes expose 1.8 million people to risk in the central zone and have caused 289 deaths since 1840. However it must be remembered that return periods for volcanic eruptions are much longer than for earthquakes of comparable threat and while floods are very frequent they are rarely fatal.

By international standards New Zealand is a windy country and there have been 11 major civil defence emergencies related to winds with speeds over 160km/hour in the last 30 years including tropical cyclones. These cyclonic storms may cause storm surges of 2m in coastal areas.

2 Vulnerability assessment
Examine the vulnerability of people and the economy to the consequences of these natural hazards. You will be asked to explain why the New Zealand Government states in their National Hazard Report, 'We find floods the most common, earthquakes potentially the most dangerous and volcanic eruptions the most under-rated natural hazard' (Tephra, Vol 13, May 1994).

3 Mitigation activities. Past, present and future
Evaluate hazard management in New Zealand which has averaged only three deaths per year from natural hazards this century. Annual losses due to flooding are over US $360 million and earthquake damage averages US $30 million. Yet it is widely recognised as a nation which has extensive hazard management legislation to reduce disaster reduction, effective disaster planning at both local and national levels, and well-funded natural hazard research projects.

1 Hazard Risk Assessment: meteorological and geological threats

New Zealand is part of the Pacific Ring of Fire and is located on the Pacific and Australian crustal plates. The most active zone of deformation is 100km wide from Fiordland to East Cape, and is most clearly seen in the South Island Alpine Fault. North Island overlies an active subduction zone, and therefore future eruptions are likely to occur at all recently active volcanic centres. There have been eight fatal volcanic events since 1840 resulting in 382 deaths. (See Figures 5.34–5.40).

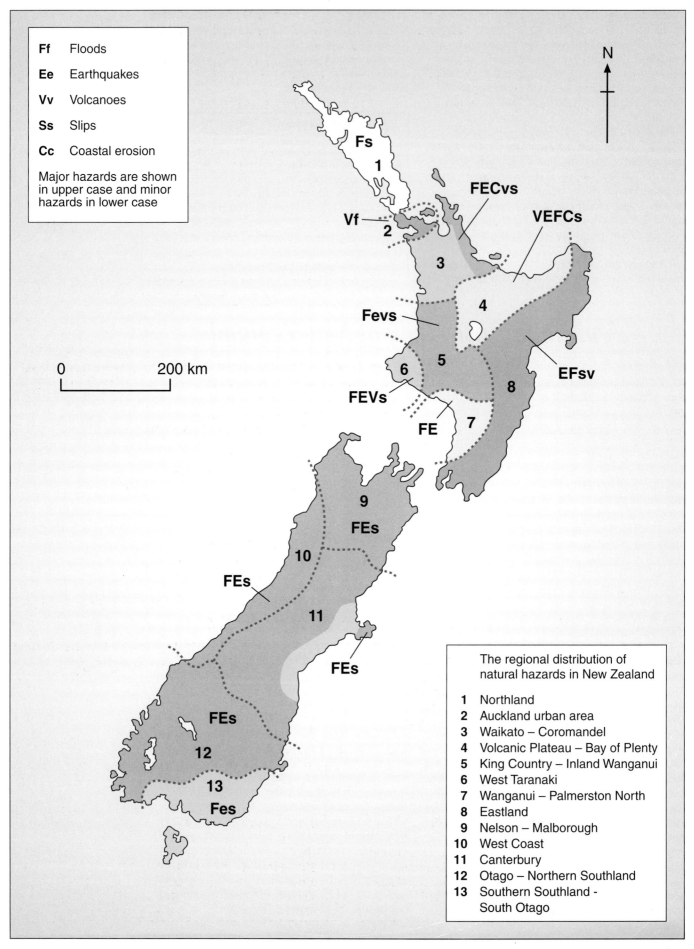

Ff   Floods
Ee   Earthquakes
Vv   Volcanoes
Ss   Slips
Cc   Coastal erosion

Major hazards are shown in upper case and minor hazards in lower case

N

0   200 km

Fs
1

Vf
2

FECvs

VEFCs

3

Fevs

4

5

6

EFsv

FEVs

8

FE

7

9
FEs

10

FEs

11

FEs

FEs

12

13
Fes

The regional distribution of natural hazards in New Zealand

1   Northland
2   Auckland urban area
3   Waikato – Coromandel
4   Volcanic Plateau – Bay of Plenty
5   King Country – Inland Wanganui
6   West Taranaki
7   Wanganui – Palmerston North
8   Eastland
9   Nelson – Malborough
10 West Coast
11 Canterbury
12 Otago – Northern Southland
13 Southern Southland - South Otago

FIGURE 5.34 New Zealand natural hazard regions

Hazards	Main areas of hazard	Effects
Floods	Coastal alluvial plains likely to receive heavy rain or snow melt.	■ Loss of life. ■ Damage to property, pasture, crops and livestock.
Coastal erosion	50 per cent of New Zealand's coastline is particularly vulnerable to storm waves.	■ No loss of life. ■ Loss of land and beaches. ■ Damage to coastal housing, roads and services.
Landslides	Much of New Zealand is vulnerable to landslides particularly: ■ areas on steep slopes with heavy rainfall and a weak soil structure.	■ Small loss of life. ■ Destruction of valuable farm land and property. ■ Silting of rivers in lowland.
Volcanic eruptions	■ The central North Island active volcanoes. ■ The Auckland and Taranaki volcanic areas are dormant but renewed activity could occur at any time.	■ Many lives have been lost in volcanic-related hazard events. ■ A renewal of volcanic activity in Auckland could be catastrophic.
Earthquakes	The most hazardous area is a 100km wide zone stretching from East Cape to Fiordland.	■ Many lives have been lost. ■ Property is often damaged even in smaller earthquakes which occur frequently.

FIGURE 5.35 New Zealand's major natural hazards

	Date	Disaster
1846	May	Landslide at Te Rapa, Lake Taupo – 61 dead
1848	Oct	The Wairau earthquake and aftershocks – 3 dead
1855	Jan	Wairarapa earthquake, Wellington, which shook both islands – 5 dead
1858	Jan	Floods in Hutt Valley – 9 dead
1863	Jul	Snowstorm and floods in Otago – about 100 dead
1878	Sep	Severe floods in the Clutha Valley with widespread destruction
1886	Jun	Eruption of Mount Tarawera – 153 dead
1897	Apr	Tutaekuri flood – 10 dead
1918	Nov	Influenza epidemic – 6700 dead
1929	Jun	Earthquake at Murchison – 17 dead
1931	Feb	Earthquake in Hawke's Bay – 256 dead, 11 000 evacuated
1938	Feb	Flash flood destroyed a work camp at Kopuawhara – 21 dead
1953	Dec	Lahar swept away bridge and express train at Tangiwai – 151 dead
1968	Apr	Cyclone Giselle – ferry Wahine sunk, over 50 dead
1968	May	Earthquake at Inangahua – 3 dead, 300 evacuated
1979	Aug	Abbotsford landslide destroyed or badly damaged 69 houses

FIGURE 5.36 (a) Some New Zealand natural disasters, 1840–1980

Date	Type	Location	Affected population		Losses
1981 Apr	Flood	Thames Valley	2250	+	$20 m
1983 Jul	Flood	Golden Bay	150	+	$5 m
1984 Jan	Flood	Southland	8000		$110 m
1984 Jul	Flood	Poverty Bay	100		$3 m +
1985 Jan	Flood	Nelson Bay	150		$1 m
1985 Feb	Flood/landslip	Thames Valley	200	(4 dead)	$10 m +
1986 Mar	Flood	Aorangi	1500	(1 dead)	$70 m +
1986 Aug	Flood	Rangiora	320		NA
1986 Mar	Earthquake	Bay of Plenty	5000	+	$1100 m
1987 Mar	Flood	Southland	700	+	NA
1988 Mar	Cyclone Bola	North Island	5000	+ (5 dead)	NA
1988 May	Flood	Greymouth	400	+	NA
1988 Jul	Flood	Palmerston North	1200		NA
1988 Sep	Flood/landslip	Greymouth	350	+ (1 dead)	$16 m +
1990 Mar	Storm, flood	Taranaki, Wanganui	200		$12 m +
1991 Jan	Flood	West Coast	130	+	$4 m
1991 Feb	Flood	Catlins	128		$5 m

NA: not available

(b) Some New Zealand natural disasters, 1980–1993

FIGURE 5.37
Meteorological threats (a)
Rapid mass movement on
the base of steep slopes,
East Cape, North Island
(affected by Cyclone Bola,
March 1988)

Figure 5.37(c) Cyclone Bola (Hazard Profile)
Widespread damage
Five people died
5000 were temporarily homeless
Insurance costs totalled US $22 million
Regional costs to the Government of US $70 million
National level Government assistance to agriculture of US $7.5 million
Estimated total costs range from US $125–150 million (1993 figures)

FIGURE 5.38 Active volcanic centres of North Island

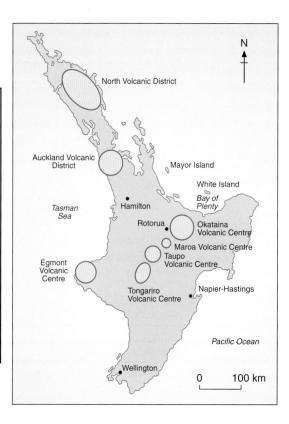

Figure 5.37 (b) Civil defence emergencies

1967	Nov	Woodville (tornado)
1968	Apr	Upper Hutt (Wahine storm and Cyclone Giselle)
1970	Sep	Dannevirke (wind)
1975	Aug	Greytown (wind, flooding)
1978	Jul	Te Aroha, Piako, Thames (wind, flooding)
1978	Oct	Invercargill, Bluff, Stewart Island (flood and storm damage)
1979	Dec	Mackenzie County, Mount Cook (wind, flooding)
1980	Mar	Chatham Islands (storm)
1980	Jun	Featherston (storm)
1988	Mar	Taranaki (Cyclone Bola), East Cape, North Island
1990		Taranaki Wariganui (Anticyclone Hilda)
1992	Jul	Masterton (storm and flooding)

STUDENT ACTIVITY 5.15

Identification of hazard risk zones in New Zealand
Is it true to say that North and South Islands experience different hazards? Try to explain why. Use Figures 5.34–5.39 to help you.

STUDENT ACTIVITY 5.16

Flooding: the main threat?
New Zealand's heavy rainfall is dependent on four factors.
1   Moisture content of the airflow.
2   Windspeeds.
3   Vertical motion which causes cooling and hence precipitation.
4   Topography which can enhance vertical motion.
Historically, floods have been the dominant natural hazard with over 50 emergencies in the last 25 years, and on average have claimed one life per annum over the last 150 years.

Many recent floods may have been caused by the long-term deforestation. This has happened steadily over the last 100 years, as trees have been removed on the steep slopes of the fertile volcanic soils to allow sheep grazing.

Consult an atlas and produce an annotated map or diagram to help explain why flooding is the most extensive potential natural hazard in New Zealand. Why is it also true to say New Zealand's wealth derives from its climate?

STUDENT ACTIVITY 5.17

Volcanic threats
Mount Tarawera in the Okataina volcanic centre erupted in June 1886 killing 153 people in what was then a sparsely populated area. It covered 7500km with 10cm of ash (Mount St Helens covered only 3000km with 10cm in 1980).
1   Identify those urban areas most at risk from volcanic activity on North Island.

In 1886 the Mount Tarawera eruption caused buildings and trees to collapse, respiratory distress, and crop destruction. The 10cm of ash also caused vehicle immobilisation, power blackouts as well as water pollution.
2   What might the impact of a similar eruption be today in this area?
3   Most New Zealanders believe the chances of a volcanic eruption are much less than those of a significant earthquake, and that economic losses will be about half those of an earthquake. Why then does the New Zealand Government believe social stress will be greater, and that economic recovery might take significantly longer?

Locations	VI	VII	VIII	IX
Kaitaia	480	2000		
Whangarei	220	1200		
Auckland	65	280	1700	
Tauranga	10	42	180	1000
Hamilton	23	92	430	
Whakatane	5	36	150	620
Rotorua	8	42	180	1100
Gisborne	10	59	180	510
Taupo	5	45	210	1200
New Plymouth	13	51	200	920
Napier/Hastings	11	62	210	640
Wanganui	5	25	120	540
Palmerston North	8	35	130	440
Masterton	12	41	130	410
Wellington/				
Hutt Valley	8	32	100	370
Nelson	6	25	88	340
Blenheim	7	26	92	360
Westport	12	40	140	580
Kaikoura	9	31	110	410
Greymouth	14	47	170	680
Christchurch	21	70	250	980
Mount Cook	19	66	240	930
Timaru	36	130	470	2400
Milford Sound	28	150	750	
Queenstown	24	100	430	2000
Oamaru	41	150	580	
Dunedin	51	200	820	
Invercargill	31	120	460	2400

FIGURE 5.39 Mean return period for modified Mercalli intensities at selected locations

Year	Locality	Claims	$(1993)
1966	Seddon	1575	2 319 000
1968	Inangahua	10 500	25 556 000
1968	Wellington	2200	1 360 000
1972	Te Aroha	1300	1 196 000
1973	Wellington/Hawkes Bay/Wellington	2300	1 482 000
1974	Dunedin	2767	2 694 000
1980	Hawkes Bay	2015	1 344 000
1987	Bay of Plenty	5039	170 571 000
1989	South Taranaki Bight	2767	113 000
1990	Southern Hawkes Bay	1267	2 822 000
1990	Weber	2632	7 577 000
1991	Westport	1997	2 865 000
1991	Wanganui	2142	2 424 000
1992	Whakatane	833	650 000
1993	Gisborne	2800	4 000 000

*Estimate

FIGURE 5.40 Cost of recent significant earthquakes with over 1000 claimants and/or $1 million worth of claims

STUDENT ACTIVITY 5.18

Earthquakes, an ever-present threat

New Zealand is very prone to earthquakes with the level of seismic activity similar to California and slightly less than Japan. From your work in Chapter 3 you should understand the processes that cause earthquakes, and how they can be measured on the Richter Scale of magnitude and Mercalli Scale of intensity. New Zealand's largest recorded earthquake was the 8.0 Wairapara Shock of 1855, but it was the 7.8 Hawkes Bay event of 1931 which had the most fatalities with 11 000 evacuated and 256 deaths. New Zealand experiences over 200 earthquakes per year, over half exceed Richter Scale 4, 10–20 exceed magnitude 5, and one exceeds magnitude 6. A magnitude 7 quake is expected every decade.

Write a brief paragraph to help explain the distribution of earthquakes in Figures 5.39 and 5.40 and identify those areas at greatest risk.

2 Vulnerability assessment: a population at risk

One of the key factors which influences the impact of a natural event is the location of the human population. The 1991 New Zealand census identified five potential risk localities for their 3.5 million residents and additionally found that 1.1 million overseas visitors spent an average of two weeks in New Zealand.

Over 1 million people in New Zealand are home-based, this includes the self-employed, retired, unemployed, children and homekeepers. There are 1.17 million households, 99 per cent of which live in conventional houses or flats. Since the 1931 Hawkes Bay earthquake, New Zealand has steadily been upgrading its building regulations. Most CBDs have been replaced in the 1960s and 1970s with new high-rise well-designed buildings. Most individual housing is of timber frame and cladding, with corrugated iron as the most popular roofing material. As a result most of the population lives and works in buildings well protected from earthquakes, excepting hazards of older chimneys and ill-secured furniture. The entire population spend half of their time at home, and two-thirds of this in bed! The second most popular leisure interest is watching TV, and 95 per cent of all households have at least one TV, and at least as many a radio. Every working day over 2 million people travel an average of 15 minutes each way to school or work, most in vehicles. The New Zealand population is, however, not homogeneous in that there are several groups of differing ability as can be seen in Figures 5.42 and 5.44.

Maori	435 000	Dutch	24 000
Japanese*	130 000	Indian	30 000
Samoan	68 000	Korean*	19 000
German*	51 000	Tongan	18 000
Chinese	45 000	Niuean	9000
Cook Island	27 000	Tokelauan	3000

*Tourists

FIGURE 5.41 Potential non-English audiences

3 Mitigation Activities. Past, present and future

The United Nations resolution 42/169 declared the 1990s to be the International Decade for Natural Disaster Reduction (IDNDR). In New Zealand this has coincided with a number of important hazard management developments:

- Significant restructuring of the agencies with responsibility for natural disaster reduction and clarification of roles.

- Improved co-ordination and integration between scientists, engineers, planners and emergency practitioners.
- The Wellington Earthquake Lifelines Project, and the recently established multi-hazard lifelines project in Christchurch (lifelines are vital infrastructure and services).
- Improved technical innovations which have improved national warning systems for extreme meteorological events.

The IDNDR is also providing a focus to help identify the key issues and areas for improvement for the latter half of the decade. The aims were:

- To improve better public understanding of the potential threat of the volcanic hazard and to publish a National Volcanic Contingency Plan.
- To improve public warning systems and encourage local councils to adopt approaches which best suit their hazards, geography and communities.
- As only one-third of the New Zealand population is considered to be prepared for a natural disaster there is a real need to improve and greatly expand community involvement and participation in all aspects of disaster reduction.

STUDENT ACTIVITY 5.19

The New Zealand population: a variable group
In 1987 all disaster preparatory material was in English. The number of people in New Zealand unable to read English may not be large, but policies intended to prepare people for disaster, or to restore confidence after a disaster strikes, need to be in a language which reinforces feelings of belonging to a caring community. Likewise, there are several groups with disabilities to whom disaster information needs to be conveyed in new ways. In 1991, it was estimated that 352 000 New Zealanders suffered from sight, hearing, mobility, verbal, cognitive or medical functional challenge.

You have been asked by the Director of the Ministry of Civil Defence to prepare a short briefing paper for the forthcoming keynote lecture to the New Zealand Equal Opportunities Forum, as part of the International Decade for National Disaster Reduction. The focus of the speech will be on the disaster preparedness for all, and must have strong specific strategies to combat the current unevenness. Briefly outline six key strategies to tackle the perceived inequality. (See Figures 5.41–5.43).

STUDENT ACTIVITY 5.20

Evaluation of national disaster reduction measures
Select any two of the listed points above and suggest what measures you would implement to improve the situation in the mid-1990s, and how these could be evaluated after five years at the end of the IDNDR in the year 2000. (Use Figure 5.44 to help you).

FIGURE 5.42 Location of the New Zealand population (hours per year)

Number	At home	At work/school	Home-based leisure	Community	On holiday	TOTAL
1.4 m	4563	2115	1613	133	336	8760
1.1 m	5613		2698	113	336	8760
1.0 m	4563	1200	2548	113	336	8760

FIGURE 5.43 Preferred media for those with disabilities

Disability	(Base)	Large leaflet	Print	Audio	Video	Visit	Workshop
Intellectual	(10)	0	0	2	5	6	4
MS	(23)	12	0	0	6	6	0
Hearing	(16)	7	0	0	7	4	0
Sight	(27)	6	14	4	0	5	5
Mobility	(33)	12	1	1	19	12	14
Schizophrenia	(22)	11	0	6	7	7	1
Totals	(131)	48	23	44	40	24	5

Mitigation activities and warnings

• Legislation

The following New Zealand statutes have major implications for natural disaster reduction.

1967 Water and Soil Conservation Act

River clearance in lower reaches. Tree planting in 'at risk' headwaters. Stop banks to protect urban communities.

1974 Local Government Act

Establish 74 authorities for hazard mapping and land use zoning.

1975 Fire Services Act and 1977 Town and Country Planning Act

New Zealand has excellent emergency services, co-ordinated police, fire and ambulance.

1983 Civil Defence Act

Civil defence is an all-hazard approach, involving the whole nation, co-ordinated by 100 staff and with a US $7 million budget.

1991 Building Act

Defines performance standards for buildings.

1991 Resource Management Act

Creation of Regional Councils to reform central and local government, with some emphasis on managing environments sustainably. All 15 councils have draft hazard plans.

1992 Health and Safety in Employment Act

To improve safety at work for employees in the event of a disaster.

1993 Earthquake Commission Act

Removing the EQC from the commercial sector and improving insurance cover.

• Mitigation plans

Catchment works, e.g. Greymouth Wall constructed in 1988/9. Revised Building Codes for CBDs and individual households. Seismic stations have been placed on important volcanic fields. Tropical Cyclone Operational Plan updated every two years from the World Meteorological Organisation.

• Research projects in addition to general hazard studies

1 **Lifelines projects** The capital city of Wellington (population 300 000) has a high earthquake risk. Lifelines reviews and attempts to reduce the vulnerability of key services including electricity, gas, water, telecommunications.
2 **Dynamic consolidation** To mitigate **liquefaction** potential in Wellington, Christchurch, Tauranga, Napier, Taupo. Research is taking place into the cost-benefit ratios of this technique and the problems of pumice sandy soils.
3 **Volcanic studies** Scientists advise that New Zealand has in excess of 20 per cent of the world's most destructive volcanoes and it is the country's most under-rated threat. Research is taking place with publications on all main volcanic fields.

• Civil defence in New Zealand

The Civil Defence Act requires all communities to have an up-to-date plan for the response to natural hazards, and this must be reviewed every three years.

Unlike the UK, Community Civil Defence is a very important aspect of everyone's lifestyle in New Zealand. Most disaster response in New Zealand is civilian, and it is expected that trained community people will provide most disaster staffing. The Civil Defence Plan is understood by all of the population to be an all-hazard approach, and on average there are three civil defence emergencies per year in New Zealand serious enough to evoke the powers of the Civil Defence Act. In the last 30 years these have mainly been floods, but the two most traumatic have both been earthquakes. The first response to local disasters takes place at household and community level, co-ordinated by trained volunteers and economically supported by the Government, e.g. refunds covering the costs of housing and feeding the displaced people. Regionally widespread disasters require Regional Defence or the national structure to be called into action. Annual national exercises are held every four years, the Minister for Civil Defence operates a specialist training school which opened in 1983. In the last decade, 10 000 participants have attended 170 events and courses. Over 50 organisations are involved in the discussions to refine the National Civil Defence Plan every year, and co-ordinate their response, e.g. Red Cross, Salvation Army, Amateur Radio Organisations. Every school and state organisation must have its own hazard management plan to include how they might operate during and after an emergency.

Local Civil Defence is organised into six sections: warden; rescue; welfare; medical; transport; and supply. Their other key function is to liaise with police, post office, social welfare, hospital, health department, fire services, Public Information, traffic control, energy services and the Ministry of Works.

• Public education and information

1 Civil Defence Organisations distribute 200 000 leaflets, besides posters, videos etc to service clubs, community groups, church groups, rest homes and schools.
2 The Earthquake Business Plans.
3 1993 IDNDR Day of 'Stop Disasters in Schools'.
4 Natural hazards are part of the National Curriculum.
5 New diploma in Civil Defence.

• Operational projects

1 System for Monitoring and Alerting Seismic Hazards (SMASH) (three new seismic stations), May 1993.
2 Egmont Volcanic Field Seismic Station Project.
3 National Post-Disaster Support for Victims.
4 Computerised register of residents who need special help in an emergency, in collaboration with Disabled Persons' Assembly and local community groups.
5 New Meteorological Service weather radar at strategic points to improve accuracy of forecasting.
6 Emergency services radio band.

FIGURE 5.44 Mitigation in the early and late 1990s

A review of the current situation in the late 90s

The Centre for Research on the Epidemiology of Disasters (CRED) measures disaster in terms of thresholds of ten dead or 100 displaced. In the 1993 World Disasters report CRED noted that for the period 1967–1992, New Zealand had on average two deaths and 425 people affected by a disaster every year. This was fourth behind the USA, Japan and India. CRED also classified New Zealand as the country with the highest spatial risk ratio to flooding, even higher than Bangladesh.

New Zealand is a geomorphologically, geologically and meteorologically unstable country where extreme natural events are relatively frequent. The settlement and human land-use patterns can transform these extreme natural events into hazards causing loss of life and property. They have a high potential to become hazards but do not always, because of effective hazard management and the low vulnerability of most sections of the population, who cope and adjust well due to their preparedness, resilience, and experiences which have led them to expect the unexpected.

Currently there are three main potential hazards:
1 Flooding: the most frequent and widespread;
2 Earthquakes: the most dangerous;
3 Volcanic events: the least frequent, most underrated.

Although all New Zealand people could be affected, because neither the population of New Zealand nor extreme natural events are evenly distributed, areas of increased vulnerability can be identified. Currently 88 per cent of the population live on 1 per cent of the land, and 96 per cent of building investment is constructed in this urban 1 per cent. The remaining rural 12 per cent of the population are concentrated in the intensive farming areas on the volcanic soils.

The most spatially vulnerable areas are as follows:
1 Metropolitan Auckland and North Island. Over 880 000 people and a very high property investment on an island with 66 volcanoes (Figure 5.45b).
2 The capital Wellington, with a population of 400 000 located in an active earthquake zone and in the Hutt Valley area which has serious flood risks (Figure 5.45a and c).
3 The Christchurch region and the Canterbury alluvial plains area, with a population of 300 000 at risk from flooding from the Waimakarri River.
4 Riverside communities on both North and South Islands that have a high flood risk and cyclone potential, e.g. Invercargill and Gisborne (Figure 5.45d).

FIGURE 5.45 4 photos of spatially vulnerable areas (a) Wellington active earthquake zone from Mt Victoria. The shoreline buildings are built on land created in the 1851 earthquake (b) Auckland. A view of the crater from Mt Eden. The Rangitoto Volcanic Cone last erupted 200 years ago (c) Houses built on a fault zone in Wellington (d) East Cape area. Deforested hillslopes were rapidly eroded causing extensive damage and flooding in March 1998 (Cyclone Bola)

FIGURE 5.46 Hazard Profiles – Kobe and Northridge

KOBE QUAKE, JAPAN	NORTHRIDGE QUAKE, LA, USA
JAN 17 1995 5.46AM MAGNITUDE 6.9 5 200 Dead 190 000 BUILDINGS DESTROYED 300 000 HOMELESS 200 BILLION US $ DAMAGES	SUBURB OF L.A. 21 miles north-west of Central L.A. JAN 19 1994 4.31AM A HOLIDAY MORNING MAGNITUDE 6.7 57 DEAD 4 500 BUILDINGS DESTROYED 40 BILLION US $ DAMAGES

In the early 1990s the New Zealand Government and population adopt six main hazard management responses. It is argued that these hazard responses are a function of perception, ability and willingness to attempt to provide some measure of control over the event.

1 Risk acceptance due to the resilience of the population and the high degree of preparedness of the population.

2 Vulnerability assessment. Assess every part of the country for its risk potential.

3 Legislation, e.g. town and country planning and building regulations to create hazard planning zones within urban areas identified to be highly vulnerable. Increasingly no development is allowed in the highest risk areas and these are left as public open spaces, and in other areas building design or height is regulated. Auckland has been mapped and has eight zones, and Christchurch 11 zones.

4 Community preparedness, e.g. civil defence and community education.

5 Improved monitoring and alerting services, e.g. SMASH.

6 Aid and insurance.

New directions – Beyond 2000

In 1998 the New Zealand Government began to transform its approach to hazard management. In the autumn of 1998 a new structure for emergency management was announced including a proposal to create a new ministry of civil defence in 1999. The thrust of these revisions will focus on:

■ Improved consultation with stakeholder representatives, e.g. local government;
■ New legislation;
■ Improved risk management systems;
■ A new field structure;
■ Improved integration and inter-agency co-operation;
■ Improved international co-operation;
■ Improved public awareness;
■ An all-hazard approach.

Central to the whole approach is the determination to learn the lessons from overseas, e.g. Kobe, Japan and Northridge, LA, USA. (See Figure 5.46).

Kobe was a community that was trusting in outside help and direction; this reliance on external sources explains the failure of an operation that took 3 days to get effectively underway. In response to the Northridge quake, the US mobilised

enormous resources, and within 48 hours 22 000 people were housed in tents around their communities and more than 1000 welfare personnel were deployed. Water tankers were swiftly brought in, and within 24 hours 93 per cent of power was restored.

The new director for emergency management and civil defence stated:

'In NZ, we are simply not large enough to have US level back-up, so what we lack in size, we have to make up for by being smarter. We have the opportunity to establish NZ as the world leader in Nationwide Risk Management, and to set new international standards.'

STUDENT TASK 5.21

How are the New Zealand Government transforming their approach to hazard management for the year 2000 and beyond? **Attempt the following essay on hazard prevention.**

'The physical processes that create hazards cannot be totally controlled, but their consequences may be alleviated by hazard prediction and prevention methods, by education and by other effective hazard management techniques.'

Explain why New Zealand is perceived as a high-risk environment, yet appears to have few natural disasters.

Glossary

Civil defence – trained community representatives providing an all-hazard approach at all stages, e.g. education and community preparedness, disaster relief.

Lifelines Project – designed to reduce the vulnerability of key infrastructural services in high-risk zones, e.g. putting electricity cables underground.

Liquefaction – loose sediments behave as fluids due to the pressure of overlying material, and consequently cannot support objects and flow swiftly.

References

Tephra, Vol 13, No 1, May 1994, Ministry of Civil Defence, New Zealand

6

CONCLUSION

Scientific interest in managing natural hazards is at a very youthful stage. It was only 60 years ago that the first systematic, policy-orientated research into integrated hazard assessment and reduction began with the work of Gilbert White in the USA. The pace did not really quicken until the 1970s, when extreme natural events exposed the vulnerability of rich and poor countries alike, and the current explosion of hazard-related research into a wide range of academic disciplines began. As we approach the end of the millennium awareness of environmental hazards has never been greater, reinforced by the decision of the United Nations Assembly in December 1989 to adopt resolution 44/236, proclaiming the 1990s as the International Decade for Natural Disaster reduction (IDNDR). The objective of the decade is as follows.

'To reduce through concerted international action, especially in the developing countries, the loss of life, property damage and the social and economic disruption caused by natural disasters.'

The IDNDR relies heavily on measures taken at a national level and all governments are called upon to formulate national disaster-mitigation programmes. The IDNDR is a continuously evolving programme and therefore the success of the decade will not be entirely known until after the year 2000.

Although global awareness is certainly increasing, is it also true that the world is becoming a more hazardous place? Are the frequency and magnitude of natural hazards increasing? Is our human society becoming somehow more vulnerable to the same incidence of hazard?

It is essential that great care is taken when we review disaster trends and we must not seek simplistic answers to these very complex questions. Evidence must be treated cautiously, as is well illustrated by this example of the West Indies. Rapid waterfront development has increased the hazard from storm surge and tsunamis, yet the increased use of masonry for house construction has lowered the threat from hurricane winds. Masonry structures however, have increased vulnerability to earthquakes. In addition we acknowledge that continuous improvements in monitoring systems and global communications tend to produce an artificial increase in the frequency of disaster detection.

STUDENT ACTIVITY 6.1

Is there a genuine increase in the impact of natural hazards?
Read the extract in Figure 6.2 and summarise the key issues raised in the article.

Study Figures 6.1, 6.3, 6.4 and 6.5. What are the main trends? Is this picture clear?

How far do you agree that the progressive improvement in the global communications system enables disasters to be reported more efficiently, and thus the apparent increase in global natural hazards is merely a media invention?

Is it realistic to look forward to a world where environmental hazards can be eliminated?

STUDENT ACTIVITY 6.2

1998 – the most hazardous year?
In the introduction to the book we suggested that 1998 may have been one of the most hazardous years for the global population, and we have asked you how you might test this hypothesis. Now you have completed your study of natural hazards, how would you modify your initial viewpoints?

A review of the IDNDR, 1990–2000

Should we be overly pessimistic? When we see natural disasters in the media we often assume few people survive. In fact, with few exceptions this century, the opposite is the case and very few disasters have wiped out the majority of the population. For example, Mont Pelée in 1902 killed 29 998 out of 30 000, Mount Huascaran in May 1970 killed most of the population of Yungy in Peru, and in November 1985 the eruption of the Nevado del Ruiz volcano in Colombia killed nearly all of the local community. Generally though, even in the other worst disasters, the majority of the population have survived and in many instances communities have been rebuilt.

Cyclone Tracy killed 64 people out of a population of 25 000 in Darwin on 25 December 1974, and even the Kobe earthquake disaster of

January 1995 claimed only 5390 lives in the central Japanese port. Most of the population of 215 000 survived. It is true that one month later many were still homeless and psychologically disturbed, and there was rampant profiteering and petty crime. Demolition charges spiralled by 500 per cent, building costs soared by up to 1000 per cent. Racism and xenophobia were rife as the Japanese media reported that foreigners were responsible for the looting, theft and profiteering. Yet the evidence from previous disasters highlights people's remarkable resilience and ability not only to survive, but to rebuild their own lives and communities.

The real future purpose for hazard management however, must be to reduce, through concerted international action, especially in the LEDCs, the loss of life, property damage, and extreme social and economic disruption caused by natural disasters. This is the stated objective of the United Nations Decade for Natural Disaster Reduction. The IDNDR has put hazard awareness high on the political agenda.

One key aim is to encourage further the trend in disaster management from a reactive strategy of post-disaster improvisation and heavy reliance on relief aid, to a more pro-active strategy of pre-disaster planning and preparedness.

However, the IDNDR is merely a signpost at the

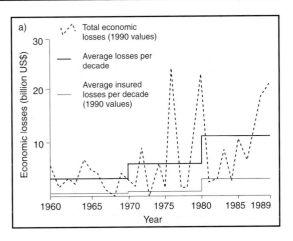

FIGURE 6.1 The world-wide increase in the frequency of natural disasters and the associated economic losses as revealed by insurance statistics, 1960–89

beginning of a long, difficult and unpredictable journey towards highly desirable goals. There are choices to be made which include the following.

1 Should technological hazards have been embraced within the IDNDR definition of integrated management planning?

2 In the LEDCs would sustainable development save more lives than the IDNDR's emphasis on hi-tech hazard-mitigating technologies?

3 To make real progress, hazard mitigation must develop more rapidly than human vulnerability. This will require profound and difficult socio-economic and political changes. Is this realistic?

FIGURE 6.2 Global disasters cause spiral of decline

Global disasters cause spiral of decline

Disasters are affecting an ever-increasing number of people in the world, causing a spiral of decline from which they are unlikely to recover.

An extra 10 million people – are added on average each year to the list of individuals affected by disasters.

Civil strife following a natural disaster is on the increase, especially on the African continent where the spread of arms is undermining law and order, leading to virtual anarchy and exacerbating famine and drought.

The trend in the number of people caught up in disasters over the past quarter century has been 'ever upwards', warns the International Federation of Red Cross and Red Crescent Societies in its *World Disasters Report* 1994.

'Today, even if those caught up in war are excluded, something in the region of 250 to 300 million people a year are affected by disasters, and this figure is growing at a rate of around 10 million a year,' the report says.

Peter Walker, head of the disaster policy department at the Red Cross federation, said the nature of disasters had changed in recent years. This was partly due to an increase in poverty, and in population density.

'We are now seeing a second style of disaster. In the past an earthquake or flood were blips on the road to recovery. We are now getting total disasters where there is no chance of a return to normality because there is often no normality to return to.'

Dr Walker said that natural disasters often triggered a much larger crisis brought about by people being already vulnerable.

The report highlights the case of north-east Brazil, where four years of low rainfall have created the prospect of a severe disaster among 12 million people in the region.

'But as so often in supposedly "natural" disasters such as drought, the lack of rains in north-eastern Brazil is merely the trigger for a disaster which could not happen if the people were not already vulnerable for a range of social, environmental and economic reasons,' the report says.

Dr Walker said the upsurge in violence in the world is hindering efforts to contain disasters. Thirty years ago there were 10 on-going wars; now there are about 50.

The Independent, 19 August 1994

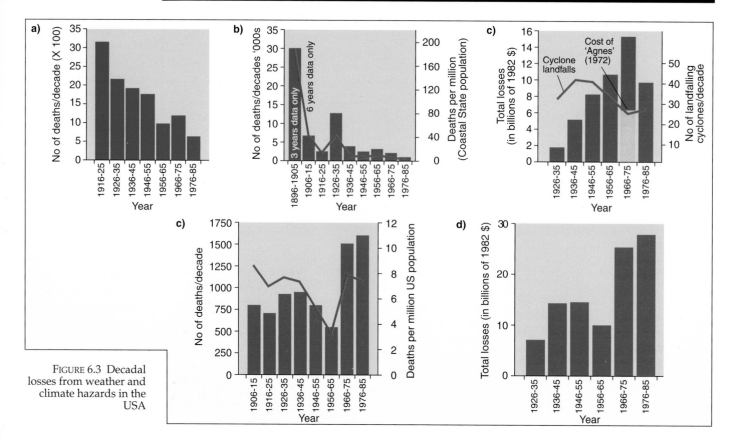

FIGURE 6.3 Decadal losses from weather and climate hazards in the USA

The correct road involves the following:

1 Shifting from research to action and the effective implementation of all the existing hazard-reducing capabilities.

2 Improved public information and education.

3 As relief aid will always be required, it must be made more effective and efficient, e.g. incentives to LEDCs who avoid hazard zone development, in the form of aid or safe refuges and equipment.

4 Rigid enforcement in the MEDCs of proven building design and land-use restrictions that are avoided because of cost and lack of stringent enforcement.

This still leaves poverty as the greatest challenge and obstacle to realising the key objective of a safer world. The most intractable problems exist in countries which are too poor to help themselves. Countries such as Bangladesh where although cyclone warnings exist, there are only safe cyclone shelters for 3 per cent of the population, and where most well heads are not covered or protected against storm surge damage, and a chronic lack of resources hampers relief efforts after the disaster. In 1991, Bangladesh had only 13 operational helicopters dealing with 10 million homeless and 150 000 deaths resulted from one of the most severe cyclones of the twentieth century in the Bay of Bengal.

The underlying cause of the Bangladesh tragedy is the extreme poverty that condemns more than 10 million people to live in one of the most densely populated and lowest-lying areas of the world, and in one of our planet's most vulnerable cyclone zones.

It is said that we live in interesting times. The reality is that short-term prospects are bleak and we are not coping well with the challenges of natural hazards at the end of this millennia. In the LEDCs the majority of the world's population are confined to live in hazard-prone high-risk environments due to poverty. Meanwhile in the MEDCs, in Tokyo and San Francisco, cities have been rebuilt on exactly the same high-risk sites. Los Angeles continues to expand in spite of the multiple hazards of earthquakes, ground subsidence, tsunamis, landslides, bush fires, drought, and smog, many of which will be compounded by global warming.

We must therefore conclude our mid-term report on the IDNDR not with 'could do better' but 'must do better'. The IDNDR must be prepared to tackle the difficult issues and seek to tackle the underlying socio-economic, and political causes if an extension of the current trend of increasing deaths and damage from natural hazards beyond the decade and into the next millennium is to be prevented.

Review of key ideas

1 Interpreting global and national disaster trends is very complex.

2 Improved communications and growing hazard awareness, especially in the 1990s, may over-estimate the real position.

3 Not only has the total number of deaths per year from natural hazards increased to over 250 000, but more critically the number of deaths per million of the world's population has also increased. Changes in both these trends are sufficiently large to suggest

FIGURE 6.4 Data from the International Red Cross – World Disasters Report (available on the Internet)

a) People killed by disaster 1972–1996 (annual averages)

	AFRICA	AMERICAS	ASIA	EUROPE	OCEANIA	TOTAL
1972 to 1976	254 051	25 259	67 148	2 089	83	**348 631**
1977 to 1981	1 512	2 486	16 631	1 861	56	**22 547**
1982 to 1986	114 415	9 925	14 690	1 757	183	**140 971**
1987 to 1991	11 686	5 994	114 990	7 560	151	**140 381**
1992 to 1996	7 595	3 104	18 305	2 352	66	**31 422**
1972 to 1996	77 852	9 354	46 353	3 124	108	**136 790**

b) People affected by disaster 1972–1996 (annual averages)

	AFRICA	AMERICAS	ASIA	EUROPE	OCEANIA	TOTAL
1972 to 1976	3 744 901	1 904 177	61 061 699	267 165	45 889	**67 023 832**
1977 to 1981	9 137 642	2 645 235	81 550 558	380 640	27 620	**93 741 694**
1982 to 1986	17 487 252	8 400 440	116 286 138	326 552	231 230	**142 731 613**
1987 to 1991	13 546 675	4 010 491	217 771 500	1 023 310	69 746	**236 421 721**
1992 to 1995	11 894 585	3 803 731	126 092 412	713 161	1 008 274	**177 541 958**
1972 to 1996	11 894 585	3 803 731	126 092 412	713 161	1 008 274	**143 512 154**

c) People made homeless by disaster 1972–1996 (annual averages)

	AFRICA	AMERICAS	ASIA	EUROPE	OCEANIA	TOTAL
1972 to 1976	44 970	381 577	2 020 205	69 200	240	**2 516 192**
1977 to 1981	213 706	190 660	1 565 719	73 441	4 722	**2 048 248**
1982 to 1986	211 758	405 693	2 440 833	17 360	24 340	**3 099 984**
1987 to 1991	396 423	349 401	9 102 567	145 557	9 627	**10 003 575**
1992 to 1996	555 858	324 252	5 566 715	54 820	32 170	**6 533 815**
1972 to 1996	284 543	330 317	4 139 208	72 076	14 220	**4 840 363**

d) People injured by disaster 1972–1996 (annual averages)

	AFRICA	AMERICAS	ASIA	EUROPE	OCEANIA	TOTAL
1972 to 1976	63	20 882	43 200	4 181	257	**68 583**
1977 to 1981	2 129	3 433	18 282	5 375	139	**29 358**
1982 to 1986	985	18 269	31 239	1 537	2 260	**54 290**
1987 to 1991	645	5 297	51 552	3 905	54	**61 453**
1992 to 1996	6 641	4 896	125 548	4 800	460	**142 345**
1972 to 1996	2 093	10 555	53 964	3 960	634	**71 206**

e) Table 5 Annual average number of people killed by type of disaster and by period (1972 to 1996)

	EARTH-QUAKE	DROUGHT & FAMINE	FLOOD	HIGH WIND	LANDSLIDE	VOLCANO	TOTAL
1972 to 1976	64 170	253 800	7 232	4 977	1 142	9	**331 330**
1977 to 1981	5 821	56	4 900	6 729	343	129	**17 979**
1982 to 1986	3 210	111 832	4 269	6 494	488	4 740	**131 033**
1987 to 1991	15 548	1 852	39 787	57 803	1 184	151	**116 325**
1992 to 1996	4 826	489	7 293	3 797	807	56	**17 268**
1972 to 1996	18 715	73 606	12 696	15 960	793	1 017	**122 787**

f) Table 6 Annual average number of people affected by type of disaster and by period (1972 to 1996)

	EARTH-QUAKE	DROUGHT & FAMINE	FLOOD	HIGH WIND	LANDSLIDE	VOLCANO	TOTAL
1972 to 1976	1 341 084	43 563 400	18 867 313	3 116 419	17 600	34 500	**66 940 317**
1977 to 1981	614 626	52 122 671	31 609 232	8 199 291	1 802	28 400	**92 576 021**
1982 to 1986	484 431	103 246 778	28 693 409	6 399 549	4 461	106 269	**138 934 898**
1987 to 1991	5 071 710	75 851 888	119 779 115	22 664 204	630 750	156 740	**224 154 407**
1992 to 1996	753 477	21 480 303	130 433 416	18 235 163	34 914	144 685	**171 081 957**
1972 to 1996	1 653 066	59 253 008	65 876 497	11 722 925	137 905	94 119	**138 737 520**

g) Table 7 Annual average number of people made homeless by type of disaster and by period (1972 to 1996)

	EARTH-QUAKE	DROUGHT & FAMINE	FLOOD	HIGH WIND	LANDSLIDE	VOLCANO	TOTAL
1972 to 1976	344 457	0	2 041 583	89 629	300	1 000	**2 476 969**
1977 to 1981	166 070	0	238 838	1 630 400	3 420	3 500	**2 042 228**
1982 to 1986	188 056	100 000	1 548 438	729 856	501 316	11 220	**3 078 886**
1987 to 1991	337 048	9 600	8 058 439	1 522 708	18 051	33 325	**9 979 171**
1992 to 1996	205 204	0	4 895 072	1 372 519	14 228	25 753	**6 512 776**
1972 to 1996	248 167	21 920	3 356 474	1 069 022	107 463	14 960	**4 818 006**

h) Table 8 Annual average number of people injured by type of disaster and by period (1972 to 1996)

	EARTH-QUAKE	DROUGHT & FAMINE	FLOOD	HIGH WIND	LANDSLIDE	VOLCANO	TOTAL
1972 to 1976	62 251	0	378	3 828	203	1	**66 660**
1977 to 1981	10 489	0	8 591	6 733	18	207	**26 038**
1982 to 1986	13 911	0	5 593	7 708	25	1 100	**28 337**
1987 to 1991	29 035	0	16 947	9 718	916	66	**56 682**
1992 to 1996	19 372	0	77 861	36 131	160	51	**133 576**
1972 to 1996	27 012	0	21 874	12 824	264	285	**62 259**

* From 1960–69 to 1986–96

(i) the number of recorded disasters quadrupled
(ii) after allowing for inflation, direct financial losses increased 8 fold
(iii) insured losses increased 15 fold

* In 1996 the annual number of natural disasters was 590
 (1995 = 579, 1994 = 597)

In 1996, Asia was the most severely affected continent with

(i) 31% of total natural disaster events
(ii) 80% of the total global casualties
(iii) 61% of the total economic losses

* In 1996 the USA suffered the most insured losses with 81% of the global total of 9 billion US $. (NB. 51 billion of these 60 billion US $ of economic losses are uninsured.)

* The number of natural disasters, and their associated socio-economic costs continue to rise, and reductions in these trends are not anticipated.

Dr Neil Britton, Emergency Management and Civil Defence, Wellington, New Zealand.

that since 1960 there has been a genuine increase taking place in disaster impact, but these are not uniform across the globe, due to uneven levels of economic development. There is also evidence of increased spatial variability in both climatic and geological phenomena. In terms of natural hazard events we live in very interesting times!

4 Broadly speaking both deaths and damages have increased in the LEDCs, whilst rising economic losses in the MEDCs have been matched by a fall in fatalities.

5 Despite the welcome fall in fatalities for some hazards in many of the wealthier countries, the global trend is probably towards more disaster-related deaths and damages. The following factors help to show why deaths and damages from natural hazards are increasing, even if the frequency of events is not growing and despite the many positive steps being taken to reduce disasters.

a) Rapid population growth in the poorest sections of the global community in the LEDCs.

b) Land pressure and ecological degradation enhances the problem.

c) Continued economic growth increases vulnerability and exposure to property damage. Property damage is now estimated to be over US $40 billion per year.

d) Technological innovation increases the potential for disaster if the technology fails.

e) Increased social expectations and demands for instant mobility in the MEDCs.

f) Growing interdependence, such that major disasters can now have global consequences.

g) Rapid increases in urbanisation. Urban populations and urban areas are more vulnerable.

In a recent World Disaster Report the International Red Cross identified the issues that will influence the effectiveness of future natural hazard management strategies.

– Within the next generation most of the world's population will live in urban areas, yet most disaster response practice and experience to date is with rural people and rural disasters. The new urban challenge will not be the megacities, but the small and medium-sized towns especially those in LEDC's, that have spread beyond their original boundaries into more hazardous areas.

– Tackling these new towns and cities at risk will critically need:

* Good governance. Effective and accountable local authorities with sound disaster preparations and urban planning, and an open democratic communication process.

* An understanding that most disaster victims will be people trapped by poverty into living on marginal lands. Unplanned cities and shanty towns do not have to be high-risk areas.

* To recognise that these concentrations are an 'opportunity' as they offer large economies of scale potential, e.g. to identify the vulnerable, implement effective preventative measures and adopt best value risk reduction.

– Identifying vulnerable people will be critical.

* High-risk sites e.g. Flood-prone areas, buildings that were not designed to withstand earthquakes.

* High-risk groups, e.g. very young/disabled/ aged.

* Those that cannot expect a rapid response.

– Prevention is now an option, e.g. land-use zoning and watershed management, moving people to safe sites, improved housing design, early warning systems, effective rapid response emergency services.

– The report concluded that best value risk reduction must be the goal. The best possible use of local knowledge and resources to reduce risks.

This must involve:

* All public agencies taking appropriate and integrated disaster prevention and preparedness measures, e.g. education, health, planning, building control and emergency services.

* Effective communication with all local people.

* Encouraging householders, community organisations, NGO's and other private enterprises to work together to reduce hazard risks. Developing solutions *with* not for them.

Poor urban areas are the most vulnerable. (See Figure 6.6).

References

World Disasters Reports, International Federation of Red Cross and Red Crescent Societies, e.g. 1998

FIGURE 6.5 (*opposite*) The Global Hazardscape 1960–1996

FIGURE 6.6 The New Urban Challenge – Tackling City Risks I.R.C. World Disasters Report 1998

APPENDIX

Study skills and Generalisations

At the end of your unit of study on natural hazards you should be capable of using your own research case studies and material from this book to illustrate the following ten points.

1 *Hazards and people* – most hazards are not entirely 'natural', but their very definition relates to their impact upon land use patterns and processes, societies and economies.

2 *Hazard classification* – hazards can be classified by their causal processes, spatial occurrence, scale of impact on human communities and activities.

3 *Causes of hazards* – tectonic, climatic and geomorphological processes can create potential hazard problems of societies and people.

4 *Understanding hazards* – the causal physical processes and natural systems need to be fully understood in order to produce effective risk assessment and hazard management.

5 *Hazard impact* – the social, economic and demographic impact of hazards can include loss of life, property, livelihood and community stress and strain.

6 *Spatial variations in hazard impact* – the degree of economic and social impact is related to frequency magnitude and spatial distribution of the hazard.

7 *Perception of hazards* – human responses towards hazards are affected by people perceptions of hazards.

8 *The human response* – people respond to hazards in a variety of ways, from fatalism or no reaction to prevention and protection. Human responses towards the way in which hazards are managed are affected by the variations in the economic resources available within a country to deal with the hazard.

9 *Hazard prediction* – increased research into hazard frequency and occurrence may allow improved prediction to reduce the impact of hazards.

10 *Hazard prevention and management* – hazards can never be totally prevented, but their consequences and causes may be alleviated by hazard prevention methods, education and hazard management techniques.

Study skills: the consolidation and application of acquired knowledge

There are two varying, but equally useful ways of consolidating your knowledge on natural hazards.

1 Brainstorming, topic webs or summaries.

2 Writing a research essay.

STUDENT ACTIVITY A.1

Brainstorming, topic summary

Firstly, for any of the ten above generalisations, carry out a brainstorming exercise to try and see which case studies and other key ideas you would try to bring into any answer related to this topic. Then produce a neat copy of this as a topic summary and try and sequence your ideas (see Figure A1).

Be sure to use a large A4 sheet of blank paper and do not worry about structuring your thoughts at first. Brainstorming should be a creative and enjoyable activity. Freed from your books and notes, you provide the key resource of ideas.

Ultimately it may be worth having such a plan for every generalisation.

Writing a research essay

Many of you will be assessed on your natural hazards work by means of a timed or research essay. It is essential then that you are well-skilled in the technique of effective essay writing.

Check the exam syllabus regulations and mode of assessment

Be sure you are clear on the exact nature of both the content you are required to cover and the exact nature of the mode of assessment including specific details of any limitations, e.g. timings, word limits and restrictions on word-processing, etc. Find out whether you must learn your whole module of work or a small section in detail.

For example, the Edexcel Advanced GCE Specification B Geography will give students two generalisations for them to research in detail up to 2 weeks in advance of their module test. The test itself will be in the form of one 80-minute student-researched long essay, from a choice of 2 titles. Candidates are advised to prepare revision notes from their research files, resources and books used during their study of their chosen module and then learn these for assessment under strict examination conditions.

It will be closed-book so students will have to revise and learn their material for the exam. Ensure

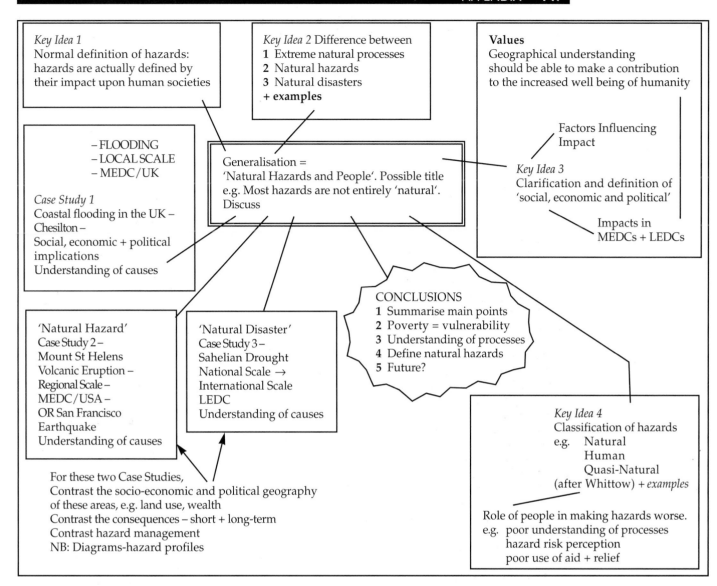

FIGURE A1 Brainstormed patterned notes or ideas web for a generalisation

you see past papers to see exactly what is required. Study the information for candidates carefully.

You should also try and see past exam papers, mark schemes and model answers issued by your exam board. They can often tell you how to obtain maximum marks, and what you would need to do as shown in the points listed below.

a) Clear opening statement of both: i) the question, problem or issue; ii) the nature of the data needed.

b) Select and apply a wide range of: i) carefully researched case study evidence; ii) maps, figures and diagrams.

c) A logical route of enquiry, and all data and examples used to illustrate specific relevant points arranged in a clear order.

d) Clearly stated conclusions with full support and justification and directly related to the rest of the essay.

e) To be well-written, using good clear English.

Pre-writing state

Whatever format your assessment takes, the golden rule for success is thorough planning at the pre-writing stage.

1 Analyse the wording of the assignment, essay title or generalisation. Identify the key geographical terms, key ideas and key command verbs.

Be sure you understand the difference between the common command words in Figure A2.

2 Brainstorm and write your topic summary.

3 Identify and collect sources of data required. Get a balance of your own sources and material provided by your teacher. Do not over-collect material blindly.

4 Make initial notes in the format of key words, concepts and phrases rather than linear sentences. Include the author, title and page references.

Essay structure and paragraphing

1 Summarise your notes.

2 Organise your notes into paragraphs with a clear controlling idea.

3 Rearrange your notes to focus on your task.

Drafting

1 Shape your notes into your draft essay.

2 Be sure at this stage you:

a) stick to the point;

FIGURE A2 Common command words used in hazard essays

Analyse	Critically investigate.
Compare	Look for similarities and differences between.
Contrast	Highlight the differences between.
Define	Briefly set down the meaning of a word or phrase.
Describe	Give a detailed account of.
Discuss	Investigate, giving evidence reasons for and against.
Evaluate	Give your evidenced judgement.
Examine	Look closely into.
Explain	Make plain; interpret and account for; give reasons for.
Explore	Examine thoroughly from a variety of viewpoints.
Interpret	Make clear and show the meaning of.
Justify	Show adequate grounds for decisions and conclusions.
Outline	Give the main feature or general principles of a subject, emphasising structure and interrelations.
State	Present in a brief, clear form.
Summarise	Give a concise account of the chief points omitting details and examples.

b) develop an argument;

c) cover all your points in a logical sequenced way;

d) look at the issue from all possible value perspectives;

e) support your argument with evidence, and refer to your source of information;

f) keep personal opinions and anecdotes out, unless you are absolutely sure of their relevance;

g) develop your conclusions as a logical follow-on from your ideas;

h) ensure your introduction outlines the topic, defines terms and presents a structure for the essay.

Editing

1 Check for factual errors.

2 Correct your English:

a) sentences;

b) paragraphs;

c) punctuation;

d) spelling;

e) clarity of style.

3 Ensure all data sources and references are properly acknowledged and you have an accurate bibliography.

Essays in examinations

If your assessment is an essay that has to be written under timed conditions in an exam room, your approach should generally be the same, but realise that the whole process is speeded up and more concentrated. There are, however, new skills and techniques that must be understood and effectively mastered *before* you enter the exam room. They are essential pre-requisites for producing a quality timed essay.

Your planned revision schedule

Ensure your files are fully organised, and that any areas of poor understanding or weak case studies are corrected prior to beginning your revision schedule. Reduce the volume of your notes by condensing them into bullet points of the key ideas, concepts, words and statistics. Use headings and side headings to structure your notes. Alternatively produce topic web revision summaries. You must

set yourself realistic targets within your revision schedule, and organise your learning into blocks of 30–45 minutes, as this is your period of optimum effectiveness and concentration, and where there is the best relationship between understanding and remembering. Avoid last minute cramming, so that you enter the examination refreshed and with a clear mind. Remember the general rule that the depth and detail of your revision will need to increase with the length of your exam.

Essay writing in the exam room

Follow the same stages and approach suggested in writing all essays, but be aware of the following basic **dos** and **don'ts**.

1 **Do** choose your question(s) carefully. Concentrate on your strengths.

2 **Do** manage your most precious resource wisely – draw up a time management plan and stick to it!

3 **Do** allow yourself adequate time to draw up a concise plan for your answer. If you must do your essay in 45 minutes allow 5 minutes, but if you have 80 minutes you can afford 8 minutes drawing up a more comprehensive and carefully considered plan. However **do not** produce a full rough draft, there is not enough time!

4 **Do** write clearly, concisely and quickly.

5 **Do** use appropriate technical terms, key words and phases and quote evidence.

6 **Do** allow a few minutes at the end to check coherence, structure, factual accuracy and your English.

7 **Do not** waffle, and **do not** answer the question you had hoped would be on the paper, but wasn't!

8 **Do not** waste time writing a plan and then ignoring it!

9 **Do not** be repetitive, especially in the conclusion.

10 **Do not** write overlong introductions.

11 **Do not** stray from the key theme.

Finally **do** be confident. If you have worked hard on your course, practised your essay writing skills and revised in detail you have every right to expect to achieve your true potential. If you have worked hard the greatest risk is failure to have confidence in your own ability.

Index